Please Live

Please Live

The Chechen Wars, My Mother and Me

LANA ESTEMIROVA

JOHN MURRAY

First published in Great Britain in 2025 by John Murray (Publishers)

1

Copyright © Lana Estemirova 2025

The right of Lana Estemirova to be identified as the Author of the Work has been asserted by her in accordance with the Copyright, Designs and Patents Act 1988.

Extract from 'Hey Now Now', written by Jonathan Petrow, Jonathan Stuart, Jason Pharr and Benjamin Nugent, published by Soundrights Music / Red Brick Songs, admin. by Bucks Music Group Ltd., Roundhouse, 212 Regents Park Road Entrance, London NW11 7RG.

Extracts from Natalia Estemirova, 'People Are Still Being Kidnapped in Chechnya', 20 October 2008, 'Militants in Power Are Annihilating the New Generation of Militants', 14 January 2009, and 'Thousands of Murderers Are Walking Free', 21 January 2009, reprinted courtesy of *Novaya Gazeta*.

Every reasonable effort has been made to trace copyright holders, but if there are any errors or omissions, John Murray will be pleased to insert the appropriate acknowledgement in any subsequent printings or editions.

All rights reserved. No part of this publication may be reproduced, stored in a retrieval system, or transmitted, in any form or by any means without the prior written permission of the publisher, nor be otherwise circulated in any form of binding or cover other than that in which it is published and without a similar condition being imposed on the subsequent purchaser.

A CIP catalogue record for this title is available from the British Library

Hardback ISBN 9781399811620
Trade Paperback ISBN 9781399811637
ebook ISBN 9781399811651

Typeset in Bembo by Hewer Text UK Ltd, Edinburgh
Printed and bound in Great Britain by Clays Ltd, Elcograf S.p.A.

John Murray policy is to use papers that are natural, renewable and recyclable products and made from wood grown in sustainable forests. The logging and manufacturing processes are expected to conform to the environmental regulations of the country of origin.

Carmelite House
50 Victoria Embankment
London EC4Y 0DZ

www.johnmurraypress.co.uk

John Murray Press, part of Hodder & Stoughton Limited
An Hachette UK company

The authorised representative in the EEA is Hachette Ireland, 8 Castlecourt Centre, Dublin 15, D15 XTP3, Ireland (email: info@hbgi.ie)

To my Mum

Contents

	Premier Jour	1
1.	Born Into a Storm	3
2.	Tell Me About War	13
3.	Baba	35
	The Paints That Quarrelled	55
4.	Memorial	57
5.	Piano on Fire	76
	How People Conquered Fear	110
6.	Three Villages	116
7.	Putin's Little Dragon	147
8.	The Headscarf	181
9.	Yekaterinburg	211
10.	15 July 2009	237
11.	The Balcony	246
12.	The Investigation	253
13.	A Promise	261
14.	A Story Without an End	267
	Acknowledgements	275

Premier Jour

'Lana, where's my perfume?' I hear Mum's voice. Squinting against the bright morning sun streaming in through the window, I am too sleepy to see her properly. The blinding light contours her silhouette.

'It's there, in the bottom drawer,' I mumble before going back to sleep. Mum rustles around in the cupboard for a few more moments, then I hear the sound of a closing door.

Or did she ask me to lock it instead? Did she say something about my French class? Did she ask me to buy bread?

I guess it doesn't matter anymore. Ten years ago, I could recall that day minute by minute, but now the details are fading.

'Where's my perfume?' Quick words with a hint of reproach. I had my own way of putting things in order, unlike Mum. I had a system. Maybe, if I'd left that goddamn perfume where it was, she would have said something else, in a different tone of voice.

'Where's my perfume?' were the last words I ever heard from my mother. She left, trailing the scent of Nina Ricci's Premier Jour behind her, and I never saw her alive again.

I

Born Into a Storm
1944–94

'She's a retard, a mutant,' the midwife announced, moments after my birth on 3 March 1994. 'Do you really want a disabled child? You're still young, you can have more. Leave this one behind.'

That's how my mother and I were introduced, in a dilapidated hospital on the outskirts of Yekaterinburg, Russia – the city where the last tsar of Russia, Nicholas II, and his entire family were executed in 1918 – thousands of miles away from Chechnya, the place that would become my real home.

'I told them to bring you to me,' she reminisced years later. 'They warned me that there had been some kind of problem during my delivery and I had to prepare for the worst. That you were damaged.

'But I knew that no matter what, I would always love you,' Mum continued. 'When they brought you to me I saw that you were a perfectly normal baby. All your fingers and toes were in the right places and your hair was black, jet black. Nothing was wrong with you.'

Lana. She knew straight away. It was a tribute to her beloved but difficult Chechen father. Lana was his favourite name. It was what he had wanted to call his second daughter, but on the day of her birth he drank so much in celebration that he had blurted out something like 'Bleahna' at the registry office.

'Lena?'

'Nah, Bleahana.'

Without further hesitation, the registrar wrote down 'Elena', an everyday Russian name. Then came the twins – my uncle and aunt, Leonid and Svetlana. I guess he was hoping that Auntie Sveta would be called 'Lana' for short, but that never caught on. So, the name came to me.

Estemirova. Neatly handwritten on my birth certificate, my mother's surname firmly establishing who would play the only role in my upbringing. I rarely asked questions about my father. Mum was always enough.

Our surname was an invention. Almost exactly fifty years before my birth, on 23 February 1944, the entire population of Chechnya and the neighbouring republic of Ingushetia was deported to Central Asia on Stalin's orders. The pretext was collaboration with Nazi Germany, a myth later debunked by historians – the Nazis never even reached the North Caucasus. Nonetheless, on a cold winter's day, Russian soldiers appeared in every Chechen village and rounded up the confused and terrified inhabitants, barely giving them any time to gather their belongings. Forced into lines, the crowds were marched to the nearest train stations. Sometimes it took hours to get there and those who were too weak or old for the journey were shot – or, as with the seven hundred inhabitants of Khaibakh, a remote mountain village, locked in stables and burned alive. Thousands of Chechens fighting against the Nazis were pulled off the front line and deported along with their compatriots.

My grandfather Hussein, who was somewhere between eleven and twelve at the time (he never knew his exact birthday), was separated from his parents and three sisters at a train station. In the old days, Chechens didn't have surnames; instead, they were known by their first name followed by their father's first name – for instance: Patimat, Badruddi's daughter from Duba-Yurt. To simplify their records, the Soviets turned people's patronyms into new surnames. Thus, the name of my great-grandfather, Astemir, was transformed into Estemirov. But, unbeknown to him, his sisters were documented as Astemirov.

At the station, still desperately looking for his parents, Hussein was forced into a cattle wagon with no water or heating and sent into the unknown, alone and scared. All deportees were despatched to the remote Central Asian steppes, Kazakhstan being the main destination. In my grandfather's case, he was being sent to the small Soviet republic of Kyrgyzstan, although no one had informed him of that at the time. It took the wagon about two weeks to reach the town where they were to settle. Although 'settle' is too generous a word, really, because nothing but hunger, disease and destitution awaited them there. The local population was told to stay away from the newcomers because they were 'bandits' and 'traitors', but luckily many Kazakhs and Kyrgyzs defied those orders and shared their food and clothes. The exact number of Chechens who perished during the deportation, or Ardakhar, is not known, but according to the most conservative estimates it was over 100,000 – a third of the population. In most cases, the bodies of the dead were tossed from moving trains by Soviet soldiers, dooming the lost souls of the unburied to forever walk the earth. Little Hussein lost contact with his family for many years, unaware that both his parents had died during the perilous journey.

I'm surprised to see my grandfather appear in the first pages of this book – it was not what I had planned, and he died from tuberculosis in 1989 before he had the chance to meet me. Yet when I think about it, it seems appropriate. He too was sucked, at a young age, into a vortex of violence and uncertainty, not knowing who he was anymore. Our family never had the chance to be bystanders to history – we found ourselves in the middle of the storm. Somehow, despite this, the branches of my family tree continued to grow and entwine. Coincidences, choices, ruthless orders and chance meetings all led to that overcrowded hospital ward in Yekaterinburg, where my mother held me for the first time. A powerful bond developed between us, an invisible thread that could never be broken. Not even by death.

History has always clung to the Chechens like a second skin. Preserving and passing it on helps us to remember who we are even when we are ordered to forget. Deportation shaped the lives of an entire generation. The collective trauma and injustice of it fuelled the fight for independence that resulted in the two wars Mum and I were caught up in. To tell you our story, I first need to share some of this history with you.

Despite its modest size, the landlocked republic of Chechnya has always been a sharp bone in Russia's throat. To understand why, one must look at a map. Chechnya lies in the North Caucasus, on the south-eastern border of Russia in a sliver of land squeezed between the Black Sea to the west and the Caspian Sea to the east. To the north is Russia, to the south is Georgia, and Dagestan and Ingushetia are east and west. Covering only 20,000 square kilometres, it creates a natural boundary between Europe and Asia, a geographical feature that no doubt contributed to the unique and diverse range of cultures to be found there. These are mountain lands teeming with different identities, languages and religions. Among them lived the Vainakh people – which literally translates as 'our people' – a name for Chechens and our cousin nation the Ingush, with whom we share a border and similar customs.

In ancient times, when the barriers between myth and reality often blurred, travellers were intrigued by this mystical faraway land on the edge of the earth. The kingdom of Colchis, where Jason stole the precious golden fleece and sailed off on his ship with the Argonauts, was located in the western part of modern Georgia that borders the Chechen republic. A few hundred miles to the north, the titan Prometheus was chained to a tall mountain by Zeus for bringing fire to humans. To add to his punishment, Zeus' eagle fed on his liver daily, only for the wounds to heal so that his torture could be repeated all over again. Whether Prometheus was bound to Georgia's Mount Kazbek or Mount Elbrus in the Kabardino-Balkaria Republic of Russia is still open to debate. Pkharmat, as Chechens called him, was not the most well-known hero in Vainakh mythology but he was worshipped as the bringer of fire and the patron of all blacksmiths. This legend of rebellion and punishment, torture and injustice, continues to echo in the Caucasus, as if the whole land has been cursed alongside Prometheus.

The origins of the Chechen people (or Nokhchi, as we call ourselves) can be traced all the way back to the Mesopotamians. The Chechen language – one of the oldest in the region – has no analogues, apart from Ingush. The Vainakh belief system is rooted in paganism and nature worship, which includes complex shamanic rituals. Islam came to the Caucasus in waves and took a long time to embed itself because of the strength of local beliefs and traditions. By the eighteenth century most Chechens had converted to Islam but their lives were still strongly guided by *adats* – a complex, unwritten code of conduct that shaped everything from social interaction to marriage proposals and neighbours' disputes. We had no marble palaces or opulent temples, nor could our austere, stone towers compete with the pyramids of Giza and other ancient marvels, but we had mountains. Towering, unforgiving mountains moulded the Chechen people into resilient farmers and agile warriors and insulated them from the outside world, helping to preserve their culture – sometimes to their benefit, other times to their detriment.

Ever since Russia's first attempts to interact with Chechnya during the time of Peter the Great, the restive mountain people have been suspicious of outsiders. And with good reason. At the beginning of the nineteenth century, the Russians launched a decades-long campaign to subdue the Caucasus, sending one army after another into the peaks, suffering a string of humiliating defeats at the hands of those they saw as savages. But the mountain people – facing repeated, devastating attacks – were gradually worn down by the sheer size of the Russian army and their inhumane methods. One notoriously cruel Russian commander, General Yermolov, became known for razing entire villages to the ground as retaliation for resistance. Finally, by the end of the nineteenth century, most of Chechnya had been subjugated. Nationalist sentiment remained strong, however, and Chechen insurgents went underground.

Why did Chechens resist conquest and integration into the Russian Empire so much more fiercely than their neighbours? The answer lies in Chechnya's culture and its geography. Chechen society had no rigid hierarchy, no political elites and no nobility. People defined themselves as *uzdeni* – free people. Instead of European-style feudalism, the Vainakh organised themselves by *teips* – clan-like kinship groupings based on land ownership rather than familial ties. While some economic inequality existed between different households and villages, the decision-making process was relatively democratic (though women were of course excluded) and power was vested in community elders. Russian colonial officials struggled to establish a nominative leader in Chechnya, because while some might take a deal and join the empire, they certainly didn't speak for everyone.

Later, during the Russian Civil War which followed the October Revolution of 1917, the Bolsheviks lured the Chechens and Ingush to their side with promises of autonomy and equality. Compared to the

White Army's old imperial practices, the Reds seemed a lesser evil. As the White Army legions advanced towards the Caucasus with the help of pro-tsarist Cossacks, the highlanders put up a fierce resistance. After the Bolshevik victory, a deal between the Commissar on Nationalities, Joseph Stalin, and the Mountain Republic's Congress created the Mountain Autonomous Soviet Socialist Republic in 1922.

When policies like *korenizatsiya*, 'indigenisation', were introduced to promote local cultures and increase literacy rates, it seemed that highlanders would finally be given a seat at the table. However, Chechen resistance was soon reignited when Stalin's dekulakisation policies expropriated land from private farmers in favour of collective state ownership. To people for whom ancestral land was akin to a holy shrine, the idea of handing it over to the state was an outrage. Land hunger had been a big issue for Chechens, but still they were determined to hold on to every acre they owned. The Communist crack-down on *sharia* laws and *adats* further alienated Chechens. It was clear that the autonomy they had been promised would never materialise. When Stalin established himself as the leader of the Soviet Union, he vowed to rid it of all insubordinate elements. In 1937, around 14,000 Chechens and Ingush – intelligentsia, rebels, peasants and religious leaders – were rounded up, executed and buried in a mass grave. My grandad was already alive by then. Seven years later, Stalin deported the entire Chechen population to Central Asia.

A history teacher before she became a human rights activist, my mother, who knew this story of repression and resistance like the back of her hand, found herself living through the latest twist in the tale.

After the USSR's collapse in 1991, tensions in Chechnya, where Mum had been living since 1979, reached boiling point. As spontaneous demonstrations broke out on the streets, new alliances formed. It was then that Mum first engaged with political activism. She campaigned for fair pay for teachers, then became involved with the All-National Congress of the Chechen People headed by a charismatic former Soviet general, Dzhokhar Dudayev, who would become the first president of Chechnya.

On 6 September 1991, the Congress – motivated by vivid memories of the deportation – declared Chechen independence, later renaming the country Ichkeria, with its own flag, anthem and constitution. This bid for independence was, unsurprisingly, not well received in the Kremlin. The then Russian president Boris Yeltsin rejected the declaration and embarked on several attempts to oust Dudayev. This only boosted the Chechen president's popularity and the cause of independence.

Though outright war would not come for another three years, these were turbulent times. Dudayev was a controversial figure, constantly arguing with his parliament about how to handle secession negotiations with Russia. Not all Chechens were in favour of seceding either; certain influential individuals benefited greatly from proximity to Russia.

There was an attempted coup d'etat against Dudayev in 1993, prompting the president of Chechnya to dissolve the parliament. The following year, Yeltsin continued to make public threats against Dudayev, who responded by mobilising the Chechen military and declaring *gazavat* – holy war. Negotiations between the two leaders broke down with neither side willing to budge.

On 26 November 1994, an armed putsch was attempted, with Chechen forces operating on the side of the Kremlin entering Grozny with Russian support. They advanced a fair way into the city before sustaining heavy losses. Thirty soldiers were captured and paraded on Chechen TV. An incensed Dudayev threatened to execute them unless Russia confessed to complicity in the assault. But by then it was too late: the Russian security council was already planning a military operation in Chechnya. If Yeltsin were to grant Chechnya independence, other republics could fall like dominoes. He wanted to make an example of this little rebellion, whatever the cost. And so began the first Chechen war.

What would become the first Chechen war was not the first conflict to break out in the Caucasus after the Soviet Union fell apart. A clash between the north Caucasian republics of Ingushetia and Ossetia came earlier, in October 1992. The dispute concerned an area called Prigorodnoye, an Ingushetian district that had been transferred to

Ossetia following Stalin's 1944 deportation of the Ingush people. Although the area was officially Ossetian, many ethnic Ingush had returned there after the deportation, despite facing constant harassment from their Ossetian neighbours who had the backing of Russian security forces. Six hundred and forty-four people, most of them Ingush, died in the fighting. It was a grim prelude to the violence that would come to dominate the region for decades.

It was also the moment that Mum found her true calling and became a human rights activist.

On 2 November 1992 a twenty-four-year-old reporter named Alexander Mnatsakanyan arrived in Nazran, Ingushetia, to write a story. The city he found was in chaos, with refugees, distraught women and military men running around everywhere with guns. In the mayhem, he spotted a young Russian woman assisting refugees. 'She was called Tanya or Natasha, or something like that. She said she was a representative of the Chechen Red Cross.' Mum (for it was her) had gone to Ingushetia because she felt drawn to help, looking for transport and medical assistance for Ingush refugees and helping them find missing relatives.

The local mayor's office had been converted into a temporary crisis centre. Mum was there one day when a desperate Ingush woman ran inside. The Ossetian military had taken her four children hostage, she explained, and had let her go on condition that she secure the return of an AMPV, an armoured vehicle bristling with weapons, seized from them by the Ingush. It was an impossible dilemma: return an armoured vehicle that could kill more of their compatriots or let the woman's children die. Mum had a different solution. She demanded an ambulance with a Russian driver, and drove with him under open fire to where the children were being held. There, she launched into a long tirade, shaming the Ossetian militants. She was a Red Cross representative, she claimed, and there would be consequences if she called her superiors in Moscow. In the end, the Ossetians released the children. Had they known that she was in fact Chechen, they would not have let her go.

'Of course, there was no Chechen Red Cross,' chuckled Alik, the young journalist who became a close family friend. 'But when you spoke with confidence and referred to friends in high places, all doors opened for you.' She used the Red Cross act many times in the early nineties. And no doubt she would have continued to do so, had she not discovered that she was about to become a mother.

In 1993, Mum was pregnant and divorced from my Chechen father. Her relationship with him was always something of a mystery to me. 'I'll tell you all about it one day,' she would reassure me, but that day never came. It's just another thing I've long since had to accept.

With a baby on the way, Mum went back to her family home in Kamyshlov in the Urals. She left behind a life that had taken her years to build: a little ground-floor flat with a library she was very proud of near Grozny's leafy Pervomayskaya Street, her friends and her beloved teaching position at the prestigious school N7 (given a number rather than a name, in the Soviet style).

She watched that life get ripped apart on a TV screen in her mother's house, while rocking me to sleep. On 11 December 1994, Russian troops finally launched their attack on Chechnya, determined to put an end to its restive independence. On 31 December, while the rest of the country was celebrating New Year, the Russian air force began carpet bombing Grozny without regard for civilian life, pulverising entire neighbourhoods to dust. Bodies were spread out on the ground, many of them Russian pensioners unable to flee to ancestral villages in the countryside as their Chechen neighbours did. That the Kremlin was indiscriminately killing its own ethnic population was ignored as little more than collateral damage.

The school Mum had taught at was used as a military base by Chechen fighters, who shot through the classroom windows at Russian tank columns inching towards the city centre down the once beautiful Pervomayskaya Street. The roof of the school collapsed and the facade was ripped apart by bullets and grenades.

I often wonder what was going through her mind as she watched grainy images of her home, a thousand miles away, being turned to ruins; the streets that she had walked now covered with rubble, ant-like soldiers running back and forth. I wonder how she reacted to photographs of hollowed-out multi-storey buildings, their basements turned into bomb shelters while the upper floors were converted into snipers' dens. What it must have been like to have the joy of new-found motherhood invaded by the pain of seeing her beloved city destroyed? Even as she held me, something was calling her back, whispering that she was needed. Torn between duty and motherhood, Mum finally made up her mind. Just before I turned two years old, she left me in the care of my grandmother, and returned to Grozny where a painted sign at the city's entrance greeted her with the words *Welcome to Hell*.

2

Tell Me About War
1996–9

'Tell me about war.' I was swinging my legs back and forth on the kitchen stool while Mum cooked dinner. I was only two when the war ended, and everything from the past existed as a shapeless, colourless nothing. Now that I was almost five, I wanted to hear stories of how we survived. When I shut my eyes and tried to remember the war, only one image emerged from the darkness: a grey dog lying in a puddle of black blood. My head bounces against Mum's shoulder as she runs with me in her arms, and the dog, still alive, its guts falling out of its stomach, looks right into my eyes. Then it gets smaller and smaller, its little body disappearing into the distance.

'I don't remember that,' Mum said, her back turned to me. 'Perhaps I didn't notice it.'

She told me about how we had hidden in basements with our neighbours as the city was bombed almost every night. Our refuge was a damp, dark, rat-infested space beneath a tower block. 'How could we ever have slept there?' I asked, appalled by the stench coming from it when we walked past. Back then, Mum told me, we had no choice.

'When we ran out of food, our neighbours and I would sneak out to forage in the middle of the night. A few times we broke into shops and grabbed whatever we could carry. And we crawled to avoid being shot at. One time, I crawled almost four kilometres while the federals (that's what Chechens called Russian soldiers) were firing guns just above my head.'

How exciting and scary, I thought to myself.

'We hid in a corridor outside the lift. Federals were bombing us all night long and you and I could barely get any sleep. That night, I was scared for us like never before. Suddenly, I knew that we had to run.

I had wrapped you in blankets and you had just fallen asleep, I didn't want to wake you but I didn't have a choice. I started shaking you but you refused to move. You said, "Mummy, I'm sleepy. I don't care if they bomb us!" I finally managed to get you up and we left in a hurry. Seconds later I heard an explosion behind us and the roof collapsed into the corridor. If I hadn't listened to my gut feeling that night, we would both be dead.'

It was a blessing, not being able to remember the horrors of those final weeks of war that Mum and I had lived through. Perhaps she rushed back with me to Grozny too soon, hearing that the bombing campaigns were over. It was difficult to get any reliable information back then.

Years later, in an interview, Mum recounted how the two of us had been caught up in shelling and what a terrifying experience it had been; her mind gripped with anxiety about what would happen to me if she was killed.

'When we walked under that shelling,' she continued, 'I wrote my sister's address on the back of my daughter's jacket, so people would know where to send her, should anything happen to me.'

The first time Mum returned to Chechnya, in 1996, she left me behind with my grandmother. When she came back to Russia to see me, a few weeks or perhaps even a few months later, she wasn't sure whether it would be just a fleeting visit. Arriving at Kamyshlov train station, she immediately spotted Baba holding me in her arms and ran towards us. But when she reached out excitedly to take me from her, I turned away and cried, 'I'm scared of this auntie!', hiding my face in Baba's armpit. Mum was a stranger to me. After all those weeks she had spent away, I'd forgotten her.

'It was the most devastating moment of my life', Mum recalled later, 'when you didn't recognise me.'

She had to spend the following days reintroducing herself to her own daughter, hoping to regain her trust. It was clear to her that her love for me and her duty to Chechnya couldn't be reconciled unless they were brought together. And so, she went back to a war zone with a toddler.

Her memories of that time must have been deeply traumatic. But she handled them in her own special way – turning them into stories full of twists, dramatic pauses, villains and heroes. Mum never let the past weigh her down. She never grew tired of telling me the story of our survival, and I never grew tired of hearing it. Yet the reality of it never really sank in. I didn't believe in death when I was four. No matter how terrifying, every tale had a happy ending: Mum and me in our kitchen with our fluffy tabby cat, Manya, next to us. If only I could go back now, to listen more, take notes and greedily consume all the details.

The First Battle of Grozny started with a Russian attack on the capital on New Year's Eve 1994 and lasted until March 1995. Survivors told stories of seeing dozens of corpses on the street and tower blocks going up in flames, people – mostly women, children and the elderly – huddled together in basements, crying and praying for the fighting to stop. As for the men, any that could lay their hands on a Kalashnikov were defending the city, regardless of prior military experience. 'Conquer the capital, win the war.' This was the rationale behind the relentless bombardment. But the city wasn't going down without a fight. Familiar with their city's terrain, Chechen fighters outmanoeuvred the Russian squads with their cumbersome military vehicles. But they couldn't protect the city from bombs. In a few short days, the streets were reduced to rubble and dogs were eating away at corpses that lay on the ground unburied.

Witnessing the carnage, human rights activists at the time pushed for peace, advocating for the lives of both Chechen civilians and the young inexperienced Russian conscripts who died for nothing. But advised by hawkish generals and officials, Boris Yeltsin refused to divert his course. According to Memorial – the only organisation that was counting casualties on the ground – at least 25,000 civilians were killed during the First Battle of Grozny. Chechen fighters eventually retreated to villages in the mountains, and the city came under Russian control. But that was just the beginning. The war that Russian military command thought would be over in a matter of weeks stretched on for more than two years and revealed the full extent of the corruption and disarray that had hollowed out the self-described 'second largest army in the world'. It wasn't just Grozny that came under attack; there was heavy fighting in all the major cities in Chechnya. Urban areas and mountainous villages alike were mercilessly pounded by artillery, causing thousands upon thousands of civilian deaths. Chechen fighters retaliated with guerrilla tactics, setting booby traps and ambushing their enemies.

Some of the most harrowing, hidden crimes committed by Russian troops – rapes, cleansing operations and secret torture prisons – would be uncovered with the help of journalists and human rights organisations in the years that followed the war. Mum played a role in this morbid task.

For those who live through war, certain words – or even an entire language – can trigger painful memories. In Chechnya, *zachistka* became a word that could curdle your blood. Even years later, those three syllables would make you want to lock your doors and pull your loved ones closer. There's no equivalent in English; the translations 'clean-up' and 'mop-up operation' don't convey the terror that word can inspire.

Zachistka was one of the Russian forces' most beloved activities, requiring the minimum use of military equipment: just a few APVs (armoured patrol vehicles) and guns, and copious amounts of alcohol. The same pattern was repeated day after day, in village after village. Russian soldiers, often drunk or high, knocked on doors (or kicked them open) and searched for males aged between fifteen and sixty-five, for a 'document check', an official part of the anti-terrorist operation. In the process, they looted Chechen homes, holding the inhabitants at gunpoint until they handed over their valuables. Anyone the federals didn't like or deemed suspicious was beaten, tortured or killed on the spot. The most unfortunate were shoved into military vehicles and taken to the illegal prisons and filtration camps. There might be anything from five to fifty kidnappings across Chechnya in any one night, and most of the men taken never returned alive. Sometimes women were taken too. While every *zachistka* was despicably brutal, one in particular came to be written into the history books in bloody ink.

On 6 April 1995, Samashki, a small farming village in western Chechnya, was given an ultimatum by forces linked to the Russian Ministry of Internal Affairs: give up all their rebels and weapons and be spared, or refuse and die. The problem was, there were no Chechen soldiers there. Under pressure from the village elders, the militants had left Samashki weeks before, to avoid putting the civilians in danger. Nor was there a large stash of guns. Any militants who had remained in the village did so without the consent of the locals. And yet on 7 April the village was bombarded with artillery fire and aerial strikes.

That same evening a squad of federals burst into the village. What happened in the hours that followed would only come to light later. For four days, neither the press nor human rights organisations such as Memorial or the Red Cross were allowed to enter. When at last they did so, it became clear that this so-called 'operation' had been nothing short of a massacre. Survivors spoke about those days in harrowing detail. The Russians had killed at least 103 civilians, among them a ninety-year-old veteran of the Second World War and a number of small children. Men were shot at point-blank range in their own gardens, their hands tied behind their backs. Grenades were thrown into the basements of homes where families were sheltering. As if that weren't enough, some witnesses testified that the federals drenched the dead bodies in petrol and set them on fire, trying to destroy the evidence. After the Russian soldiers left, the villagers found empty alcohol bottles and syringes scattered on the ground. Despite all the evidence and independent cross-examined interviews, the Russian authorities vehemently denied the massacre. To this day, not a single perpetrator has been charged. Such brazen impunity paved the way for a series of heinous crimes committed against the Chechen civilian population. Just five years later, a similarly horrific village massacre occurred at the hands of a different Russian squad.

When the story of the Samashki massacre hit the international news it sent shockwaves through the West, and the pressure on Yeltsin to end the war continued to mount. Violence had now spilled over into Russia as well. On 14 June 1995, Shamil Basayev, the infamous Chechen field commander who had made a name for himself during the war as a ruthless tactician, led a squad of 195 militants to the Russian southern city of Budyonnovsk, about 110 km north of Chechnya. Without much resistance, the militants entered the city, seized several administrative buildings and occupied the local hospital, taking around 1,500 civilians hostage. In return for their release,

Basayev had demanded the withdrawal of Russian troops from Chechnya and the start of the peace process. Ignoring pleas from the hostages, Russian forces tried to storm the hospital several times, resulting in over 100 civilian deaths.

In the end, Basayev negotiated a safe return for himself and his squad, on condition that he would be surrounded by a human shield made up of volunteer hostages. A group of journalists, MPs and activists signed up for this risky mission, among them familiar faces: Sergey Kovalyov (a negotiator between Basayev and the Russians) and Oleg Orlov. These volunteers boarded buses along with armed militants, in the full knowledge that Russian forces might sacrifice them all at any moment in order to destroy Basayev. Their journey to Chechnya stretched for several days and upon arrival, the militants were greeted as heroes and the hostages that made up the human shield were unharmed. In the following years, Oleg spoke often about his experience in Budyonnovsk and highlighted that he was never ill-treated by his captors, although he frankly expressed to them his disdain for their methods. Although this daring endeavour was seen as a success by many Chechens, it didn't bring an end to hostilities – and learning from their humiliation, Russian law enforcement began refusing to negotiate with terrorists, even if it meant saving innocent lives. Meanwhile, the president of Chechnya, Dudayev, was in hiding, moving locations every few days to avoid being killed. He continued to pass on orders and give interviews to journalists. In one of them, held in 1995, he made a somewhat prescient prediction – foreseeing that Russia would not stop after invading Chechnya: 'There's going to be a bloodbath in Crimea ... Ukraine will clash with Russia once more. While Ruscism exists, it will never give up its ambitions.' On 21 April 1996, Dudayev was killed in a guided-missile strike after Russian secret services detected his use of a satellite phone.

The final phase of the war started on 6 August 1996 when around 1,500 Chechen fighters infiltrated Grozny and attacked the 12,000 Russian troops stationed in the city. They captured several strategic targets, including the airport, the Khankala airbase and the headquarters of the Federal Security Service (FSB) and police. Despite their numerical advantage, the Russian troops couldn't repel the attack and within several hours Grozny was back in Chechen hands. Judging by Mum's stories, we were in the city during this time. The image of the grey dog dying in a puddle of blood must have come from those final weeks of war, along with my nightmares, my hatred of low-flying planes, and the way that fireworks will send me into a frenzy.

On 19 August, Chechen fighters faced an ultimatum: surrender within forty-eight hours or face another barrage of bombardment and destruction. Thousands of civilians rushed from the city, but some 70,000 remained, enduring yet another wave of bombing raids. But the mood in the Kremlin was shifting; it was becoming clear to many that this war was unsustainable. By then, President Yeltsin's health had declined and he was eager to disentangle himself from the bloody mess he'd created. A ceasefire was ordered on 20 August 1996 and two days later Russian troops began to withdraw from Chechnya. On 30 August, after the signing of the Khasavyurt Accord, the first Chechen war ended with Russia's humiliation. Chechnya was de facto independent, with talks to follow. The number of civilian and military casualties on the Chechen side has been estimated at somewhere between 50,000 and 100,000. And it wasn't just Chechens who were killed; this total includes around 35,000 ethnic Russians who lived in the republic. More than a third of Chechens became refugees, most settling in refugee camps in neighbouring Ingushetia, eager to return home at the first opportunity.

In 1997, following a presidential election, Aslan Maskhadov, a commander who had been pivotal in securing Chechnya's military victory, became the third president of Chechnya. In those interbellum years, Chechnya existed in a semi-legal vacuum, not recognised by its neighbours as a sovereign state. The region was politically divided: the popular Dudayev cast a long shadow even after his death, making it difficult for Maskhadov to muster the same degree of authority. Shamil Basayev, the military commander, demanded to be involved in political decision-making.

By the mid-nineties, Basayev had pivoted to Wahhabism, a more radical and puritanical strand of Islam that had arrived from Saudi Arabia, along with opportunistic mercenaries looking for a new war. After coming second in the presidential election, he was given the premiership as a consolation prize. But as so often turns out, military men, especially ones who resort to hostage-taking, don't make good politicians. Endless in-fighting descended into violent clashes between opposing factions, often between moderates and religious fundamentalists. Basayev and other militants started recruiting disenfranchised, empty-bellied youths, many of whom had lost their loved ones. Their 'training camps' were more like Boy Scout organisations; the majority of young men who turned to them went for the camaraderie and a bowl of soup rather than religious sermons. Wahhabism, a stark departure from traditional Chechen Sufi practices embedded in mysticism and tomb worship, didn't find overwhelming support in Chechnya; nor would it replace the traditional *adats* that governed society. Most people wanted peace, not jihad.

With the exception of a small number of corrupt profiteers who turned economic catastrophe into a lucrative opportunity, Chechens were impoverished by the war. Some 80 per cent of the region's economy and infrastructure had been destroyed, and little was done to rebuild it. Russia ignored the terms of the Khasavyurt agreement and refused to transfer funds to rebuild the republic that it had decimated. Taxation was non-existent, and education and healthcare, the foundations on which society rests, were severely underfunded. When I eavesdropped on Mum's conversations, they were peppered with words like 'privatisation' and 'Wahhabis' and a list of names that sounded like spells: Maskhadov, Dudayev, Yeltsin, Lebed, Udugov, Basayev, Khattab-Raduyev-Gelaev-Grachev . . . This was a period of uncertainty, when nothing worked. Gunshots were still heard every now and then, as weapons were in abundance. Not every street was reduced to rubble, but you could hardly find a building that wasn't scarred by bullets and missiles.

Life went on, even in the ruins. Once Mum's school, N7, had been patched up, she returned to work as a history teacher, although her salary was paid infrequently, if at all. Despite still looking like a building used for target practice, the school managed to retain some of the best teachers. Sometimes, when my kindergarten was closed, Mum had no choice but to take me along to work with her – as long as I promised to be quiet. Her teenage students, buzzing with excitement at the sight of a chatty toddler, fought over who got to hold me. It was also a great excuse not to go up to the blackboard for a presentation: 'Sorry, Natalia Husseinovna, I can't move. Lana is sitting on my lap!' That's how students address their teachers in Chechnya, using their full name followed by a patronym. To her friends and colleagues, she was Natasha. I was so used to hearing these names, that I started forgetting to refer to her as 'Mum'. She used to always laugh about it:

'Every night before bed you would turn to me half asleep and ask, "Natalia Husseinovna, would you be so kind as to bring me some water?"'

Our tiny, just about habitable flat was a ten-minute walk from the school. That's where my first proper memories were made, in a quiet, leafy neighbourhood that still bore the marks of recent hostilities. The architecture was a mix of uniform tower blocks, surrounded by more traditional houses with gardens. The level of physical damage that the buildings had sustained varied. Our nine-storey *devyatietazhka*, for instance, was in relatively good shape, apart from multiple bullet dents and a couple of bigger holes where missiles had struck. The building opposite, which was identical to ours, was missing several upper floors and was charred completely black on one side. Even the children's slide which survived in the yard between the tower blocks was disfigured; rusty and covered in bullet holes, it resembled a cheese grater. I could see it clearly from the balcony of our home. The balcony's glass windows had long since been shattered, so my mother made do with plastic film. Sometimes, local youths would gather below, strumming guitars and occasionally playing with the odd Kalashnikov. When they were feeling particularly boisterous, shots were fired in the air. Mum would lean out of the window, frustrated:

'Could you stop shooting right this moment?' she would order sternly. 'My daughter is trying to sleep!'

Our home was sparsely furnished, minimalist in the truest sense of the word: a sofa bed for Mum, a chest of drawers that housed a Soviet-era black-and-white TV, my bed in the corner and a tiny shelf where all five of my toys lived. Next to the shelf Mum hung a small painting given to her by an artist friend, a small oil landscape in muddy brown colours depicting a traditional Chechen obelisk-like stone tower – a *bow* – standing next to an ancient family house. The most cherished objects in our flat, three crystal flutes with a pattern of cheerful blue forget-me-nots that had, astonishingly, survived the war, were shut away in a cupboard in the corridor. Originally a set of four (one didn't make it), they were given to Mum by my grandfather Hussein. We had so little back then but every item – every piece of clothing, every kitchen utensil we owned – was special, imbued with utilitarian or symbolic meaning. Losing any one of those objects was like losing a part of yourself.

Mum told me that when we entered her Grozny flat in 1996, she discovered that her home library had been burned down to the very last book. Her collection, which she had accumulated over many years, and which included some pre-1917 Revolution editions, was more precious than all her other belongings put together. Heartbroken, she vowed to never amass books again. But soon enough new piles started to sprout from every corner of our home. By 1998, some important additions had been made to this new, smaller book collection: children's fairy tales.

Mum passed on her love of books to me. Sometime after I turned four, she gave me the best present imaginable, worth more than all the Barbie dolls put together – she taught me to read. Every night we would snuggle up in bed together, each with our own book. As Mum read silently, I slowly whispered the letters until they turned into coherent words and sentences. One day I finally learnt the trick: if you don't open your mouth, everything still makes sense! From then on, I never felt lonely because wherever I went, I would bring along a book or two for companionship. And since our black-and-white TV showed only two channels, books became my main form of entertainment. With every page, words turned into colourful scenes right before my eyes. I watched the golden cockerel from Pushkin's fairy tale fly across the room. The asphalt-covered yard outside my window became an exotic ocean, the rusty bullet-ridden slide a pink island to be explored. My mind was bursting with storylines and characters who were as alive to me as my family or my kindergarten friends. Mum added to my treasure chest of fantasies with fairy tales of her own invention and characters from history – the victories of

Caesar and Alexander the Great. I was so inspired by the latter that for years I dreamt of one day owning a black horse that I would, of course, name Bucephalus. But for the time being, I was happy with my own little collection of toys, all five of them. Ginger Doggy and Pink Kitty were particularly special to me.

The appearance of Ginger Doggy in my life was a true miracle, because I made him up. Anyone willing to listen to a four-year-old girl would hear that 'If I behave well and don't act up, Ded Moroz [Russian Santa] is going to give me Ginger Doggy for New Year, maybe even beforehand!' I believed in him with all my heart. I thought about him constantly, imagined myself carrying him everywhere with me. I don't think that I ever wanted anything more than that Ginger Doggy.

Finally, the celebration for New Year (the main winter holiday in Russia and, by default, in Chechnya) came around at Mum's school and, being the teacher's daughter, I was allowed to attend as a special guest. I vaguely remember a crowd of schoolchildren and their parents who filled out a small unheated gym. Sometime later Ded Moroz entered, and I had to sing a song or recite a poem in exchange for a gift from him. I immediately started to show off my talents. Ded Moroz responded by playing a joyful, thunderous chord on his accordion, right in front of my face. He must have wanted to accompany me, but seeing his red-painted face so close up terrified me and I burst into tears. Mum took me in her arms and I buried my face in her neck, crying. 'Look, Lanusya,' she said soothingly – I still hear her voice decades later – 'there's Ginger Doggy!' I turned my head in disbelief and saw that it was true: Ded Moroz was handing me a soft toy with a yellow velvet belly, curly ginger wool and black beady eyes hidden behind a fringe. I stroked his fur and held him tight. It was somehow obvious to me that doggy was a boy. *How did he know what I wanted?* I wondered, looking back at the terrifying figure of Ded Moroz.

I suspect that Ginger Doggy was not really the fruit of my imagination come to life, but rather the result of a plot carefully implemented by Mum. Earlier that year, when Mum and I were visiting relatives in a nearby village, my uncle brought home a cute black-and-brown puppy, a Caucasian shepherd mix. I was convinced that the dog was mine, and no one dared to tell me otherwise. I named him Chudik and played with him endlessly. For days we ran around the dusty backyard together. I secretly fed him meat and even held a tea party, dressing the poor puppy up in a bonnet. Soon it was time to go back to Grozny and leave the puppy behind. I can't remember whether I cried when I hugged Chudik for the last time but for many years I considered him my dog 'from the village'. In the end, the memory of Chudik was replaced by my new obsession: Ginger Doggy.

After the New Year's party, I brought Ginger Doggy home and put him on the top shelf next to Pink Kitty. The two liked each other instantly and it was decided that they should be a couple. Since they were the best-looking of my toys, it was only natural that they should be king and queen of the toy kingdom. In March, on my fifth birthday, Ginger Doggy and Pink Kitty had their first child: I was given a small toy puppy and named him Prince Tuzik. I decided that all of my toys would have fixed names and personalities. No one was ever allowed to change them. 'We don't go around changing our names and stories every day,' I reasoned. 'So why should my toys be any different?'

Mum and I may have built a little oasis for ourselves, but even as a young child I wasn't entirely oblivious to my unstable surroundings and the trauma I had endured. On the surface, I'd forgotten about the war. But my imagination had a dark side. I was less frightened by the sound of gunshots or armed men than I was by dark and supernatural beings – the ghouls and monsters I thought were lurking in the shadows. Sometimes, they stepped out of my nightmares to haunt me and I found it hard to distinguish between dreams and reality.

'Mummy, I have something sitting inside my head but I don't know if it really happened or if I dreamt it.'

'What is it?'

'So, I was with Madina and Marem near the tower blocks. We had gone out to get some sweets. But then someone started shooting and we had to run into the building and hide in a corridor. We climbed to the first floor and there was this picture, which I could see through a glass door, of the three bears from the Goldilocks fairy tale, all wearing Russian shirts.'

'They are called *kosovorotka*.'

'Yes, them. The mama bear is wearing red, the daddy bear, blue, and their little son, green. And they're all smiling. But then the picture comes alive and it starts moving towards me, closer and closer. And the bears have these terrible scowls . . . And then we have to decide whether to run back towards the bullets or to stay there with these scary bears. I can't remember what happened after that. Do you think it was a dream?'

'The bears definitely weren't real. I can tell you that much.'

Mum was more interested in the shooting part. If it really happened, she would have to tell off the two teenage sisters Madina and Marem, students of Mum's who sometimes babysat me, for taking me too far away from the house. Their parents were our next-door neighbours, and during the years that bombs fell on Grozny we would share the basement with them, listening in terror to the whistling of approaching missiles. War bonded people who otherwise wouldn't have much in common – nothing brings you closer than the need to survive.

The bears continued to haunt me after that, always a two-dimensional trio confined by a frame, always moving towards me. They were a new addition to my pantheon of nightmares, the darkness monsters. Inside the abandoned, windowless three-storey building that was visible from our balcony lived a group of scary *babaikas*. Just like the bears, they were flat, and though not quite as terrifying, there were lots of them. They were the blackest shade of black, with sharp, angular features, pointed, bat-like ears and yellow glowing slits for eyes. As long as I didn't go near the building, I was safe from them. But still they hid behind my eyelids and whenever I squinted hard I could see the glow of their yellow eyes.

But the one monster I couldn't escape, the one who kept returning to me night after night, was the Tall Pale One. I would see him out of the corner of my eye, in glimpses because I was too scared to take a proper look. He would tower over me in my little bed, his head touching the two-and-a-half metre ceiling of our studio flat and, though half of his pallid face was hidden by a hood, the thin line of his lip was turned up in a distorted smile. Whenever he appeared – always without warning – I was paralysed by fear, letting out mute screams. He would stand next to my bed, never uttering a word. After several seconds I would manage to break through the barrier and yell

'MAMAAA!' In three jumps, she would be there, wrapping me in a hug with one hand and wiping beads of sweat from my forehead with the other. Then she would carry me to her side of the room, to her sofa bed, where she would guard me from the monsters.

'You know,' she told me later, 'when your nightmares got very bad, I gave you a choice: you could either sleep in your bed with a night light or you could sleep next to me with the lights off. You always chose to sleep next to me.'

And though I was always afraid of the dark, my mother's magic powers kept the Tall Pale One and the other monsters away.

'It doesn't matter how little money you have, as long as you can disguise it,' Mum lectured me while applying glossy burgundy lipstick, most likely the only one she had. This was our ritual: I would watch her get ready in the morning, and when she had finished, I would say, 'Don't forget to do *mhua mhua*,' pursing my lips to make what I thought was a blotting sound. 'Thanks for reminding me, Lanusya,' she replied every time, and elegantly blotted the excess lipstick on a tissue. Sometimes she did it by giving me a big kiss on the cheek, leaving a pinkish imprint on my skin.

No matter how dire our financial situation was between the wars, Mum made sure we always looked well put-together. Her secret was an old sewing machine and battered copies of the fashion magazine *Burda*, which included sewing patterns. Scraps of fabric bought at the market and even old gowns were transformed into sartorial miracles: a chic navy two-piece skirt suit with a square collar, a gorgeous midi-length wrap dress with a matching headband. Mum even made me a green satin princess dress covered in frills and tiny handcrafted red roses. We didn't have a lot of clothes but everything we owned was well-fitting and looked expensive. Rumours of Mum's sewing talents spread through the neighbourhood and soon she was sewing skirts to make a little extra money. From time to time our flat was crowded with shy adolescent girls who twisted and turned while Mum took their measurements.

All dressed up, we would head to the only remaining patisserie in the city called Stolychnyi for a glass of juice and a slice of cake, our sacred Sunday tradition. It was never too busy; there were rarely more than two or three tables occupied. Stolychnyi seemed like the fanciest place in the world to me and, stepping inside in my finest outfit, I always tried to behave like a lady, remembering Mum's instructions: 'Sit up straight, keep your elbows off the table, chew with your mouth closed.' But something more delightful even than the cake was to be found in the corner of the patisserie: a beautiful fish tank with real golden fish. Mesmerised, I would glue myself to the glass and watch as the fish darted indifferently from one corner of their little blue-and-green world to another. It is one of my most magical memories from that time.

'I could have bought a hunk of meat with that money,' Mum would tell me. 'My friends scolded me for spending it on cake. But it was more important to me that you had a normal childhood.'

I was entirely convinced by the illusion of normality that my mother painstakingly sustained, and was turning out to be a very happy-go-lucky child. Many truths only became clear to me when I was older: that the school had stopped paying teachers' salaries and we survived only thanks to Mum's work as a private tutor and a seamstress; that Mum would often give up her meals so I could eat; that she waited for me to fall asleep and then cried alone in the kitchen.

Sometimes she would take me along to her tutoring jobs and I had a peek at posh interiors with large TVs and polished cabinets that occupied an entire wall. I sighed, looking at beautiful Barbie dolls and luxurious plastic palm trees, and politely accepted sweets from the generous parents of Mum's pupils. I'm not exactly sure how they managed to afford such a different lifestyle to ours, but Chechens are quite entrepreneurial. Some found a way to make money, once the fighting stopped. Mum pretended not to notice the plastic bags full of snacks that some women sneaked inside her handbag. But they weren't all for me. At home, Mum tutored children from poor families who struggled at school, helping them with whatever subject they found most challenging and feeding them whatever modest meal she had made the previous day. Throughout our years in Grozny, we were always bumping into her students in the markets and streets. When they saw her, their faces would light up with sincere smiles: 'Natalia Husseinovna!' they would gasp, 'It's been so long!'

'You were our favourite teacher! So strict but also fair! Remember how you kicked me out of the classroom for chatting?'

'Oh, and remember when Lana snitched on us when we cheated in a test?' Mum replied that this was nonsense and I never told on anyone. She was perfectly capable of detecting cheaters all by herself.

Mum had so many jobs that I never understood how she found time to do them all. She didn't always manage it perfectly. She forgot to pick me up from kindergarten a number of times and left me with neighbours for longer than I wished. On top of her busy schedule of teaching, tutoring, sewing and caring for me, she also volunteered as press secretary for an organisation with an impossibly long name in Russian – the Prisoners of Filtration Camps – *and* made documentaries for a Grozny TV channel. On days when there was no kindergarten (which happened often) and the neighbours were busy, Mum would take me on her rounds, to school, to tutoring sessions, to her office. 'Natasha's little tail' friends and colleagues would call me, laughing, whenever they saw us together, hand in hand. We had relatives who would have been happy to look after me, but they were far away, in the rural villages. Besides, I never minded sitting in a corner with a book. As long as I was with Mum, I was content. I loved all the attention from teachers and students I got when she took me to her school, and all the free fried *belyashi* with mince I was given by the cafeteria cook.

The atmosphere was very different at the Prisoners of the Filtration Camps office, where I was also left to my own devices. I would wander the narrow, dungeon-like corridors while Mum had meetings. People often stopped me, moved by a child's presence, and I would return with presents: sweets, chocolates, sometimes coins. One time, I saw a moustachioed man with kind eyes in one of the rooms. He invited me in and sat me on his lap, cracking jokes. 'Are you my dad?' I asked him bluntly. He shook his head with a smile. 'Lanusya, there you are!' Mum suddenly appeared in the doorway. She apologised to the man on my behalf and as I climbed down, he slipped a small banknote discreetly into my hand. That must have been the last time I confused a man with a moustache for my father. After that episode, he disappeared from my mind almost entirely.

As if mimicking that sombre place, Mum's demeanour was very different at the office. She rarely smiled during the long conversations she had with the streams of men and women who came and went. One thing that Mum and her colleagues repeated in whispered conversations and that stuck in my mind like a burdock sticks to a dress was 'PAP1'. At first it didn't mean anything to me, but it gave me a strange sensation when I repeated it to myself again and again until it stopped making sense. One day, I tagged along with Mum and a cameraman called Kazbek on a trip to get footage for one of her documentaries, and as we drove Mum whispered, 'Look Lanusya, that's PAP1.' I raised my eyes and saw a large car park in front of a bus depot. *So that was all that mysterious, terrible word referred to? A bus depot?*

We parked the car on the abandoned lot. 'Wait in the car,' Mum instructed, and she disappeared behind the gates with Kazbek. There was not a soul around. All I could see was an empty asphalt yard behind the fence. As the minutes ticked by, I began to grow anxious: why had Mum gone into that place? When would they come back?

Inside, Mum and Kazbek were busy filming. Despite its unremarkable exterior, the bus depot had housed one of the most notorious illegal prisons in Chechnya. The copies of the documentaries Mum made must have been lost or erased but she saved all the handwritten notes from her interviews and typed them up on an old typewriter at the Prisoners of the Filtration Camps office. The yellowed pages with frayed edges describe PAP1: 'This is a former motor transport business, but in January 1995 it became a giant monster that wrapped its tentacles around the whole of Chechnya. It suddenly gripped its unsuspecting victim in a death choke and dragged it here, to its greedy belly.'

The bloodstained cellars that Mum and Kazbek visited had once been occupied by prisoners. The script continued: 'It was very difficult to get out of here, very difficult to stay alive. Victims came here in broad daylight and late at night with their hands twisted behind their backs or bags on their heads. The cells opened their beastly mouths and terrible instruments of torture began to break bones, destinies, lives . . .'

Russian troops might have withdrawn from Chechnya (for the time being) but their bloody legacy remained. Officials claimed the 'filtering' system was simply used to separate militants from civilians. In reality, federals seized people indiscriminately, from their homes or in the middle of the street, and detained them under invented pretexts such as missing identity papers. Detainees were taken to checkpoints, stripped and searched for tell-tale signs of their connection to the rebels, such as bruises on the shoulder that indicated having carried a Kalashnikov. They would then be transferred to filtration camps, where they would be humiliated, beaten, tortured for weeks and sometimes months on end, until eventually they were left spitting out their teeth along with confessions for crimes they had never committed. Many didn't make it out alive and were buried right there at the camp, in the graves dug for them by other prisoners. Those who survived emerged from PAP1 with horrifying tales of dark, cold chambers and sadistic interrogators. It was these testimonies that my mother collected, asking the victims, 'Tell me about the war.'

Mum's documentaries humanised the survivors of these camps, reminding you they could have been a neighbour or a loved one. There was a story of two teenage brothers who were picked up as they were playing in the street. One had an old rouble in his pocket, which the federals took to be a sure sign of cooperation with the militants. There began an odyssey that carried both brothers through various detention centres, including PAP1. They were released without any identification papers, then moments later detained again by another squad who brought them, once again, to PAP1, much to the amusement of their drunken captors. A father and a son were kidnapped together, beaten and then forced to lie on top of each other to make space for more prisoners. A married couple, Hedi Daudova and Yakub Dudayev, were imprisoned and tortured at the Khankala airbase. Yakub was accused of being related to President Dudayev, his wife 'charged' with providing medical assistance to the militants. The federals, my mother's notes reveal, derived a sick pleasure from beating the husband and wife in front of each other.

One subject of Mum's documentaries that left a particularly strong impression on her was a young bedridden man named Ruslan Dzhapkayev. His injuries at the hands of the federals had left him crippled for life, and he confessed to her that instant death would have been a better fate than what he'd been put through:

> These institutions were called filters, designed to identify militants, but it seems to me that those who worked there were also filtered,

in order to select the ones most cruel, mentally deranged, completely devoid of humanity. And then these men were armed with such instruments of torture and murder that they became real monsters, who could only be flattered by comparison with animals.

For the victims, sharing their stories publicly required an unfathomable amount of courage. The harrowing accounts that Mum collected were compiled into an impactful but dark anthology of human suffering. At least 200,000 people passed through the filtration camps during the first Chechen war, and the crimes of their captors went unpunished. Preserving the testimonies of those who lived through this hell was the first step in pursuing justice. Mum wanted to expose the extent of the horror that had been inflicted on innocent Chechens. She believed that a story well told could soothe, educate and even save lives.

Sometimes I eavesdropped as she conducted interviews; she couldn't stop me. Other times I tuned out entirely, distracted by a book or colouring pencils. After a while, I became so inured to hearing survivors' accounts in the background of our lives that when I met someone my first question would be, 'Were you ever a prisoner of a filtration camp?' I believed it was something of a rite of passage.

Mum and Kazbek took their time filming at PAP1 while I waited in the locked car, surrounded by deafening silence. I started to panic. When at last they reappeared and got back in the car, there was a strange mood hanging in the air, as if the dark spirit of that awful place had attached itself to us. Not knowing how to process my deep unease, I resorted to throwing a tantrum after hitting my head slightly on the car window. This broke the tension, as both Mum and Kazbek tried to console me, thinking my injury worse than it actually was.

To reward me for being a brave girl – and because Kazbek needed a few more aerial shots – Mum led us to the rooftop of a nearby charred building. A concrete fence that came up to my shoulder marked the edge, and Mum lifted me up so that I could get a better look over it. I still remember the nervousness that overtook me as I cautiously glanced over the grey cityscape, Mum's hands gripping my sides. It wasn't the height or the crumbled tower blocks with shattered windows that scared me, nor was it the blackened, rain-drenched pavements or the naked trees, or even our proximity to a place that used to be hell on earth. What daunted me was the emptiness of the streets, as if someone had scooped all the people up and made them disappear so that the three of us were the only ones left alive. And then, what was that, flashing in the window below? Was it the yellow glow of the *babaikas'* eyes? I started to cry again.

'Don't be scared, Lanusya, we'll go now,' Mum reassured me, pulling me back from the ledge. 'But shall we maybe record a little music video while we're here? Let's sing your favourite song!'

I stopped crying instantly and composed myself. If there was one thing that I loved more than reading and making up stories, it was singing at the top of my voice. Specifically, I loved to sing that song everyone knows from the movie *Titanic*. Kazbek pointed to where I should stand, pressed record, and suddenly the anxiety, the confusion, the shadow of PAPI and its victims all disappeared. I was just a child again, delighting my mum with my singing.

I watched the video for the first time several years later. I am standing in a red-and-white striped dress decorated with ribbons, singing 'My Heart Will Go On' by Celine Dion. I don't know the words and don't speak any English, so I make it up as I go along. When I get to the chorus – 'Once more you open the door', which in my rendition sounds something like 'Ye shmooshen de doo' – I belt it out, my voice reaching a high-pitched scream. Mum loved my performance of the song so much that she requested I repeat it often, complete with passionate mispronunciations. Her colleague from school, the English teacher who actually knew the words, was an even bigger fan. Whenever I remember that day, this is what springs to my mind: the rooftop, the striped dress and the song, not the fear I felt looking across the half-abandoned city.

This chaotic interbellum period lasted only three years. Chechnya was now independent, but it was also economically devastated, politically fractured and highly unstable. An abundance of guns and mass unemployment is never a good mix and the incumbent president Aslan Maskhadov didn't have a firm grip on power. Skirmishes broke out between the micro-armies of competing warlords. Racketeering and kidnappings for ransom became commonplace. One of the most notorious warlords, Arbi Barayev, and his gang were responsible for the kidnapping of four foreign telecommunications engineers, three British men and a New Zealander. All four were subsequently found dead; they had been decapitated. These horrific acts of violence, as well as inflicting anguish on the victims' families, made international audiences cool towards the plight of Chechen independence. Mum was bitterly disappointed by most local politicians, whether they were pro- or anti-Russian. She thought that ordinary Chechens, many of whom had lost loved ones in the fight for freedom, deserved far better.

Meanwhile, the Russian military command was itching for payback, still sore at being humiliated by a bunch of rebels. In August 1999 a Soviet KGB spy and former head of the Federal Security Service or FSB, Vladimir Putin, became acting prime minister – a firm right-hand man to the decrepit and perpetually drunk Boris Yeltsin. He was part of a group that sought to seize back power from the oligarchs who dominated Russia during the nineties and to restore the pride of the Russian state. Putin was presented with his opportunity when, the very same month, a military squad headed by Shamil Basayev invaded Dagestan, Chechnya's neighbouring republic. This move, which no one saw coming, made Basayev a hated figure both in Dagestan and Chechnya. Only a small, ideologically driven group of fanatics were in favour of the incursion.

The Russian response would mark the beginning of the second Chechen war. A spate of apartment bombings that occurred between 4 and 16 September in Moscow – which killed more than 300 people – were blamed on Chechen terrorists, though no group has ever claimed responsibility and there were rumours and circumstantial evidence that pointed to the involvement of Russian security services. Some saw it as a deliberate, coordinated effort by them to create a climate of fear that would trigger the war with Chechnya and bring Putin to the presidency. These suspicions were fuelled by the arrest of three FSB agents on 22 September by local police in Ryazan, after they were found to have planted a suspicious device, resembling the ones that had been used in the bombings, in the basement of an apartment block. The next day, the head of the FSB claimed that this had been an anti-terror drill and that the suspicious device had simply been filled with sugar. The agents were released, and Kremlin officials praised the vigilance of the residents, while simultaneously ordering the aerial bombardment of Grozny that marked the beginning of the second Chechen war.

Faced with the spectre of another war, Mum decided to return with me to the safety of Yekaterinburg. She didn't want me to have to live under bombs again. In mid-September, she scraped together a ludicrous sum of money for train tickets departing from Stavropol, a city about 400 kilometres from Grozny. By then, passenger trains weren't running from Chechnya. We left via the so-called road of life, the motorway used by thousands of refugees to escape.

We left everything behind – our flat, our new collection of books, even Manya, the cat. My grandfather's crystal flutes were neatly wrapped in rags and left with the neighbours once again for safekeeping. Until we returned.

3
Baba
1999–2000

The Kremlin had learnt from the disastrous result of the first Chechen war, and changed its tactics. They clamped down on reporting that painted Chechens in a sympathetic light and exposed the cruelty and ineptitude of the Russian army. Grotesque myths and misinformation were intentionally spread, about a so-called genocide of Russian civilians in Grozny, about Chechen militants playing football with the heads of enemy soldiers. By the time the second war broke out, in 1999, the state-controlled Russian media was running constant propaganda stories that portrayed all Chechens as crooks and terrorists. Those seeking refuge in Russia were not welcome. It wasn't hard to stir up this hostility, in part because of the terror attacks conducted by Basayev and his militants, but mostly because racist and xenophobic attitudes towards the 'other' were deeply ingrained in Russian society. In major cities, especially Moscow and St Petersburg, 'persons of Caucasian nationality' – in other words, anyone with dark eyes and hair – were racially profiled by the police and forced to produce documents. Beatings and false imprisonment by law enforcement officers became the norm.

As my mother and I made our escape by train, Chechen passengers were ordered out of the compartments, along with their luggage, at every stop, even in the middle of the night. Everyone else was left in their seats. Local authorities and the police knew that refugees were leaving the warzone in droves, and so with crazed enthusiasm they conducted 'bomb searches', ransacking bags and helping themselves to whatever they fancied as they went. Hints were made that Mum would have to pay if we wanted to continue our journey. So, she did. And again, and again, until our modest savings were heavily depleted.

A lady pushing a cart full of snacks and drinks back and forth through the train kept trying to persuade Mum to buy something. 'I kept saying no,' Mum remembered later. 'Then she put a packet of crisps into your hands, hoping that you would ask me to buy it. You gave me such a pitiful look but all I could say was, "Lanusya, we really don't have any money." That woman grabbed the packet back out of your hands, cursing both of us.' By the time we arrived in Yekaterinburg, I had had nothing but little scraps of food. Mum hadn't eaten for almost two days.

When Mum and I arrived on Auntie Sveta's doorstep, suitcases in hand, no questions were asked. Without hesitation, Sveta and her husband, Andrey, took us in, making sure we felt welcome and comfortable. Both scientists, they lived in battered, multi-storey accommodation provided by their research institute – academic careers were not as financially rewarding as racketeering in this new Russia. Their tiny flat had just one bedroom, which belonged to my cousin Sasha, and Auntie Sveta and Uncle Andrey slept in the living room. There was barely an inch of space left but, endlessly generous, Auntie Sveta offered us Sasha's bedroom, moving him into the living room with them. This sacrifice was made in a casual, matter-of-fact manner; making a big deal of it would have been considered almost embarrassing. That was what family was for.

The very next day, sporting a full denim outfit (courtesy of Sasha's hand-me-downs), I was learning to roller-skate outside on the pavement, which was slippery and glistening after a rain shower. Mum was running behind me with her arms outstretched, ready to catch me if I fell. With every burst of laughter, the tension from our journey seemed to lift from my body. Nothing bad could happen to me here as long as Mum was beside me.

The days that followed were filled with family reunions and expeditions to the nearby gold- and auburn-hued woods. At a picnic with all of my cousins and aunt, I insisted on shedding my bright overalls to dip into a freezing river, and I splashed in the water until my lips turned blue. For the time being, the war was contained within the black box of the TV, far, far away. Mum must have felt a sickening sense of déjà vu, watching helplessly as events unfolded on the screen while I played with Sasha in the other room. The Russian reports never used the word 'war', instead referring to a 'counterterrorist operation' that would crush the rebels in a swift series of targeted offensives. That's how the Kremlin tried to sell it.

Mum knew the only way to find out the truth about what was happening was to go back, and it wasn't long until she started questioning, *What am I still doing here now that my child is safe?* Mum was by this time an experienced activist and journalist, adept at operating a camera and asking people the right questions. She could put her skills to good use on the ground in Chechnya. And besides, we'd left in such a hurry that she hadn't managed to sort out the flat. What if something happened to it? She would only go for two weeks, three at most. Auntie Sveta would be happy to look after me while she was away.

At the start of October 1999, only a few short weeks after we had arrived at Auntie Sveta's, Mum made her way back to the war zone, not knowing what awaited her there.

Years later, when I was trying to find out what exactly Mum was doing in Chechnya during those weeks, I came across an old notepad. Mum wasn't one to keep a diary; most of her planners were reserved for names and addresses accompanied by the occasional dry two-sentence descriptions. But this one was different. Words etched in red ink on its crumpled old pages, obviously written down with a sense of urgency, described one of the most despicable war crimes committed by the Russian army in Chechnya: the infamous air strike on Grozny market on 21 October 1999, which killed at least 118 people.

The pages told of how, sometime after six o'clock in the evening, Mum had boarded a bus near the former Central Post Office in Grozny, planning to visit a friend and return home before dark. Market day was coming to an end, and she was accompanied by women with heavy bags. Suddenly, as the last passengers boarded the bus, there was 'a terrible roar, and a huge brown cloud flew right at us'. Mum describes how she and the other passengers jumped off the bus and ran towards a nearby bombed-out building: 'The man who was one step ahead of me fell. The first-floor remnants of the old brick building sheltered us from death. There was darkness all around – the air was grey with specks of dust.'

The explosions continued, and those taking cover under the rubble asked each other where the nearest hospital was. My mother knew it was just a block away, but, she wrote, 'Do we dare move?'

A twelve-year-old girl was brought in. She was screaming, and her face and hands were covered in blood. 'Finally,' Mum wrote, 'the darkness cleared a little and we stepped out into the street.' The man who had fallen in front of her was still lying face down. 'Did he fall so hard?' my mother wondered.

We started to shake him, then we turned him over and lifted him up. His head tilted back, his eyes rolled up. The entire back of his jacket was wet. I couldn't understand why, because there was no rain. I just couldn't believe he was dead. Three metres away there was a jeep filled with people wearing military uniforms. We asked them to take him to the hospital, but they ignored us. I looked inside the ruins again and saw a man dressed in brown camouflage. The camouflage was barely visible because the whole of his back was one bloody wound. That's when I started running!

Mum tried to stay close to the walls of the houses, but didn't know from which direction the next strike would come. She was out of breath, her lungs clogged with brick dust. By pure chance, she had witnessed one of the most infamous moments of the conflict.

She later learnt that the missile that had landed near the bus station had done less damage than the others dropped that day – two had exploded near a maternity hospital and another had been dropped on a village mosque. In the market, where women sometimes traded long into the night, the death toll was at its worst. It was high, too, in the village of Kalinin, where people had been gathered for prayer. The missile that had struck the maternity hospital killed fifteen women and thirteen newborns.

We took around twelve wounded and dead to the city hospital, N9. There were about seventy-five dead and more than 150 wounded. So many women! Five girls were brought from the village of Kalinin. They had been struck when they were fetching water.

In total across the different sites, at least 140 civilians were killed that day, and around 400 were wounded. To Mum's anger, the story presented on national Russian TV sounded very different. The military command and politicians spoke of 'targeted military strikes' that were designed to eliminate rebels and spare civilian lives. At the same time, it was claimed that the attacks were 'terror acts' carried out by Chechens, and the market itself was an arms den. This wasn't a coherent cover-up but an array of contradictory, implausible explanations. Most Russian journalists, bar a few, parroted the official line rather than challenging it. While Western powers condemned the missile attacks and human rights organisations recorded the testimonies of survivors, the Kremlin was waging its own information war, breaking into a chorus of lies. There would be no repeat of the first Chechen war, when free media ran the narrative. 'That evening,' Mum wrote, 'I stood in front of the TV and, just like the day before, I was choking, this time not from dust but from bewilderment and rage.' She had managed to get out of Grozny and spend the night in the neighbouring city of Nazran, in the safety of the neighbouring Ingush Republic.

Following the missile attack, tens of thousands of refugees flocked to the borders of Chechnya. An official order issued by General Vladimir Shamanov, aptly nicknamed 'the butcher' for his cruel and illegal conduct of the war, forbade civilians from exiting the war zone. Russian media alleged that a 'safety corridor' was being set up at a checkpoint, Kavkaz-1, near the border with Ingushetia. This was another lie. When exhausted, hungry families, in a haphazard column of vehicles, reached the border, they were attacked from the air by a fleet of SU-25 jets. The strikes, ordered by Shamanov, caused havoc, prompting the terrified people to abandon their cars and run for shelter. According to one survivor's account, whenever someone attempted to run back to the road and rescue the wounded, they were shot at by snipers. The nearby hospital was without electricity and running water, its supplies so depleted that locals had to ransack their homes for bandages and antiseptic. At least twenty-three people were killed that day, among them a young woman who was eight months pregnant and five children. It was a cold-blooded massacre. By then, Chechen president Aslan Maskhadov had sent a peace proposal to the

Kremlin, but it was rejected. Calls for Western intervention fell on deaf ears.

Meanwhile in Yekaterinburg, Grozny was beginning to seem like a dream. A few months can seem like a decade to a five-year-old, and I soon started to forget the names of our neighbours in the city I had left behind, and even the Chechen language. For some reason the only Chechen word that stayed firmly in my mind was *gant* which means 'chair'.

Mum returned from Chechnya in November 1999, and we looked forward to celebrating the New Year – the beginning of a new millennium – together in snow-covered Yekaterinburg. My days were simple then. I would not start school for another year, so when the rest of the family was at school or at work, I had no other option but to follow Mum everywhere, including to a new place with a mysterious name: Memorial.

My first memory of Memorial is of a pair of square masks, carved in black granite, one looking forward and the other back. The monument stood in the corner of the largest room in the office, and the faces seemed to watch you wherever you went. Perhaps that was the sculptor's intention, as it was dedicated to the victims of Stalin's repressions. Both tribal-style masks captured an expression of mute sorrow. It is no wonder that, as a sensitive child, I always wanted to direct my gaze towards more cheerful objects. During one of the New Year's office parties, Mum persuaded me to pose in a pretty red dress in front of the masks and the result was a rather funny photograph of me forcing a smile through clenched teeth, as if I'm expecting the statues to attack me from behind at any moment.

Memorial was created during perestroika, a period of increased openness and liberalisation, by a group of prominent dissidents. Their goal was to document evidence of state repression during Communism. The branch of the organisation I was first introduced to in Yekaterinburg was just one in a vast network that spread all over post-Soviet Russia, with its main headquarters in Moscow. As Russia became a democracy, at least in name, the need for holding the government to account only increased. The human rights branch of Memorial sent out missions to conflict zones along all the seams of the former empire – Transnistria, Nagorno-Karabakh, South Ossetia and, of course, Chechnya. I often wondered how many times Mum crossed paths, during that time in Yekaterinburg, with her future colleagues Oleg Orlov, Alexander 'Sasha' Cherkasov and others.

The people of Memorial were fearless, throwing themselves into the heart of any action. Mum's future colleagues were near Chechnya from the first days of the second war, but getting in was tough. At a certain point, only people registered at Chechen addresses were allowed to enter through checkpoints, after thorough passport checks. Memorial needed local activists who knew the situation on the ground. Since Mum was already freelancing with them and had risked her life to gather information about Russian war crimes, her name was at the top of their list. Soon, she would go back to Chechnya, this time as a full-time Memorial employee.

I remember sitting quietly in the common room of the Yekaterinburg Memorial office, flipping through the books. The most accessible one I could find was an illustrated *Declaration of the Rights of the Child*, which stated that every child is entitled to their name and nationality, to a free education and to special assistance if they're handicapped. But the pictures were boring and there weren't enough of them anyhow. When my patience ran out, I would sneak into the corridor and peek through the door of Mum's office to see if she could come and play with me. But she was always busy talking to people. She was always very serious there.

Mum warned me that she would soon have to go back to Chechnya. But not until my sixth birthday, she promised, which was still three months away. The year 2000 began in the most delightful way, with presents for the New Year. I was given a blonde Barbie named Jessica; she came with a smaller doll called Mindy – they were mother and daughter, just like Mum and me. Mum also had a fur coat made to keep me warm in the harsh Ural winter. The seamstress was slow, and I remember wishing that she'd never finish her job, as though that would mean that Mum would stay. When the coat was done, a cosy brown thing with drawstrings on the hood shaped like tiny mushrooms, it made me look like a teddy bear.

The most meaningful present Mum gave me was a book she'd written herself. 'Take care of it,' she told me, handing me a file of A4 pages with a tangerine-coloured cover, tied with a gold ribbon. On the front she'd written 'Mum's Fairytales' and inside was every bedtime story she'd ever made up for me. As she prepared to return to the war zone, she wanted to make sure a piece of her would stay with me. I treasured the book, but at the time, though I was embarrassed to admit it, my favourite parting gift of all was a bubble-gum-pink stroller for Mindy.

The day Mum went back to the war, in March 2000, the world was covered in snow. After dropping me off in Kamyshlov at my grandmother's, she boarded a train, heading back into the unknown. Hand in hand, Baba and I walked alongside her carriage, watching her face in the window as the train picked up speed. This time, I would not forget her.

Granny Klava – Baba, as we called her – was different then. A woman with a no-nonsense attitude, she was short and stocky, with hair cut in a bob that she hid beneath a triangular headscarf. She was deaf in both ears, so that I had to talk loudly into her hearing aids to be heard. Sometimes she used to say that she became deaf after she'd caught a terrible flu, other times she blamed the mill where she used to work. I never found out which was the real reason.

Like my grandfather Hussein, Baba had lived a very hard life. Born in Kamyshlov in 1930, Klavdia, or Klava for short, was a younger sister to two brothers, Sergey and Leonid. Her youngest brother Boris was born a few years later. Kamyshlov was a typical Urals town, built alongside the river Pyshma, with pokey wooden houses, a church and mud tracks for roads. Klava's father had been killed in strange circumstances when she was three years old: her mother, Elizaveta, only discovered his death when, out looking for her missing husband, she saw a woman selling his blood-stained clothes at the market. When the Second World War started, Klava was eleven. Her older brothers enlisted right away, Leonid adding a few years to his age to be eligible. Sergey, who was working on a hospital train, went missing in action in 1941. Leonid was killed near Stalingrad in 1943. Meanwhile, life in the Urals during the war was cold and hungry. Klava and Boris shared one pair of shoes between them and wore them in turns as they scoured the frozen fields for potatoes. After one of these outings, Boris became ill with pneumonia and perished in weeks.

By the time the Soviet Union was celebrating its victory over Hitler, all that was left of Klava's family was her and her embittered mother, who never missed a chance to bully her daughter. Without an education certificate – Klava had abandoned her studies after middle school, tired of her classmates laughing at her ragged clothes – she started working at the mill that would become her job for decades.

Aged twenty-seven, Klava was considered nearly a spinster, her bad hearing damaging her marriage prospects. Other than recounting old grudges against neighbours, she didn't much like to dwell on the past, but from Mum and her siblings I managed to piece together most of the story of how she and Hussein had met. After being separated from his family during the deportation, my grandfather ended up attaching himself to a group of petty criminals. We don't know much about the time he spent in Kyrgyzstan, exiled and alone; he never spoke about it. Mum and later my aunt filled in the blanks. A brawl broke out between the criminals who had 'adopted' Hussein and another group of men at a restaurant. Knives were involved. The trouble was their rivals turned out to be no ordinary individuals but KGB agents. It was decided that Hussein should take the fall as he was a minor, though he had not started the fight. Perhaps they thought he would only spend a couple of years in juvenile detention. The boy was sent to serve his sentence in a small provincial town called Kamyshlov in the Ural region, about 200 kilometres from Yekaterinburg, where, half a century later, I would be born. The years stretched on for Hussein. We can only speculate as to why his sentence kept being prolonged. Was it because of that line in his passport that said he was a Chechen, an enemy of the people?

Several years later, still in prison, Hussein started corresponding with a Russian woman called Klava. Letters between inmates and women from the outside were encouraged by the prison administration because if the epistolary romance led to marriage, those men had somewhere to go once they got out. A family man, they reasoned, is less likely to return to a life of crime. Shortly after his release, sometime in 1957, Hussein and Klava got married. By the age of twenty-four or twenty-five, he had spent most of his youth in prison. He had lost his homeland, his family, his language and even his first name –

for convenience, people called him Andrey, dropping the foreign-sounding Hussein.

To borrow from Tolstoy, the Estemirov family was unhappy in its own way. The family – two parents, four children and their grandmother Elizaveta – occupied two small rooms with no amenities on the first-floor of a shabby wooden apartment block. Those suffocating rooms turned into a battleground between the spouses, with verbal abuse often turning physical. Hussein was a drunk like most men in forgotten Russian towns, stumbling home with shaking hands and empty pockets. He was a womaniser too, most likely due to his natural charisma and 'exotic' dark features, which made him rather dashing. During those fights, all four children used to jump between their parents and shield their mother from fists, while the house was would shake with the screams.

Natasha, the eldest, was a shy girl, tall and lean like a tree, with delicate wrists and ankles. She had fantastically expressive eyes, malachite-green like her mother's. Her oval face with high cheekbones was framed by wavy light-brown hair. She rarely smiled in photographs, but seriousness suited her somehow. Whenever the home situation became too much to bear, Natasha would escape into books and nature. The Ural forests of ancient, aromatic pine trees stretch for miles and miles. They are dark and luscious, and rich with gifts; all four siblings and their friends would disappear into them for hours at a time, foraging summer berries to eat and to turn into sweet jam back at home.

'God is in nature,' Hussein used to tell his eldest daughter whenever he took her to the forest, pointing out birds and rare plants. He taught her how to throw a knife so that it thudded into the thick pine trunks. Natasha didn't like weapons but cherished those rare moments with her father when he wasn't drunk or angry. 'He could have been a great man,' she reminisced years later. 'He may not have had much of an education, but he was very intelligent. And he was always trying to learn more, he loved to read.'

Hussein passed on his love of reading to Natasha. She would often be found hiding in a corner where no one would bother her, her head buried in a book. History books interested her most of all. Sometimes she would defy her father's orders – he felt she was too young for such serious topics – and steal an old volume on Peter the Great from the top shelf. The tales of great men, wars, political drama and intriguing customs must have been a thirst-quenching escape from a dull, troubled reality. She turned to the living for stories too, pestering her grandma Elizaveta to tell her about the olden days. Elizaveta was something of a local witch and fortune teller, who read fortunes with the help of a pillow. Once, she helped an aggrieved family whose horses had been stolen by pointing out the exact location on a map where the thieves were hiding them.

In 1956, Soviet leader Nikita Khrushchev allowed the Chechens and Ingush to return to their homes from Central Asia. However, they were strictly prohibited from talking about the deportation of 1944. Upon their return, they found their homes occupied by new inhabitants – mostly Russians, but also people of other ethnicities from the North Caucasus. Hussein's three sisters were all married with children when they found their little brother again. By that time he had spent at least six years in prison, in the faraway Urals. Exactly how they reconnected was unclear but once the family was in touch again, visits followed. The sisters sent 'envoys' to Kamyshlov in the form of various uncles and cousins who travelled by motorbike over 2,500 kilometres, all the way from Chechnya. The town was a welcome pit stop on the way to various *shabashka* – low-paid construction jobs that Chechens left for in Russia because there was no work back home. Hussein and Klava hosted them all in the tiny flat, conjuring extra sleeping places out of thin air. Whenever they had enough money – which was mostly due to thrifty and hardworking Klava – the entire Estemirov clan travelled to Chechnya for a visit.

They even tried to move back, when Natasha was about seven. But the stay only lasted a few months since there were no jobs available. So the family packed up and returned to Kamyshlov.

Then, when Natasha was in her late teens, the Estemirov household was shaken up all over again when Hussein decided to move back to Chechnya on his own. Lack of job prospects or a clear plan didn't deter him. His sisters would be thrilled to have their youngest brother, the only surviving man of the family, back by their side, and

45

they would help him settle in. For Hussein that ancestral voice, the ghost of a childhood cut short, was calling.

'Nonsense,' Klava would protest decades later when asked about this. 'He owed everyone money, that's why he took off. For weeks after he was gone, I had neighbours knocking on my door demanding I pay them back. Well, I told them it was not my debt to settle and they should pay a visit to Andrey in Chechnya.'

Natasha followed her father to Chechnya a few months later.

I always wondered what it was that prompted her to follow him there and make the choice to become a Chechen. Had those few months, when she was seven years old, left her with such an impression that she found herself aching to return? Or was it the mysterious, magnetic pull of the homeland that is especially pronounced in the psyche of Chechen people? Or the beauty of the landscape and the temperate climate, with its mild winters and fruit-bearing summers.

I think it is most likely that she fell in love with the people. Her aunts had welcomed them with open arms when they moved, exuding warmth. Natasha had met a whole host of cousins of a similar age to her, with whom she had become fast friends and exchanged letters for many years afterwards. In contrast to the grim surroundings and dysfunction that she had left behind in Kamyshlov, Chechnya radiated hospitality and joy. Natasha gravitated towards the kindness of her extended Chechen family like a flower reaching towards the sun.

So, confronted with the prospect of being forced to teach in a remote Siberian town as part of a mandatory Soviet work assignment, she packed her few belongings in a bag and followed her father to Chechnya to continue her studies at Grozny State University.

There was, of course, another side to the culture – a rigidity born of conservative tradition, gossip and gender inequality. Neighbours had whispered when they had moved there about the strange Nokhchi-Gaski, 'Chechen-Russians'. She struggled with the impossibly difficult Chechen language, and never quite managed to shake off the label of 'that Russian woman'. But that didn't stop her feeling an affinity for her people. Where there was ugliness and injustice, she believed, there was always the potential for beauty, a way to make things better. It's why after choosing Grozny that first time she found herself drawn back there again and again, braving the bullets and bombs while leaving me with Baba for safekeeping.

Baba still lived in the same tiny flat where she'd raised her four children. The house had been built as basic, temporary accommodation in the early 1950s but it still stood over forty years later, housing twelve families. I can still summon the specific scent of that building when I close my eyes – a mixture of dust, wet wood and smoke.

As none of the flats had a bathroom, toilet, running water or heating, Baba had to carry water from a pond fed by a running stream about a kilometre away. There were toilets in the backyard, behind the rubbish bins, and the two combined brewed an unspeakable smell that not even sub-zero temperatures could suppress. For that reason, and because the area behind the bins was the local drunkards' favourite spot, Baba set up a bucket in her flat that was emptied once a day. As for washing, once a week we took a trip to a local *banya*, public baths with plenty of hot running water. There was a wood burner in the living room that doubled as a rubbish incinerator. In the bedroom, two beds stood along the walls with large carpets hanging above them, for warmth and decor, as was standard in ex-Soviet homes. There were no telephones, and letters from Grozny took months to arrive. The flat was big enough for the two of us, but I did wonder how it had accommodated a family of seven in the past.

In the weeks following Mum's return to Grozny, Baba and I developed a routine. That March was particularly cold and the streets were wrapped in thick layers of snow. Each morning we would get up and venture out for groceries, walking through empty streets and backyards. Kamyshlov is a small provincial town, lost in the plains of the Urals. As I remember it, it was always rundown and unkempt. Walking from Baba's home on the outskirts of the city, we would see pretty houses built in a traditional Russian style, painted in bright colours and decorated with intricate carvings. But as we got closer to the town centre we'd find five-storey concrete houses scarred with deep crumbling cracks. The supermarket was a grim-looking pale-blue building with bars on the windows and a very specific Soviet smell ingrained in its large refrigerators: boiled sausage and chlorine. I secretly liked it. Baba picked the groceries carefully, chatting to the cashier, and once she was done, I would get a lolly and a poppy-seed bun. Afterwards, we would make our way home, a slow journey that was interrupted every ten minutes by Baba's acquaintances. While she spoke, I would skip around impatiently or disappear into a nearby playground, walking past the drunks huddled together on benches or wandering through the streets, swaying from side to side.

Baba waddled, hands crossed behind her back, and because of her gait we called her Granny Duck. I jumped around beside her, telling her whatever nonsense was in my mind. I worshipped my grandmother because I thought that she believed my tall tales – a quality always appreciated by children with wild imaginations. I invented the most unbelievable stories, usually involving family members and talking animals.

'One time,' I would begin, 'Uncle Andrey, Cousin Sasha and I went for a walk in the woods. I got lost and fell into a deep pit, but somehow managed not to break a single bone! The snow protected me. And then, Uncle Andrey finally found me, but he didn't have a rope to throw. So instead he chopped down a pine tree and quickly made a ladder. And I was saved!'

While telling the story, I would sneakily watch Baba's face. *Did she buy it?* Baba puffed, groaned and looked at her feet, giving no reaction – that means she believes it! My stories gradually became more fantastical:

'Once, Sasha and I went down a mountain on a sledge for three hours and we met talking penguins! And bandits captured us, so we had to smooth talk them and run away.'

Excited, I would make faces and swing my arms. 'Stop messing about,' Baba would mutter every now and then. Finally, a familiar-looking house with three entrances would appear ahead of us. We were home.

When I look back at that strange period of my childhood, it feels as if Mum and I were separated for years. I dutifully waited, occupying my pre-school life with all sorts of things – books, secrets, temporary friends and dark corridors with spooky tales. Every day was like the last and, since I didn't know how clocks worked and never looked at a calendar, time for me was a hazy concept. Where was Mum? Shouldn't she be back by now?

At night, I buried my head in my pillow, trying to remember her face. She would appear for a second and then dissolve in a golden cloud (as when you rub your eyes and then look at a blank wall). I was beginning to forget what she looked like. Only the soft glowing warmth that she radiated remained clear to me. She wasn't my mother anymore, she was an enchantress, a mirage always just out of reach. It was as if my old life had been a dream, and now there was just me and Baba and nothing else. When I missed her particularly badly, I reread her fairy tales.

One day, Baba came into the room with a long-awaited letter from Mum. In it, Mum had written to say that my father had been killed in the war. My six-year-old mind couldn't comprehend that he was gone, simply because to me he had never existed; my parents had separated before my birth and we never spoke of him. If I closed my eyes and tried to summon up a memory of his face, all I saw was a thick black moustache. Sometimes, for a second, I would see an image of a tall, smiling, olive-skinned man, but something told me that this could have been one of my mum's colleagues from the television station.

Later that night, Baba had one of her little gatherings, a circle of girlfriends sitting around the table, playing cards and drinking vodka. Such parties didn't happen very often, but when they did, I hid in the smaller room and waited for everyone to leave. Though they were only a bunch of harmless old women, they still frightened me when they drank. I hated the absurd way drunken people acted, their foggy gaze, the contrived sentimentality. Saying goodnight, Baba gave me a kiss, muttering through tears, 'My poor little orphan! No father, no mother! It's just the two of us now!' I covered my ears and refused to listen to her – what does she know, she's just tipsy! Sober Baba would never say such things. I ran back into the small room and buried my head in the duvet. Through the thick mass, I heard the old women singing sad, old songs from their youth. Lying with my eyes open, I tried again to conjure up Mum's face, only to be interrupted by another thunderous chorus from the next room. Her image evaporated, leaving an all-consuming loneliness. I felt the weight of it in every cell of my body. Was she ever coming back?

Then came the nightmares. The Tall Pale One began to haunt me again, standing silently by my bed with his sinister smile. But there were new monsters too. I would wake up screaming in the middle of the night and dive under the duvet, shaking. In the darkness, everything was a threat – the chair standing in the corner, the wardrobe, the chimney. What terrified me most of all was the coat rack; at night-time it turned into a huge black ghost, covered in rags. I couldn't sleep on my own and begged Baba to share the bed with me. But even when she was next to me, I would tremble in fear because the moment she started to snore I was vulnerable to the monsters. I would move close to the wall and cover my head with a pillow, leaving only a little hole to breathe through. Sometimes I entered a strange in-between state, when my body was asleep but my mind was awake. In those moments, I couldn't move a finger, my whole body was paralysed. 'Mummy, Mummy!' I would scream, but no sound would come out. A few years later, a girl in the village told me that that sort of thing happens when an evil jinn sits on your chest in your sleep, and the only way to prevent it is to say a special prayer.

Baba noticed that I was getting worse and decided to act. After taking counsel with her friends, she went to a local priest and returned with a little bottle of holy water. She summoned me to the kitchen and told me to stand right in front of her. After saying some prayers, she filled her mouth with holy water and spat it all over my face. She repeated the procedure three or four times. Unamused, I sat quietly through the ritual and, after Baba was done, I went back to the room and dried my face thoroughly with a towel. It's hard to tell whether the holy water was responsible, but gradually the nightmares disappeared. I accepted that Kamyshlov was now home, and found a way not to be miserable there.

But this didn't stop me from watching the news from Chechnya fanatically every evening, hoping to see Mum on screen. For a six-year-old, much of it was hard to understand, and the boring men in grey suits often sent me to sleep, but nonetheless I waited. I remember seeing Putin for the first time, in what must have been the first year of his presidency: a young-looking man in a camouflage jacket, being swallowed by a crowd as he stepped out of a helicopter. I didn't think he was very serious, as he wasn't wearing a grey suit, but I had a feeling that he was somehow important.

Whenever images from Chechnya appeared, I would move closer to the screen, studying every detail. I watched men in military uniforms firing machine guns and screaming orders. I watched the streets of Grozny being demolished, and struggled to remember what it had been like to live there. My only goal was to make sure Mum was still alive. When the images flashed past too quickly, I would become furious and bang the table with my little fists. I looked at every face, searching, hoping. Night after night, Baba would find me glued to the screen. She gave up trying to send me to bed on time. I couldn't miss a single news programme – what if I did and they showed Mum that day? This was a vigil.

And then, one day, watching a man in Chechnya give a speech, carefully scanning every face in the crowd, I suddenly saw a woman in a black jacket, standing about a metre from the speaker. I gasped – it was Mum! Her face was serious and white against the dark sky, her gaze cast down, her lips tightly pressed together. She looked sad, or focused, never raising her eyes, although my entire being screamed for her to look up. And then, before I could memorise her face and figure, she was gone, like a ghost dematerialising. I sat transfixed, unable to take my eyes off the screen, although the news had moved on. Had it really been her? Yes, without a doubt. She was alive; she was well. I was euphoric, and triumphant that my stubbornness had paid off. I had told myself that if I waited long enough, she would appear, and she had!

The snow was almost gone now. I scraped the last of the slush from the ground and squeezed it with bare palms, turning it into dumplings. Underneath the white crust grew fresh green grass, which made a perfect condiment for my snow dough. I lined up all the dumplings in a perfect line and quietly admired my work.

I was with Dima, a local boy of the same age, whom I had reluctantly befriended. We mostly hung out outside; Baba didn't like it when he visited our flat and I didn't enjoy going to his – his dad and older brother were always drunk. It wasn't really a friendship but a temporary alliance between two lonely children who had little in common. We played tic-tac-toe with a stick in the sand and occasionally mixed with equally bored neighbourhood kids. They teased us, calling us bride and groom, which we both fiercely denied. One day, guided by the spirit of adventure, Dima and I decided to follow an abandoned railway track that led all the way into the forest. When we finally returned, tired and covered in mud, Baba gave me a serious telling off and even slapped me. She had been worried sick.

Soon the summer came. Gone was the jacket, the hat and prickly woollen socks. The grass outside sparkled in the sun and the walls of Baba's flat started smelling of raw wood again. But the true indicator of summer was the abundance of babushkas on the streets – every bench was occupied until the next cold spell. They would sit there for hours, lazily exchanging the latest news, gossip and complaints. Sometimes they would fall quiet, having nothing more to say, and simply soak up the sunshine. Baba's favourite spot was a large wooden table with two benches on either side, located in the centre of the yard. From there you could see the entire backyard and a bit of the street. It was the perfect hunting spot for gossip! With Baba's permission, I drew figures on a corner of an old newspaper, quite content with my little corner of the bench.

'Who's that? I haven't seen her before,' I heard someone say, but paid no attention. Soon all the babushkas, my own included, grew animated. I finally lifted my eyes from my doodling to see the latest victim of their gossip. It was a young, slender woman with short dark hair, dressed in a long off-white dress. Half of her face was hidden behind large sunglasses. 'Where is she from?' I thought. 'Not from here . . .'

Walking slowly towards our bench, the woman stopped, bent to her knees and removed her sunglasses.

'Mama! MAMA!' I screamed and ran towards her. I hugged her tightly and buried my head in her hair. There it was, the happiest moment of my life. That warm embrace that I'd been longing for and the sound of two hearts beating next to each other. Even now I see it, when I close my eyes – my mother in her light summer clothes, kneeling to be my height. After a while, we broke the embrace and started to make our way towards Baba's flat. I refused to let go of her hand.

This was no brief visit. Mum had arrived determined to take me back to Chechnya, to rebuild our lives there. In the constant push–pull she felt between duty to others and her love for me, motherhood had won.

'I'm not letting her go!' shouted Baba to my mother. 'You're not taking her back to the war!'

I tensed up. The whole time they were arguing, I was sitting on my mum's lap, as if I was an extension of her body.

'Lanusya, please, go to the bedroom and pack your things,' said Mum calmly.

I walked slowly towards the bedroom, looking back anxiously at Baba. Then I sat on the bed in confusion. What should I pack? Clothes? Should I leave my toys behind? I had hardly any possessions, and I was ready to leave with Mum this very second, leaving everything behind. I could hear shouting through the closed door but couldn't make out the words. Moments ago, I'd been the happiest girl in the world but now everything seemed scary and uncertain. What if Mum were to decide to leave me with Baba and go away again?

'What the hell is this? Have you been feeding my child with this vomit?' I heard through a crack in the door. Then there was a loud banging noise, followed by the sound of liquid being poured.

After what felt like a very long time, the shouting stopped. And Mum seemed to have won the battle: I was going back to Chechnya. As we packed my bags, Baba sat at the edge of the bed, looking lonely and confused.

'Come here,' she said and sat me on her lap. 'Was it really that bad living with Baba? Why don't you stay with me?' This last, forlorn attempt to dissuade me from leaving made me feel very awkward. Of course, I felt sorry for my Baba, but that feeling was completely overshadowed by the prospect of living with Mum again. Mum spared me from having to find a way to answer by telling me to get changed.

Mum and Baba made up in the most Russian way possible – they went to Baba's allotment to dig out potatoes. I 'contributed' by burying my hands in moist soil and making figures with it. From where I was sitting, I could see her perfectly. Dressed in old tracksuit bottoms, with her stubborn lock that escaped a white headscarf, Mum looked like the most beautiful woman in the world. I looked and looked, mesmerised by her – real, made of flesh, not a mirage or a memory.

That evening we had fried potatoes with onion, and the next morning Mum and I caught a train to Yekaterinburg. Baba walked along the platform and waved at us, wiping tears away with her handkerchief. I watched her as she grew smaller and smaller. Then, she was gone.

The Paints That Quarrelled
by Natalia Estemirova

A girl placed a blank sheet of paper in front of her, opened her box of paints and wondered,

Which paint should I take first?

'Pick me!' shouted the red paint. 'I am the most beautiful! I can draw poppies, apples, a wonderful sunset!'

'But what about me?' objected the blue paint. 'Who else can draw the sky, cornflowers and bluebells?'

'And who, besides me, will draw the sun at noon?' asked the yellow paint indignantly. 'And chickens, and pears, and sunflowers? I should be the first!'

'Ah, just who do you think you are?' came the voice of the green paint. 'How will you draw your poppies, cornflowers and sunflowers if they don't have green stems and leaves? You must choose me first!'

'No, me! No, me!' the paints shouted together. They all rushed to reach the paper, chasing and pushing each other, until a large smudge appeared on the page.

'Ugh, what a mess!' the girl exclaimed, and threw the paper in the bin.

The colours went quiet. They were very much ashamed of their behaviour.

The girl grabbed a new sheet of paper. None of the paints argued, and soon there appeared a green meadow with bluebells, cornflowers and poppies. There were chickens, and frogs that hopped among the flowers, and butterflies that fluttered over them. Above, the sun smiled sweetly.

A blue cloud appeared, wanting to burst into tears, but, seeing the happy scene below, she cheered up, dropping only a few raindrops. And then all the colours joined hands and ran across the page, making a rainbow.

4

Memorial

2000–1

I started school on the first day of September 2000. Mum decided I should begin my formal education aged six rather than seven, like most children in the country. Clutching a bouquet of flowers for the teacher, I wore an improvised uniform of a black skirt and a matching vest over a white turtleneck, my hair tied with a big white bow. Even my tights (white, with a pattern of the English alphabet) were specially chosen for the occasion. I posed for the obligatory photo by the school gate and then for another one with Mum, both shot on our Kodak film camera. No one would have guessed that this impeccably dressed mother and daughter were, technically, homeless.

I had never imagined I would start school in Nazran, Ingushetia, instead of Grozny in Chechnya. I was excited, impatient to show off my reading skills, but nervous too. What if I didn't understand what anyone was saying? The Ingush language was similar to Chechen, but I still struggled to make out full sentences. My Chechen was also somewhat lacking after a year in the Urals, a mishap that Mum had attempted to mend by sending me to spend the remainder of the summer with relatives in various villages. That summer I had begged her repeatedly to let me visit Grozny, but she always replied that it wasn't safe enough yet, that the federals were shooting at people all the time.

The battle for the city lasted for three months, between December 1999 and early February 2000. As it came to an end, most of the insurgents fled to villages in the mountains, and then into the dense Chechen woods where only locals knew their way around. This is why young men who joined the militants were described as having 'gone to the woods'. From then on, Chechen fighters adopted guerrilla tactics, carrying out devastating surprise attacks on the Russian military. The federals retaliated by targeting any Chechen they could find – most of them innocent civilians scraping for survival.

On her way to collect me from Yekaterinburg, Mum had made a stop in Moscow to visit Svetlana Alekseevna Gannushkina – a respected human rights activist with a dissident background. Svetlana was the head of the Civic Assistance Committee, an NGO that helped refugees, migrants and victims of war with everything from humanitarian aid to language classes and children's books. For Mum, this was the start of a decades-long partnership. Sitting on her red sofa and sipping black tea, she told Svetlana Alekseevna about everything she'd seen and heard during her hellish trip back to Grozny.

From the first day of the war, civilians seemed to have been the prime target of the Russian army. When a barrage of cluster bombs hit the picturesque village of Elistanzhi, killing eighty-five locals and refugees, it was not separatists who perished but innocent women and children. Mum told Svetlana about the missile strike on the Grozny market that she'd witnessed, the bloody scenes at the maternity hospital, the aerial attacks on refugee columns. And then, digging through the holdall she had brought with her from Chechnya, she produced a small plush toy. It was my beloved Pink Kitty (the wife of Ginger Doggy, with her fluffy white tail). To Svetlana Alekseevna's bemusement, Mum asked for a pair of scissors. Then she turned Pink Kitty upside down and started carefully undoing the stitches on her belly. Searching in the white cotton stuffing with her fingers, she extracted several tiny videotapes.

On those tapes was evidence of war crimes and human rights abuses committed by the Russian army, testimonies from survivors, and hours of footage of a destroyed Grozny riddled with makeshift checkpoints and tanks. She had smuggled the tapes through multiple security checks, getting into trouble only once when a Russian officer took a liking to the toy and wanted to 'confiscate' it for his daughter. Mum pleaded with him, telling him how much I missed the toy and how desperate I was to be reunited with it. He bought the story. She used Pink Kitty on her missions many times, until one day she handed her over to me, declaring that she had earned her retirement and a new name – Mata Hari – a Dutch femme fatale who became a famous spy. Once she returned to Yekaterinburg, Mum took the tapes to a local TV station, hoping that they would use them for a story. According to my Auntie Sveta, they did air some of them, but after that all the tapes mysteriously disappeared without trace.

Back in Ingushetia, after weeks of searching and sleeping on a sofa in our friend's home, we finally found a place to live – a small room in a flat split between three Chechen families. But that tiny place, with a handful of furniture and nosy, obnoxious neighbours, didn't feel like home. Nor did my school, where a young, well-meaning teacher tried but failed to keep me engaged, and I sneaked in my own books to read under the table every day.

Memorial, Memorial, Memorial. I heard that word so often then that it felt like a song playing on repeat in the background of my life. Memorial was for Mum – and became for me – a home away from home. After picking me up from school, Mum would take me to a nearby café for piping-hot *chebureki* – fried calzone-like pastries filled with mince and onion. I would tell her all about school as she listened closely, throwing back her head in an outburst of laughter whenever I said something funny. If I caught sight of the golden tooth hidden in the far corner of her mouth, I knew that the joke was good. After lunch, we'd go to her office.

It was located on the second floor of an unremarkable commercial building in the centre of Nazran. Inside, there were four rooms divided by flimsy walls, a small kitchen and a large open space with shiny white tiles that were so slippery you could slide on them.

Memorial was much more than a workplace – it was a social club and a 'training camp' for independent journalists and fresh-faced activists alike. For them, Ingushetia was a jumping-off point for undercover trips into Chechnya. To me, though the Memorial office back in Yekaterinburg never felt particularly welcoming or warm, here in Nazran both Mum and I quickly became part of the team. Perhaps it was because of its proximity to our homeland, or because we shared more in common with the people who worked there, who were from the region themselves.

'You know what I used to call it?' reminisced Mum's colleague and friend Eliza Musaeva, 'Rick's Café Americain. From Casablanca, do you remember?' With her raven-black hair and refined features, Eliza looked like an old Hollywood movie star, our own Ingrid Bergman. 'Everyone used to stop there – journalists, lawyers. Whether you were looking for information or just a cup of tea, it was a great place to be.'

Whenever Mum's colleagues weren't busy, which wasn't very often, they were happy to chat to me and crack jokes. A mix of Chechen and Ingush nationals, they operated like a tight-knit family. I gravitated towards their warmth, eavesdropping on harmless gossip, chattering away with the young women and flying paper planes with Mum's boss, Oleg Orlov, whenever he came down from Moscow. A few months into our time in Nazran, I even got a job at Memorial, complete with a handwritten employment contract in a brazen act of nepotism – fifty roubles a week for doing the dishes.

But the real mission that brought all those brave, compassionate people together was a dangerous and sombre one. On the right-hand wall of the office, next to the staircase, hung a large board with black-and-white photos of Chechen men who had been 'disappeared' by the federals during the war. Sometimes, in quiet moments, I studied the faces of those people, knowing they were gone forever. Somewhere between three and five thousand people were disappeared during the second Chechen war, over the course of just one year. Memorial was there to document and investigate war crimes and human rights abuses, to offer legal assistance to victims and give them any other help they needed, such as applying for disability benefit or compensation for destroyed homes.

It was the only organisation that kept an accurate count of the number of civilians killed during both wars. This would have been impossible without the Chechen and Ingush activists who stayed on the ground, risking their lives to collect information. Chechens could enter the republic without any special permits if they could show their residency papers. Mum made the two-hour drive from Ingushetia to the war zone several times a week, each time following the news of yet another harrowing *zachistka*.

But there was one in particular which stood out. At first, we heard only rumours. Dozens of petrified refugees passed on bits and pieces of information as they crossed the checkpoints. Something terrible had happened in the village of Novye Aldi on 5 February 2000.

Then, there was a video, which was not for the faint-hearted. The grainy images showed bodies carefully laid out on the floor. The camera zoomed in on glassy eyes, on a blood-encrusted stump in place of a nose, on yellowish brains pouring out of the back of a scalp. The bodies were mostly male, both young and old, in bullet-ridden, blood-stained clothes. Then there were two women, lying next to each other. One of them had vine-like bruises crawling out of her collar all the way up to her chin, staining her neck ink black.

To watch those videos on a computer screen, choking on tears and suppressing a gag reflex, was hard enough. To film that macabre scene with a steady hand, to interview the traumatised, half-crazed survivors, must have been deeply traumatic. But to have lived through that horror, to have looked down the barrel of a gun and watched loved ones be ripped apart by bullets, was inconceivable.

Mum had first spoken to the survivors in Novye Aldi in early March 2000. She had only recently joined the Memorial office in Nazaran, and I was still living with Baba in Kamyshlov. As soon as she'd heard of the massacre, she headed to Chechnya, one of the first human rights activists to do so since the start of the second war. She was one of the few people who could have done it: being a Grozny resident, she could claim that she was going back to check on her flat, and being a woman, she could pass through all the checkpoints with relative ease. Seeking out the survivors in Novye Aldi who were willing to talk, she asked them to tell the world about the horror that had been inflicted upon them. Their stories were eerily similar to the 1995 Samashki massacre.

Novye Aldi, a village in the suburbs of Grozny, had already suffered from intensive aerial attacks throughout late 1999 and early 2000. At the beginning of the war it had 27,000 inhabitants, but by February, just six months later, that number had dwindled to just 2,000. Anyone who could afford to leave did so. Those who lacked the money to escape, or who were taking care of the sick and the elderly, were forced to remain. Chechen rebel fighters passed through the village but never stayed behind for too long, in part because the villagers begged them not to.

At the time, the Russian command was conducting a secret military operation, codenamed 'wolf hunt', the aim of which was to lure militants out of Grozny and into fields laced with mines. On 3 February a group of village elders headed towards the Russian military-command office, holding up a white flag. The federals nonetheless opened fire on them, hitting an ethnic Russian in the group who later died from his injuries. The elders begged the federals to stop the aerial raids and shootings, assuring them that the village was not harbouring any militants. Miraculously, the federals complied and the next day, 4 February, a squad was sent to conduct a document check in the village. This was done without any violence, but as the soldiers were leaving, they warned the locals that the next batch to arrive would be 'real beasts'.

The next day Novye Aldi turned into hell on earth. Those 'real beasts' were soldiers from the Russian army – a subdivision of the St Petersburg and Ryazan OMON – special forces unit.

At midday, the village was surrounded by several APCs (Armoured Personnel Carriers). For the next few hours, several squads of soldiers dressed in camouflage proceeded to kill, rape, torture, loot and set houses on fire. The most ruthless were said to be in their thirties and forties, most likely contractors. They were notorious for being more vicious compared to civilian recruits, since war was their career choice.

The eyewitnesses' accounts read worse than any horror story. Aset Chadaeva, a young woman who worked as a nurse, recalled how her neighbours kept bringing wounded people in to her. She saw a nine-year old girl, Leyla, rolling around on the ground, screaming that her mother had been killed. Aset ran into the neighbour's front yard and saw Leyla's mother prostrate in a pool of blood. There were bodies everywhere – on the streets, in the allotments, inside houses. Aset noticed soldiers returning to finish off people who had survived being shot, including eighty-year-old Rakiyat Akhmatova.

Survivors recalled the smell of blood that lingered in the air for hours after the massacre. Body parts were left hanging from fences and trees. Just as in Samashki, the federals threw grenades inside basements, tearing to pieces whoever was sheltering there. They held villagers at gunpoint, demanding money and valuables, and those who couldn't produce the required sum were shot. Even the dead weren't spared: the federals went through their mouths, tearing out gold teeth. Other victims, including two elderly brothers, Abdula and Salman, were burned alive inside their own homes. Survivors noted that soldiers were drunk and red in the face, stumbling about, swearing and shouting, 'Where is the money?' Several women were raped. This was the worst imaginable offence in Chechen society; to this day, it is impossible to tell how many women suffered at the hands of soldiers in this way, because the topic is simply taboo. That video of the dead woman, her neck blackened from bruises, will haunt me forever. I may have grown up ingesting other people's pain through overheard stories, photographs scattered on desks and printed reports that Mum never bothered to hide but watching the footage felt entirely different. It made it more real.

The defenceless villagers, many of them elderly, had nowhere to go and nowhere to hide. Once the soldiers had left with sacks full of loot, exhausted from the slaughtering, the villagers gathered to tend to the wounded and wash the bodies of the dead. At least eighty-two people were killed that day, and thirty-two more were missing. Some of the human remains – charred bones – were collected in large metal pots. According to strict Chechen custom, burials must happen as soon as possible, preferably on the same day. But it was decided that the funerals in Novye Aldi should be postponed until all of the forensic evidence was collected for the official investigation. On 9 February, one of the villagers filmed the video that was only shown to the rest of the world a month later. They wanted justice. But when the survivors and their families filed reports to the military prosecution office, the authorities refused to launch an investigation. That's why for the victims, the European Court of Human Rights became a last resort for some form of justice. Mum and her Memorial colleagues were instrumental in gathering the evidence that allowed them to file their cases and in 2006 and 2007 the ECHR ruled that the Russian state was guilty of human rights abuses and a failure to investigate the murders.

As a six-year-old, I was vaguely aware that something dark had happened at Novye Aldi, but the name blended with all the other villages in Chechnya I'd never been to. Aset Chadaeva, who spent a lot of time in the Nazran Memorial office helping with the case, was to me simply Asya, a lovely, chatty young woman who asked me about school. It seemed like real life was happening there, in Memorial. When Mum was away in Chechnya, I did my homework in the office's kitchen and listened in to the conversations that went on around me, accidentally memorising the recurring list of places where bad things happened: Novye Aldi, Chernorechye, Starye Atagi, Katyr-Yurt, Starye Promysla, Shuani. Looking at a gigantic map of Russia that hung in the office hallway, I saw how tiny Chechnya was and wondered how it was possible that there were so many towns and villages on such a small piece of land. How could so much bad stuff be happening in so many places at once?

Most days of the week, Mum went back and forth between Grozny and Nazran. Each time, she brought news about our old neighbours, about our flat that had a massive hole in the balcony, about my toys that she had managed to recover. When she was away, one of her colleagues had the task of helping with the school run. On one occasion, everyone forgot about me. I stood in the schoolyard with my pink backpack looking for a familiar face, but no one showed up. My form teacher, who was very understanding, asked me to wait until all her classes were over so she could take me back to her house. While we were having tea, her brothers found the Memorial office and returned with Mum's colleagues, who looked deeply embarrassed. After that, it was decided I should switch to a school closer to our home, and to Memorial. That way, it would be easier for everyone to look after me, until the day Mum finally decided to take me with her to Grozny.

The road between Nazran and Grozny cuts through unremarkable flatlands lined with farms and small villages. In peaceful times, the drive takes just over an hour. When I was a child, travelling this route felt like a perilous quest that stretched on for hours. The federals were the monsters that you had to get past, sometimes for free, sometimes for a bribe and other times paying the price of your life. The dungeons were the checkpoints scattered along the road, growing more frequent the closer you got to Chechnya. Despite these obstacles, Chechens couldn't help but go back and visit what remained of their homes, boarding overcrowded *marshrutkas*, ancient minibuses.

On a cool autumn day, sometime in November 2000, Mum and I boarded a *marshrutka* at the Nazran bus station. I was wearing my winter boots lined with black fake fur and Mum was carrying two red-and-blue chequered plastic holdalls. This surprised me. I didn't understand why we needed those large bags, the kind usually used by market sellers, when we were only going away for a couple of days? Once we'd taken our seats – to my disappointment Mum didn't let me sit by the window, in case there was shooting – she carefully placed the bags in front of me and asked me to rest my feet on them. 'Make sure you don't open them,' she warned.

Soon the minibus was full and off we went. We were stopped at every checkpoint, and each passenger had to hand over their passport for a mandatory document check. Our journey was delayed still further each time we had to pull over to let the federals pass in their endless *kolonny* – columns of military vehicles that stretched and wriggled like a mud-coloured viper. To pass the time, I made a game of trying to identify every type of vehicle: APCs, IFVs, Urals – sometimes there was even a tank. Mum showed me how to duck and cover my head in case I heard gunshots.

At the third checkpoint, the door of the minibus slid open and the shaved head of a Russian officer appeared in the doorway. His eyes scanned the passengers.

'Are they going to check our bags *again*?' muttered a woman in Chechen, but she didn't dare protest.

My mother leaned close to me, whispering in my ear, 'Listen to me, Lanuska, when the soldier gets closer, I want you to cry as loud as you can, okay? And say that you're scared. Don't move your feet off the bag, whatever happens.'

'Okay,' I agreed without thinking. I was a little scared anyway.

The first soldier walked away, but before we could breathe a sigh of relief, an older officer took his place and began studying our passports carefully. He was about to climb onto the minibus, when Mum whispered, 'Now, cry.'

I scrunched up my nose and let out a low-pitched wail. My love of acting came in handy because in that moment, I convinced even myself. 'I'm scared of this *dyadya*,' I whimpered through tears, pressing my boots into the rustling plastic of the bag.

'Don't cry, *devochka*,' the officer mumbled, seeming embarrassed. 'We're just doing our job.' Perhaps the fact that I spoke in perfect Russian helped him see my humanity because he retreated and slapped the door of the *marshrutka* twice. We were good to go.

'Well done, my little helper!' Mum said, squeezing me tight.

Once the minibus had entered the city, we were greeted by rows of destroyed buildings. There was nothing for the eye to rest on, just concrete ruins against the white sky. In 2003, Grozny would be declared the most destroyed city in the world by the United Nations. What struck me then was how colourless it all was, as if someone had bled every bright shade from the cityscape. It was hard to believe that people still lived there. Stepping back into my mother's arms, I whispered, 'What have they done to my home?' But, in reality, the year I had spent away from Chechnya had wiped most of my memories of the place, and I struggled to feel anything. This was no longer my city.

Where roads had been cleared, there were more checkpoints. Every half a mile or so, you would see them, ugly unnatural constructions with stripy black-and-white barriers covered in dirt. Some of them had been converted into improvised military stations, cubes of rough grey cement with tiny window holes, sandbags stacked into surrounding defensive walls. They puzzled me: why were the federals so scared of us? After all, we had no weapons. How many men were in there: ten, twenty? It was impossible to tell as they never came out together.

When we finally reached the friend's house where we would be staying, Mum asked me to go to another room so she could unpack her bags. Curious, I spied on her through the gap in the door, wondering what could be so precious that Mum didn't want it discovered. As she and her friend talked in hushed tones, she removed items from the unzipped mouths of the chequered holdalls. Warm clothes, scarves, shoes . . . so what was all the fuss about? But then she pulled out several packs of syringes wrapped in thin plastic and dozens and dozens of tiny cardboard boxes. Medicine! Buried under layers of donated clothing was life-saving medicine that the Russians wouldn't allow across the Chechen border. Mum had smuggled it in, and I was a great decoy. I was proud of the part I had unwittingly played in this operation.

During my first school year in Ingushetia, Mum found it increasingly difficult to find childcare. She had no family in Nazran, no money to hire help, and our neighbours, who also happened to be our landlords, could not be trusted – they timed how long we spent in the kitchen and the bathroom and were generally very gossipy and mean. Mum had to leave me behind often – called away to document the never-ending stream of human rights abuses in Chechnya. Finally, at the end of autumn 2000, when all other options were exhausted, she was forced to send me to stay with relatives. In a refugee camp.

During the war, Ingush president Ruslan Aushev had accepted into his tiny republic over 300,000 Chechen refugees. The camps that had sprung up were now more like towns. Khaki-coloured tents were set in long, neat rows against a barren landscape. Mum's cousin Tabarik was living in the camp near the town of Karabulak, with her husband and eight children. They stayed in their large house on the outskirts of Grozny throughout the first war, but at the outbreak of the second war they left Chechnya. Their area was heavily bombed and they couldn't risk their three older boys, now nearly men, being kidnapped by federals. Dozens of young men in their neighbourhood were disappeared during both wars.

Because they had no relatives outside of Chechnya, Tabarik and her family had no choice but to live in a tent. It was large, with several transparent plastic holes for windows and a wood burner in the middle, which doubled as a heat source and a stove. All around the inner wall of the tent were makeshift wooden benches for sleeping and sitting on. White sheets hung from the ceiling, separating the male and female areas. I slept in a row with the three or four other girls and women. Each night, once the big overhead lamp went out, you could hear a discordant choir of snores. Since all of us children were on school holidays – my cousin's school was set up in several shipping containers – we were left entirely to our own devices. In the mornings, we roamed around the outskirts of the camp, playing games and collecting anything that looked remotely interesting. There was so little greenery, the camp seemed to exist in a desert, lined with brown dusty roads and bald hills. Some of the hills also served as a dumping ground for industrial waste – rusty scrap metal piled high in mounds. One of our favourite ways to entertain ourselves was to run at full tilt down these hills. During one of those races, I tripped, hurtled to the ground and rolled down the slope. When my terrified cousins found me, I was screaming my head off. My right leg was red with blood, a sharp piece of metal sticking out of my right knee. Touching it was extremely painful, so all I could do was weep while Makka and Khava half carried me back to the camp. The metal wasn't removed from my leg until hours later, when somebody finally managed to fetch a medic. I still have a small bug-like scar on my right knee as a memento.

Our second favourite activity was making soup: the more ingredients, the better. We used everything we could find – weeds, occasional dandelions, stones, dirt and paper. Khava would light a fire and we would mix all the ingredients together with water from a puddle and generous portions of sand, in place of salt. Staying at the camp was exciting and new.

At the end of the week, Mum would come to pick me up, and my cousins would stay behind, carrying on with their lives in this non-place. I would go back to the little room in Chechnya that I shared with only one other person, while my ten relatives crammed into a single tent. I returned home from Karabulak with hair full of lice and pockets full of junk. Mum would sigh, run to the pharmacy to fetch special shampoo, and dispose of my collection of rusty metal. On one occasion, I remember Mum emptying a big plastic bag on the floor, watching scraps of metal and little stones hit the floor, her temper rising.

'What is this?' she asked in a stern voice that was just a few decibels away from being a shout. 'Why did you bring this rubbish home?'

I studied my shoes and mumbled a reply, anticipating a row. 'It's . . . soup.'

She was not impressed.

Some will perhaps raise an eyebrow at my chaotic upbringing. In times of war, normal rules don't apply, especially when you want to stay together as a family. Mum was brilliant at being a mother, but it wasn't what defined her. I loved her and she loved me and that was what mattered most. Her love enveloped me like a soft cloud that cushioned me from every blow. But it wasn't all sweetness and light; Mum could be strict and short-tempered, sometimes unreasonably so. One time she threatened to throw out all my Lego if I didn't clear it away, and when I didn't immediately follow her orders, she scooped up all the bricks and threw them in the bin. She would often shout at me and didn't tolerate disobedience. But just like her, I was strong-willed and set in my ways. Mum told me off for how I behaved, not for who I was. I was a loud, quirky child with a wild imagination, bursting into impromptu songs in the middle of the street and acting out plays. Mum always respected my individuality and encouraged me to be creative. She laughed at my antics and played along; it must have been a much-needed relief from the horrors of her job.

I treasured every moment we had together. When I fell ill with jaundice in December 2000, during my winter holidays, it ended up being the best thing. In a strange coincidence, I was diagnosed on the same day that the Memorial office welcomed a group of honoured guests from Moscow, which included one of its founders, Sergey Kovalyov. The whole office was buzzing with excitement and though I wasn't feeling well, I persuaded Mum to take me along. I was especially excited to meet Kovalyov, having heard Mum talk so much about him. When he finally appeared, I saw a small, soft-spoken man wearing large glasses with thick lenses. He made a short speech but I couldn't hear anything. Stepping closer, I bumped into a tall man with dark curly hair. He turned around and looked down at me. 'Oh . . . hello little girl,' he said, amused. 'And who do you belong to?' He had probably not expected to see a child present at a discussion about war, kidnappings and human rights violations.

'I'm here with my mum, she works here,' I replied, pointing at Mum who looked over at us, and seemed very pleased. We chatted while Mum tried to snap a quick photo. 'Do you know who that is?' she asked after he had moved off. 'It's Boris Nemtsov. He is a politician but a good one. He has been speaking out against the wars in Chechnya. He is very brave.' I was chuffed that such an important man had spent several minutes talking to me. 'Hang on, Lana,' Mum said suddenly. 'Come to the window, let me see your face in the light.'

I stepped closer to her and she lifted my chin with her hand, inspecting my face.

'Aah, Lanusya,' she gasped. 'You're all yellow, even your eyeballs. We must go to the hospital right this moment!'

Among the photographs that were developed sometime later, there is one that captures that day perfectly. In the background there is a crowd of people, including Sergey Kovalyov and Boris Nemtsov, half turning away. In front of them stands an exhausted-looking six-year-old with two pigtails and an unmistakable pale-yellow tinge to her face, which clashes with her emerald-green, hand-knitted jumper. We dashed to the hospital and after several tests the doctor insisted I should be admitted immediately.

Spending two weeks over the winter break at the hospital with an intravenous drip in my arm might not sound like much fun, but Mum was with me the whole time. 'What a brave girl you are, Lanusya,' she told me. 'Only six years old and not afraid of big needles.'

She slept in the same room, only leaving to make food and check in with her colleagues. Then she would return with delicious meals – meatballs, soup, pasta – which she brought in large glass jars because we had no Tupperware. Food had never tasted so good. On New Year's Eve, the nurses allowed us to leave the hospital for a while. That night, when we returned to the ward, we found, to my joy, that Ded Moroz had visited, bringing me the nicest gifts: a portable radio and a bag with doll make-up. Mum and I celebrated, welcoming in 2001, the Year of the Snake according to the Chinese calendar, with non-alcoholic champagne.

In the early days of the new year, our visits to Chechnya were becoming more frequent. I finally got to return to the Memorial office in Grozny, which was run by the formidable and impossibly cool Lida Yusupova, probably the only woman in Chechnya who wore trousers. Pity the man who would dare to comment, though – Lida had a sharp tongue and a fearless attitude, the kind of attitude required to direct a human rights centre in the middle of a war. I was entranced by her.

On 28 February, we were staying with Lida's family on the outskirts of Grozny. It was Mum's birthday and I was adamant that she should buy a pineapple for herself. God knows why, but I had decided it would be festive if she could find such an exotic fruit in Chechnya.

'Lanka,' she laughed. 'Something tells me that YOU want a pineapple!'

'Mum,' I replied in exasperation. 'It's a present I want you to buy for yourself as if it's from me. Because I don't have any money yet.'

'I'll see what I can do.'

Mum had a difficult day ahead of her. There had been rumours going around for a while about a mass grave near Khankala, one of the most sinister Russian military bases. Because the whole area was cordoned off, anyone who tried to get closer to look for their relatives risked being shot or kidnapped. There were intermediaries who were willing to sell a body to the family of the deceased for an extortionate price, but not many could afford it.

By the end of February, bereaved families had made their way to the small holiday villages near Khankala – called 'Rainbow' and 'Health' in a morbid twist of irony – where their loved ones were said to be buried. Once the digging started, dozens of men and women flocked in, hoping to identify sons, husbands and brothers, studying every scrap of decomposed clothing for clues. The corpses, in various states of decay, were everywhere, some buried in shallow graves but many just left on the streets and in the little holiday cottages. Most bore signs of torture, their hands tied behind their backs. Some were missing ears – a popular trophy among federals – and most were missing teeth, sometimes the entire front row. Some bodies were mined to make sure that whoever came back to retrieve them stayed there too. Quite a few bodies were completely unrecognisable because they had been half eaten by dogs. There were around two hundred dead, most of them killed during the first year of the second war. This was the kind of place where the missing men from those black-and-white photographs on the wall of the Memorial office ended up. Kidnapped, held in secret prisons, tortured, executed and then their bodies, unwanted evidence, tossed unceremoniously away. At the time, I could only guess at the agony that their families experienced.

Mum was present at the exhumation of these mass graves, carefully recording every testimony. She filmed the bodies after they had been laid out in rows in plastic bags. In one of the shots there is a man wearing a gas mask, because of the smell. Behind him is a woman, looking for someone – she holds only a small corner of her headscarf over her face, to protect herself from the stench.

Some of the bodies were beyond recognition and there was no effort on the part of the Russian authorities to organise DNA testing. The nearest forensics office was far away, in Rostov-on-Don, outside Chechnya. As for the investigation, it stalled and went nowhere.*

When Mum returned to Lida's house that evening, I noticed for the first time that she seemed subdued. It was as if she had been crushed between two heavy plates. I rushed to say happy birthday to her. She was sitting on a stool, still wearing her boots, her coat unzipped. Her face had a misty sheen of sweat covering it like clingfilm and it was drained of colour; it was almost the same shade as her off-white turtleneck.

'I can't shake off that smell,' I remember her saying to Lida. She couldn't even climb into a hot bath and wash away that awful day because there was no running water. She sat there, gazing into space, until I came and gave her a hug.

Suddenly, she snapped out of her trance. 'Oh, I have a surprise for you. Look in the bag.'

I dashed towards a plastic bag standing by the doorway. It took me a few seconds to rummage through it and to my amusement, my fingers found something bristly inside. I pulled out a pineapple, like a giant yellow pinecone – it was just how I imagined it. I'd never held a pineapple in my hands before. I had requested it almost as a joke, like all those fairy-tale characters that make impossible requests to test each other. But somehow, Mum made magic happen. I held the

---

*Years later an email account belonging to one of the FSB officers involved was hacked, revealing his links to this mass grave and other war crimes. In private correspondence, the officer boasted about his service in Chechnya and how at the start of the second war he had participated in *zachistka* in Mesker-Yurt village close to the Khankala base. His name came up in relation to multiple kidnappings of Chechen men whose corpses turned up in the Health holiday village, and many disappearances after that. The officer calls himself Igor Strelkov; it's also the name remembered by relatives of his victims. His real name is Igor Girkin, and in 2022 he was sentenced to life imprisonment *in absentia* for using a BUK missile to shoot down Malaysian Airlines flight MH17, a passenger plane full of civilians, above eastern Ukraine.

pineapple in both my hands and brought it back to Mum. 'Mama,' I said pompously, 'I would like to congratulate you on your birthday and give you this wonderful pineapple that you bought yourself!'

'Thank you for such a wonderful gift,' replied Mum with a smile, playing along.

I have a photograph from that day. We are sitting around a table laid with snacks, fizzy drinks and a fruit bowl. Mum is to the right of her friends, pale and exhausted from the horrors she'd seen that day. She's looking down with a weak smile, while I'm beaming and holding the pineapple. I still wonder how she managed to find this exotic fruit in a city that barely had electricity.

We moved back to Grozny carefully, step by step, as if crossing a minefield. Mum went first and I followed, hopping from one relative's house to another. When she finally felt the time was right, at the start of April 2001, she told me that we would be leaving Nazran and moving back to Chechnya. I'd be finishing the final term of my first year in the Deshi-Yurt village, where Mum's cousins could look after me while Mum was sorting out our living arrangements in Grozny. I was ecstatic because I would see much more of my cousins, Diana and Selima. And I would finally make proper progress with my Chechen; there is nothing more embarrassing than opening your mouth to say something and not being able to remember half the words. That's how I changed school for the third time in my first year. I had become like a sturdy little cactus, growing and thriving wherever I was planted.

Compared to elsewhere in Chechnya, Deshi-Yurt was prosperous; it hadn't been bombed and still had electricity. Neat red-brick houses stood behind slender walnut trees, giving the false impression that the war hadn't touched this corner of Chechnya. But the truth was that many households were missing a member – a son, a father, a husband – who had been disappeared by federals. Our relatives had so far been spared but, just in case, they sent their eldest son away at the start of the second war.

I started attending the local school in Deshi-Yurt in mid-April 2001. Each morning, on my half-hour route, I had to walk past a Russian military post stationed in a former kindergarten building. It was covered in camouflage nets so that you could never see who was inside, but I knew it was full of soldiers. Those here didn't seem too bad. In the evenings they would go out in groups to nearby shops to stock up on crisps and cigarettes. They even paid, rather than looting. Still, whenever I passed their military base, I was terrified that they would think I was a terrorist and shoot me. Just in case, I sang a popular Soviet song loudly to identify myself as I walked by:

> *May there always be sunshine*
> *May there always be blue skies*
> *May there always be Mummy*
> *May there always be me!*

One day, as I sang, a muffled sound came from the military base. I couldn't believe it at first and moved closer to the thick concrete wall, straining my ears. Could it be? Some federal was singing along with me from the other side! I never saw his face, but he knew all the words as he joined in the chorus. In a bizarre turn of events, a seven-year-old Chechen girl sang an anti-war song together with a Russian soldier. I wondered if he knew the rest of the song that I continued to sing quietly from a safe distance:

> *Down with all war!*
> *We want no more.*

Nineteen years later, long after the Russians were gone, some construction workers started doing work on the site where that military base once stood. As they started digging, they discovered an unmarked mass grave filled with human bones and shreds of clothing. The pro-Kremlin authorities ordered the locals to quietly bury the remains and forget about ever finding them.

I was still living with my aunt in Deshi-Yurt when another school year started. It had been a good summer by all measures – I'd visited all my relatives in every village and improved my Chechen dramatically; and I'd seen the sea for the first time because Mum sent me away to a summer camp in Sochi, in Southern Russia on the Black Sea. The camp was a fantastic experience, except on the first day when a boy from my group nearly drowned – most Chechen kids didn't know how to swim. And I developed a very embarrassing and obvious crush on a thirteen-year-old boy that everyone teased me about.

In the last days of August Mum came to Deshi-Yurt bringing good news: we were moving back to Grozny. She'd found me a school already and even signed me up for piano lessons. I eagerly packed my few belongings and we sat down for a final meal with my aunt and her family.

After dinner, we gathered around the television to watch a soap opera. My aunt was flicking through channels when suddenly I heard my mother yell, 'Turn up the volume!' As I looked, two tall buildings were engulfed in a cloud of white smoke. The next shot showed a plane flying directly into one of the towers, which looked as though it was going to split it in half. People on the ground were screaming, covered in what looked like grey snow. I wondered where it was – perhaps Moscow?

'Mama, mama!' I nudged her, wanting her to explain what we were seeing. She didn't reply. The buildings were in New York, the news presenter said.

Mum sat very close to the screen, eyes widened in horror, a hand covering her mouth. Tears were streaming down her face – this is my first ever memory of her crying. She never let me see her vulnerability, only her anger. And she was crying for people we didn't know, a whole continent away. Of course, I felt sorry for them, but I couldn't understand why it was such a big deal. Why was everyone suddenly so upset when we had our own war? What was so different about those people?

5

Piano on Fire
2001–4

I stood in front of the damaged facade of a ground-floor balcony, its thick cement shredded by shells. Our little flat had seen better days. Before we'd fled in 1999, this had been home, but now it was uninhabitable – the blackened walls pockmarked with dents and bullet holes; the floors covered in broken glass, plaster and rubbish. It was a miracle the tower block was still standing at all. But our corner flat had been an easy target. 'We'll fix it up as soon as we have enough money,' Mum declared, surveying the damage. She was always an optimist.

By late 2001, the first phase of the second Chechen war seemed to be over. It had been the kind of war that you see on the news – daily bombings, gunfire amid ruins, mountains of corpses, explosions and scared civilians hiding in basements. The Russian authorities, looking for legitimacy, outsourced their political and military strategy to a 'native' collaborator, someone who knew the local context and was embedded into Chechen society. The choice fell on the former Chief Mufti of Ichkeria, Akhmad-Khadji Kadyrov. During the first war, he was an ally to President Dudayev and fought by his side against the Russian troops. In 1999, however, Kadyrov switched sides and abandoned the cause of independence, claiming to be concerned about the rise of Wahhabism. One year later, he was made the head of the pro-Russian administration in Chechnya by Vladimir Putin. His appointment marked the beginning of the 'Chechenisation' of the conflict – when compliant locals were recruited to military and political positions on the Russian side. Emboldened by his new-found power, Kadyrov began to form his own private militia, starting with family members and fellow villagers.

Chechnya was now under occupation, its capital demolished by carpet bombing. What used to be a modern Soviet city – not too showy but pleasant and green – was reduced to a grey and beige mess of debris, littered with the skeletons of buildings. The tower blocks in the city centre were hit the hardest, since that was where the heaviest fighting took place. Outside the city centre, many Chechens opted to live in detached homes so they could grow their own produce in small kitchen gardens. This saved them from starvation during both wars, but the bushes and fruit trees were no protection, and almost every one of those quaint little houses bore shell holes or a damaged roofline. The iron gates that hid them were burnt and rusting.

Yet when the people crawled out of their basements and returned from the refugee camps, they began painting and fixing, putting what they could back together. Some fences still bore hand-painted signs that read *People live here!* – talismans against opportunistic looters and the Russian troops ravaging through abandoned neighbourhoods. Now, some of those signs began to disappear beneath fresh coats of bright green paint. In springtime, a riot of lilac bushes sprang up between the wounded buildings, filling the air with a heavy fragrance. Nature found its way into the ruins.

Since our own flat remained uninhabitable, Mum had managed to rent, at the end of summer 2001, a one-bedroom flat on the fourth floor of the same building. To reach it, you had to pass a massive hole that gaped in the middle of one of the landings, artfully concealed by three wooden planks that moved whenever you stepped on them. The flat itself was in a relatively good condition. It was furnished with old-style Soviet items like a massive dark veneer wall unit and a musty sofa that squeaked when you sat on it. Although there was a small bedroom at the back of the flat, Mum and I shared the sofa because we wanted to be close to each other. Besides, a mysterious smell lingered in the other room, the source of which was never discovered.

There was no electricity or running water in the whole building, or pretty much all of Grozny. When Mum was free from work, we did all the things families do during a power cut – we tackled jigsaw puzzles and played board games – except our power cut was permanent. Mum hated the smell of kerosene lamps, so we used wax candles, and when it got dark I did my homework or read by their flickering light.

One day, Mum surprised me with a new book about a little boy who found out he was a wizard. We cuddled together in bed as she read it out loud. From the very first pages, I was engrossed. I impatiently grabbed the book out of Mum's hands so that I might read ahead. The story of the wizard-boy, whose name was Harry Potter, became Mum's and my little secret. So far as I was aware, no one else in Chechnya had read it. Mum loved *Harry Potter* just as much as I did. For months after reading *The Philosopher's Stone*, I would see Hogwarts in my dreams, and imagine mounting a broomstick and flying high up in the air. 'Maybe when you turn eleven, you'll receive a letter from Hogwarts,' Mum said, 'and then you can learn how to become a witch.' I would have to wait another four years for my eleventh birthday, but I warned her that I would only attend Hogwarts if they opened a school in Chechnya because I couldn't imagine leaving my mother for months on end to study in a boarding school, even a magical one.

For now, my magic power was carrying heavy buckets of water to the fourth floor, water we collected from patched-up pipes with handmade taps on the side of a garage. Mum would grab the larger buckets, leaving the smaller ones to me, and we would tramp up and down the four flights of stairs two or three times to get the water we needed, which we'd pour into a large plastic tank in the flat, carefully rationing it out over several days. Although some Chechens drank what we called 'raw' water just as it was, Mum always used a water filter or insisted we boil it first. Some people came up with ingenious ways of delivering water to their flats. Our upstairs neighbours created their own pulley system, with a plastic rope. They would attach buckets to a metal hook and slowly lift them to their windows. These contraptions didn't last long, though – ropes tended to fray and buckets fell dramatically, splashing those unfortunate enough to be underneath and drenching the hanging washing on their way down. Mum and I preferred the traditional way. The hassle involved in getting water made it a precious commodity, and we used every drop. We lived sustainable and environmentally conscious lifestyles before it became trendy – laundry water was used for floor mopping and, after that, for flushing the toilet. For months, my poor mother had to hand-wash all our laundry, leaving her with burgundy-pink blisters all over her knuckles.

For me, the best part about living in the same building as our old flat was our neighbours. While I reconnected with my friend Kameta, Mum quietly chatted to Kameta's parents in the kitchen, asking them how they had survived, who they had lost. Kameta had changed since the war; it was as if her personality had hardened. Perhaps it was something to do with the fact that she was a year older than me and a middle child, always ordered around by her teenage sister, always expected to look after the younger one. I still called her my best friend, and we spent a lot of time together, playing in her flat or in the yard outside. But something told me that we were only saying it out of habit, and that maybe, when I wasn't around, she was pledging allegiance to some other girl.

In Chechnya, neighbours were a second family. Gossip and slander were commonplace, as were petty conflicts that sometimes erupted into screaming matches. But there was a deep sense of community and, in times of need, you could always knock on your neighbour's door, whether it was to ask for an onion or to shelter from gunfire. It was normal to pop in for tea without warning and stay a while, until the intervals between yawns became shorter and shorter.

After one such visit, Mum came home with a small plastic sack. 'Look,' she said, peeling away layers of rags, 'do you recognise them?' Then she produced three flutes with a familiar pattern of blue forget-me-nots. She placed the flutes safely behind glass, on the shelf of a cabinet, and suddenly this little flat really felt like home. In the few weeks that had passed since we'd moved into our rented home I had fallen in love with Grozny again, seeing past the ugliness that had been inflicted upon it. And Mum did everything in her power to bring normality back into our lives; she bought new bedding and a porcelain tableware set with golden rim and a pattern of pink roses. She even promised that we could get a cat soon, the ultimate symbol of home. But nothing she did could conceal the fact that we were living in a war zone.

*

The federals' khaki uniforms, and the Kalashnikovs that hung at their sides, became a familiar part of the cityscape. During the daytime we could go about our business as long as we complied with the 8 p.m. curfew. After dark, federals ruled the city and anyone found out on the street could get into serious trouble. The curfew specifically targeted young men of 'terrorist age', who were picked out by Russians and disappeared into the jaws of the Khankala prison. In those days, civilian men left their houses as little as possible – even during the day – for fear of being kidnapped, and women would often accompany their male family members to work or university, hoping that their presence would deter the federals. At night, fuelled by cheap vodka, Russian soldiers would open fire out of sheer boredom, often hitting residential buildings. We were used to hearing the clatter of bullets in the background, but on one particular night the gunfire appeared to be getting closer and louder. Suddenly my heart was beating out of my chest. I was acutely aware of the danger we were in. Tears followed, but not for long because Mum was already dragging our mattress into the windowless hallway, where we would be safe. Throughout the autumn of 2001, this night-time scene would be repeated once or twice every few weeks: Mum and I huddled on the hallway floor, her wrapping me in a hug and gently swaying from side to side, singing songs in my ear while I consoled in turn my stuffed racoon Yenny, who must have also been very scared.

Because of the endless gunfire, Mum never bothered installing glass in the window of the flat. Instead, like many Chechens, she opted for a clear plastic film that was easier to replace. Sometimes, in the morning, we would find stray bullets on the floor that had made their way through plastic – little 'gifts' from the federals. Mum always wanted to keep them as souvenirs, but whenever she forgot about them, I would chuck them in the bin; I had had enough of gunshots at school. Sometimes it seemed as if someone was firing Kalashnikovs right outside in the schoolyard, because our classroom windows – which were glassless too – faced a busy street.

'All right, children, close your textbooks,' my form teacher Rosa Arbievna would instruct in her calm, even tone. 'Climb under your desks and clasp your hands behind your heads. No need for panic.' We obeyed without delay. Some of the kids cried, others giggled, as if it was an adventure.

One autumn evening, Mum and I were visiting friends in the neighbouring district of Ippodromny and she lost track of time. When we finally left, it was twilight, though it was not yet seven. The air was fresh from recent rain, and I was jumping enthusiastically through puddles in my wellies. Suddenly, I found myself knee-deep in water – my left leg had disappeared into a wily manhole disguised as a puddle. Giggling, Mum pulled me up and I poured the muddy water out of my boot.

The sky turned dark blue and, with no streetlights, the trees began to look like monsters. To get home we had to pass a major checkpoint, and as we approached Mum told me to hurry, and to keep quiet. I sensed tension in the way she was squeezing my hand. The military base looked ominous against the dark sky. Little window cracks emitted a dull orange light, and the muffled sounds of music and chatter came from within. Mum gripped my palm even tighter and picked up her pace. Suddenly I heard laughter and, on top of the checkpoint – by now a few metres away – tiny, wobbly figures appeared.

'Faster, faster,' Mum hissed.

My heart pounded. Then, suddenly, the ground beneath me began to explode and my ears were ringing from loud gunfire. Someone was shooting at us and laughing. Dozens more were laughing along with him.

'LANA, DON'T MOVE!' Mum screamed. And then, turning her face towards the federals, she shouted, 'HEY!'

I froze and watched in horror as bullets hit the ground in front of me at terrifying speed, leaving tiny traces of smoke. Then I started screaming.

'HEY!' she went on yelling. 'Stop it immediately! I have a child with me! Stop it, you bastards!'

The shooting stopped. My knees were shaking and my hand throbbed with pain, because of how tightly Mum was gripping it. I felt so weak that I wasn't sure if I could make it home. We were still standing where we were, as if our feet were glued to the spot. Mum kept shouting at the federals, shaming them for what they did.

'Reveal yourselves, you cowards! COWARDS!' she screamed. 'Look at the woman and child that you almost killed. She's seven years old!'

The soldiers went silent and retreated into their base. The music stopped too. The sky was now pitch black.

We walked home, shocked and shaken. My sobs were interrupted only by the sound of water squelching inside my boot, but it didn't seem so funny anymore. When we arrived at the flat, Mum made some tea and we nestled in bed together. I was still trembling. 'I think what you need is a fairy tale,' Mum said. 'Remember my story about fear, and how we must conquer it?'

'Will you tell me again?'

And she did.

The next day I went to school as if nothing had happened.

The thirty-minute walk to school took us down Pervomayskaya Street, a long avenue flanked by beautiful strong trees. During the first war, this street had been the site of one of the first major battles between Chechen and Russian troops. Miraculously, most of the trees survived the shelling and made up for the disfigured and charred residential blocks on each side of the road. In the mornings, the air was fresh and clear, laced with the smell of damp earth and rotten leaves. As we walked, Mum would hold the handle of my heavy pink backpack to take the weight off my shoulders.

The only way to have a happy childhood in such a precarious setting was by holding on to everything that was good and bright and new. Anything painful or unpleasant, I papered over with stories of magic kingdoms, elaborate plots that my mind concocted every day, from the minute I opened my eyes. I was a resident of two worlds – the one that was imposed on me and the one that existed inside my head. On my walk to school, I would tell Mum about the dreams I'd had the night before. That morning, I told Mum about my dream of owning a golden retriever called Jack. We would make a superhero duo and would sneak into the Khankala prison to steal the keys of the unsuspecting federals. I would be wearing roller skates, naturally. Together Jack and I would release all the men from the torture chambers, and they would rise up and fight the federals, kicking them out of Chechnya once and for all.

'I really ought to record these stories on tape,' Mum laughed.

On my morning walk along Pervomayskaya Street, there were many more children like me on that walk – some with parents, others without. There were also bomb defusers in full body armour, walking on both sides of the street, poking the ground with long sticks. I wasn't sure how bomb defusing worked, but I'd developed the idea that the moment the soldier found something he would instantly explode and kill whoever happened to be walking near him. I tried not to think about that and continued talking nonsense and making up stories for Mum's entertainment. But every day the same image ran through my head as we were walking to school: the swearing, the explosion, bloodied earth flying everywhere, severed limbs, people running and screaming, others just standing there in shock.

At the end of the avenue, on the left, stood a monument to the deportation that was erected during Dudayev's administration and somehow survived both wars. I could see a statue of a hand holding a dagger floating behind the gates that surrounded the memorial statue. But at the junction, we turned right and ten minutes later arrived at the school gate. School N41 was considered one of the best in Grozny prior to the wars and was conveniently located close to the city centre. Opposite it stood what used to be a sports stadium. The chalk of the running tracks was still visible, and students were sometimes allowed to use the space for PE.

At the entrance of our school, visitors were confronted by collapsed walls and a roof that had been resting on the ground since the late nineties. It was hard to believe that those ruins could be used at all, but every day a crowd of fresh-faced children entered through the rusty gate. Mum would wave me goodbye and continue her journey to Memorial, walking past the stadium and down Victory Avenue.

Rosa Arbievna was enthusiastic but firm. She did her best to disguise the sorry state of our classroom, which was missing both a door and glass in the windows. Instead, there was plastic film similar to that which we had in our home. It let in light but didn't insulate the room very well. When the weather turned, my classmates and I kept our coats on all day and puffed cold air from our lungs, pretending we were smoking cigarettes. The missing door never bothered us either, until the day when the corridor suddenly filled with loud barking and, out of nowhere, a pack of stray dogs ran into the classroom, running around the rows of desks as though it had been choreographed. Everyone in the room, including my teacher, froze, unable to move or say a word. After circling the room several times, the dogs ran back outside, in the same order, where they continued to bark. The room exploded into laughter.

Apart from the occasional shooting scare and the stray dog incident, school N41 was quite ordinary. It may not have been the first choice for Mum – the one closest to our flat had been destroyed in the war – but it would do. I loved learning and I hated missing school, which tended to happen because of Mum's unpredictable work. I made friends fast and even became a teacher's pet. But my strongest memories of my time at school N41 are of a boy called Zelim I developed a crush on – a perpetual childhood habit. He didn't feel the same way about me, but that didn't deter me from following him around and coming up with schemes to ensure he broke up with his girlfriend, Makka. He kept giving me mixed signals (or so I thought). For Teacher's Day in November, he agreed to participate in a two-person play in which he was the narrator and I played a monkey puzzled by a pair of reading glasses. The play was a success and I thought that our thespian experience would bring us closer but, alas, he always went straight back to the desk he shared with Makka. The worst part was that Makka was a nice, friendly girl who didn't even protest when one day I sat in her place, boldly moving her belongings to my old seat.

Not knowing how to express my feelings, I would pick fights with Zelim, which inevitably ended up with me hitting him with a textbook. To me it was common knowledge that boys pulled girls' hair and girls hit boys with textbooks. Only Zelim never pulled my hair. I thought that everything was going well and gave him small tokens of affection – mainly old toys from chocolate Kinder eggs that I wasn't interested in anymore. Then one day, after school, a girl from my class sprinted towards me. She stopped to catch her breath and muttered:

'Lana . . . run!'

'What do you mean?'

'Zelim's mum is here and she's very angry! He told her that you've been beating him up, so she came to school to spank you!'

Looking over at the school gate, I saw a very cross-looking woman going from child to child. Clearly, she was asking them about my whereabouts. There was no time to think; ignoring my pounding heart, I started running away from school and didn't stop until I reached a tall tree with thick branches – the perfect shelter. I leapt up it like a squirrel, imagining that Zelim's mum might grab my ankle at any moment. I wasn't sure I would be hidden in the leafless branches, so instead I tried to make myself as flat as possible against the smooth tree trunk – I really didn't fancy a spanking from a strange woman. As I clung to that tree I thought about my relationship with Zelim and where it had gone wrong. At first, I felt betrayed:

How dare he run to his mummy and complain that I'd been bullying him when I was just being playful? What a coward, he's not a real man if he can't handle a little teasing! True . . . but he's only seven years old. So? He's a boy! Boys should be strong and able to withstand anything. I would never go and complain to my mum, I would fight back! But that would be unfair because I'm a girl and boys can't hit girls.

I felt very confused. Over the course of my tree therapy session, a half-formed revelation came to me: *Boys have feelings and they get hurt too. It's not right to hit them for no good reason! Oh, I've made such a fool of myself, following Zelim around like a dog. Everyone is probably laughing at me. And now, here I am, sitting halfway up a tree, hiding from his mother.*

I stayed there for a long time, to make sure that I was safe. Then, I carefully climbed down and headed home, cheeks burning. I would not be telling this to Mum.

The next day, I was unusually quiet. No one mentioned Zelim's mum to me, to my great relief. I knew what I had to do and it wasn't going to be easy. After the bell rang, I walked up to Zelim's desk and tapped him on the shoulder: 'Can we talk?'

'Listen,' I began, when the last of our classmates had disappeared behind the door frame. 'I've been really mean to you. I shouldn't have hit you for no reason. I promise that I won't do it again and that I'll stay away from you. Deal?'

Zelim looked as if he didn't know what to say. After a moment, he smiled and nodded. I stretched out my hand and he shook it, then I swiftly turned around and left the classroom, swallowing salty tears.

With that chapter closed, I rushed to nurse my broken heart at my piano lesson, five floors up in a building in the centre of the city. There, I'd be greeted by my Russian music teacher, Larisa Sergeyevna, a petite, patient woman in her early sixties, with short salt-and-pepper hair. She showed me how to spread my fingers across the keyboard and made me repeat the same sequences of notes again and again. I loved the idea of being able to play but hated the amount of practice required. Too bad, because every night Mum would lead me into the bedroom of our flat – a room we rarely used because of its odd, damp smell – which housed an old, out-of-tune piano. While my hesitant fingers moved across the keys, Mum would stand behind me with a candle in her hand, lighting up the room. If I stumbled over the notes, she tried her best to help me, though she had never learnt an instrument herself.

'Maybe you should play this note instead – is this a *ti*?' she would suggest.

'Mum, it's a *la*,' I would sigh in response.

Piano lessons were part of Mum's plan to turn me into a 'proper lady'. Requirements for this included speaking at least one European language and playing a musical instrument. A proper lady – according to Mum – must have perfect posture, excellent manners – no elbows on the table – and be polite, educated and well-read. She is principled and proud, and she never gossips. Mum was determined that war was not going to impede my progress, but her dreams of making an accomplished pianist out of me came crashing down when my music teacher moved back to Russia to live with her daughter. With a heavy heart, she sold us her beautiful piano for just four thousand roubles – a little less than a hundred pounds in today's money – because she couldn't take it with her. Mum promised she would take good care of it. I overheard her whispering to her friends that my teacher had implored her to carry on with my piano lessons because 'Lanusya has perfect pitch, and a real musical gift'. I wished that Mum would praise me to my face, but she thought it would make my ego grow too big, which would be very unladylike. People like us couldn't afford to be snooty. I wish I had remembered that when I decided to reject almost an entire box of humanitarian aid.

Gummanitarka, aid that came from relief funds like UNICEF, became a lifeline for Chechens trying to make it through the winters.

The coveted boxes contained anything from clothes and shoes, to books, household items and tinned food. The same familiar items of *gummanitarka* clothing could be seen across the city; it was common to see men and women wearing the exact same black jacket. Sometime in January 2002, *gummanitarka* arrived at our school. Lessons were delayed as my classmates and I were handed our own personal boxes of aid, and we hurried to open them. I tried on a warm navy jacket and was eyeing up the pair of wellies in my hands when it suddenly hit me that most of my classmates were trying on all the same things – jumpers, coats, boots and backpacks. I hated the idea of having matching outfits with the other girls! And what about that awful cardboard box? I didn't want to be seen carrying it all the way home, it was so large and clumsy-looking . . . I wrinkled my nose. Going through my new possessions, I set aside a jumper in a bright turquoise shade which was unlike all the others, a plastic carrier bag and a pair of socks. I gave the rest to a girl from my class who accepted them happily.

'We're not *that* poor after all,' I reasoned on my way home, swinging the carrier bag with the jumper and socks inside.

That evening, when Mum came back from work, I rushed to show her my new *gummanitarka*. She was surprised: 'Is that it? Only a jumper and a pair of socks?'

'Well, there was more . . .'

'What do you mean?'

I got a serious telling off from Mum that night. As much as I didn't want to believe it, we *were* poor, just like most Chechens. Mum could barely afford to buy me a new winter jacket. I had only two pairs of jeans and Mum had only one coat. We barely ever ate meat. I quickly realised I had messed up.

Mum was determined to get the stuff back and so the next day, to my deep embarrassment, she came into school with me. I pointed to the girl that I had given the box to and Mum went to speak to her. After a couple of minutes, she came back, barely able to contain her anger. 'Can you imagine,' she exclaimed. 'She gave the box to her mother, who is selling it all at the market right now! What a scammer! I'm going to get it back.' With that, Mum left the classroom, leaving me in a state of high anxiety. The whole situation was getting out of hand.

That evening, Mum came home empty-handed. She had confronted the woman at the market, but had been told that all the stuff was already sold. 'What a silly monkey I have for a daughter,' she said. She didn't even shout, which somehow made it worse. The truth was that back then I still hadn't fully comprehended that we were living through a war, trapped inside its malevolent dome of violence and destruction. It didn't occur to me that all the 'bad' things that made up our lives – the need for humanitarian aid, the lack of electricity and running water, the checkpoints, the gunfire, the mines, the curfew, the kidnappings, the ruins that surrounded us – could be arranged together into a jigsaw that spelled out WAR.

Life went on despite everything. Every morning I went to school, then either to piano class or Memorial. Afterwards I would take a bus home. I did all this on my own from the age of seven. Sometimes, I would hang around in the office a little longer, and if Mum had a chance to get off work early we would pop into the central city market to pick up some groceries. The busy bazaar awoke at around 7 a.m. with armies of women dragging their trolleys from every direction and setting up their stalls. It was the same market where Mum had witnessed the horrific aerial bombardment in 1999 that she described so vividly in her journal. Now it was the commercial heart of the city, where women in patterned maxi-skirts and headscarves haggled over sacks of potatoes and flour, men with lined, tired faces held out cardboard signs that read *Looking for work*, and small children did what children do everywhere – tugged at their mother's sleeves, begging to be bought a treat. The whole place looked like a small city with a maze of narrow streets made up of tents and stalls covered in blue tarpaulin. It was hard to navigate these rows in bad weather as the whole place turned into a sea of moist, deep mud that squelched unpleasantly under your feet. In some places, wooden planks and cardboard were laid down to act as bridges over the muddy puddles. Amid all the grime, framed by tower blocks in various states of dilapidation, there was sometimes a sudden flash of unexpected elegance – a bridal stall selling virgin-white dresses adorned with intricate lace and embroidery. The dresses that weren't covered in cellophane quietly swayed in the wind, waiting to be picked by some shy, small-waisted girl surrounded by a squad of bossy matrons.

No, I didn't think much about living in a war zone because my mind was filled with much more important things: decisions about what to buy at the bazaar with my pocket money, fights and reconciliations with friends (and Mum), fantasies about magical worlds. And, apart from a few setbacks, there was more and more light in our lives – quite literally. Sometime in early 2002, slowly, electricity reappeared, in our neighbourhood and then in our tower block. Light returned to our kitchen first, and then flickered through the rest of the flat. Initially the power was very weak, so we could only use one electrical device at a time. If I wanted to turn on the vacuum cleaner, for instance, I would have to switch off the TV. From time to time, the electricity would disappear for a few days, but we knew it would eventually return, and each time it did it came back stronger. When the electricity began to be less fickle, Mum bought our very first washing machine from a brand called Fairy. Alas, whenever the power was too weak Fairy lost her magic and stopped mid-cycle.

One evening, shortly after the electricity had become strong enough to have the TV on, I was struck by something unexpected when flicking through the channels (we only had about four). I came across a Russian TV channel that was showing a story about Chechnya. As always, it wasn't really about us – it was about a made-up place where every Chechen was a terrorist and danger was hiding behind every corner. There was a higher-ranking officer on screen, a colonel perhaps, going on and on about something, holding up a magazine. The camera panned in on the cover, which showed a soldier wearing a Kalashnikov on his chest and an army cap on his head. The magazine was called *My War*.

'"My War",' I repeated to myself. How odd it sounded . . . I was revolted. It felt wrong somehow, although I couldn't put into words why. The possessive 'my' suggested a tenderness, as if the soldier was talking about his girlfriend, or his motherland, not a force that was tearing apart people's lives. How could a war belong to someone? Was this why they acted with such impunity, because they felt as if they owned war, as if they had tamed it like a pet? The magazine's title was sick, twisted. That evening, I understood something about the federals. It was *their* war, not *mine*. A simple thought, really, but an important one. To them, it was a job, a game, a way to pass the time, even an old pal. We never chose this war, the choice was made for us by these men in camouflage, staring at me from the TV screen.

Gone were our quiet family evenings, now that power had returned to our home. Instead, Mum would spend hours typing away on her laptop, often bringing work into bed. I grew used to falling asleep to the soft glow of the screen and the rhythmic tapping of the keyboard. We didn't do jigsaw puzzles anymore, but flat renovation became a new hobby. It turned out that Mum had been setting aside small sums of money for months, and one day she announced that we were going to install a new front door on our damaged ground-floor flat. The eight-year-old me was indifferent, but I went along to have a look: it was a decent metal door with a lock and a peephole. As Mum and I navigated the rubble of what used to be our narrow covered balcony, I spied on the neighbourhood kids playing in the yard and poked my fingers through the holes in the cement balcony wall. The next day we came back with brooms and swept away the mess, sneezing and coughing, spraying the rooms with water to settle the dust, filling bag after bag with rubbish and taking them to the skip. Whenever we took a break, sitting down on the bulging plastic bags, we talked about all the design possibilities for the flat. Maybe we should turn the covered balcony into an office. Or we could fill it entirely with plants and hang up a parrot cage, creating a real jungle. Maybe we should turn the kitchen into my bedroom and paint it blue, because pink is boring. And when we have guests to stay, which we always do, Mum could sleep with me. After our years of staying with friends and family, of cheap rented rooms and communal living, it was thrilling to sit on those plastic bags in our very own home and dream about the future. As soon as the rooms were cleared, Mum paid someone to bring my new piano to the flat, where it sat temporarily in our hallway. As it was dropped off, I lifted the lid on the keyboard and played a melody with one finger. Mum hired builders to patch up the walls – to fill the holes and dents with cement and smooth them over. There was still a long way to go but we were getting there. I couldn't wait to move in.

In September 2002, N7, newly renovated, opened its gates for hundreds of students once more. It felt very symbolic that I would now be attending the same school where Mum had once taught history. It was also just a short walk from our flat. On 1 September I arrived in my new personal uniform, a plaid red-and-green skirt with a green blazer, looking as if I'd just transferred from a private school in England. The outfit was out of place in the sea of children dressed in more traditional white tops and black bottoms. As I moved through the crowd of students, inhaling the smell of fresh paint, I wondered who would become my next best friend. The children in my class were all a year or two older than me because I'd skipped a year, but also because it was normal to have students of different ages in the same grade: in our class of nine- and ten-year-olds we even had a pair of fifteen-year-old twins. War had shaped children's lives as much as it had their parents'. Forced to shelter from bombardments in basements or flee their homes altogether, our education had been interrupted again and again. It was rare to find a class without any orphans; in my grade, four children – including myself – didn't have fathers, and one girl had lost both her parents.

On the first day of school we were greeted by our form teacher, Nadezhda Viktorovna, a Russian lady with dyed mahogany hair. She and I started on a friendly note; she was pleasantly surprised by my general knowledge and reading skills. But several months in, things began to sour.

At the start of February, Nadezhda Viktorovna asked all the girls in the class to stay behind after school, giving us a conspiratorial wink. 'As you know,' she started, 'on 8 March, we will celebrate Women's Day, and the boys are already preparing something special for you.' This Soviet tradition had survived in modern Russia and, by default, migrated to Chechnya too. What began as a march for better working conditions for women, over a hundred years ago, had turned into a celebration of stereotypes about 'the fairer sex', accompanied with sad-looking carnations and chocolates. 'I was thinking', Nadezhda purred, 'that we could organise a little celebration for our boys for Defender of the Fatherland Day on 23 February.'

I was stunned by this. I thought I had misheard her.

'But Nadezhda Viktorovna,' I interjected, '23 February is the anniversary of our deportation. Can't we celebrate the boys on another date? In my last school, we did so on 12 April, Cosmonauts' Day.'

'That was your last school,' the teacher replied coldly. 'Here we celebrate on 23 February, with the rest of Russia. We must congratulate our future defenders.'

'Not on the anniversary of the deportation!' I was getting angry, and my voice started trembling.

'In that case, I will personally ask the boys not to give you a gift on Women's Day!'

'I don't care about that!' I yelled back, furiously shoving pens into my pencil case. 'I will not celebrate on the day my grandfather was deported from Chechnya!'

Fuming, I grabbed my schoolbag and stormed out of the classroom, attempting to slam the door on my way out – but failing because of how old its frame was – and ignoring the threats Nadezhda Viktorovna shouted after me. Adrenaline coursing through my body, I tried and failed to choke back my tears. Every Chechen was brought up hearing the stories of the Ardakhar, how we were forced to leave our homes with no time to even gather our belongings, how we starved and perished on the way to Central Asia. There wasn't a single family that wasn't touched by the deportation. I wiped my eyes with my shirtsleeve all the way back to our flat.

When Mum came home that evening, I sat on her lap and gave her an account of my run-in with Nadezhda Viktorovna. 'I would have done exactly the same thing, Lanuska,' she reassured me, stroking my hair. 'I'm so very glad that I have such a brave daughter. I'm going to go to the school tomorrow and have a word with her. To celebrate the day of the deportation in Chechnya is shocking.'

The next day, she took Nadezhda Viktorovna aside after school and spoke to her for several minutes. What was said between them remains a mystery, but my teacher returned with a saccharine smile on her face. After that, she seemed to have forgotten about our row, though Mum insisted that I skip the Women's Day celebration that year. She worried that Nadezhda Viktorovna would carry out her plan to humiliate me by depriving me of a present. Instead, we celebrated with our upstairs neighbours, who put on a huge spread. Mum wore her beautiful navy skirt suit and I donned a strawberry-patterned dress that she had made for me, reusing one of Auntie Sveta's old skirts.

A month later, Nadezhda Viktorovna turned up to our classroom with a small cardboard box. Inside was a stack of papers that bore an emblem – a bear walking underneath a Russian tricolour – and the words 'United Russia', whatever that was supposed to mean. On the back of the papers there were three words: 'War', 'Peace' and 'Referendum'.

'Children,' our teacher called out, 'we have been asked to have a little vote in our classroom. What do we say to war?'

'No!' we responded in unison.

'And what do we say to peace?'

'Yes!'

'And what do we say to a referendum?'

We weren't sure about that one. The class fell silent: everyone was too embarrassed to ask what a referendum was.

'A referendum will help bring peace,' prompted Nadezhda Viktorovna. 'And we all want peace, yes?'

'Yeees!'

'Then write down the answers as I told you and hand the ballot papers back to me.'

Ignoring my doubts, I complied with the order and wrote 'No-Yes-Yes' on the piece of paper. 'Referendum' sounded like a Latin word, which in my experience could only mean a positive thing, perhaps because I grew up listening to snippets of ancient history from Mum. But she wasn't too happy when she got home and I told her about our vote.

'Why did you sign that rubbish?' Mum grilled me. 'Was there anyone else in the room apart from your teacher?'

'Yes, there was a young man and a woman. But they didn't say anything!'

'Do you know what United Russia is? It's Putin's party. He's using this sham referendum to stay in power.'

She explained to me that in countries with proper democracies, a referendum is indeed a good thing that allows people to make decisions collectively on serious matters. But in Chechnya, a republic that didn't even have a proper government, the results would be meaningless. I had just turned nine, and didn't know much about politics, but I knew enough to hate Putin. I hated him with all the powerful earnestness that was reserved for bullies and the villains in books. And now I felt grubby.

'Never sign anything you don't understand, Lanusya, okay? Never.'

The real constitutional referendum took place on 23 March 2003, with an impressive 95.97 per cent turnout, of which 95 per cent voted for a new constitution that incorporated Chechnya into the Russian Federation. The results were as fake as a Gucci logo on a Grozny girl's headscarf. Many Chechens wouldn't have even known that there was a vote – we were too preoccupied with surviving shelling and *zachistkas*. In October of the same year, Akhmad Kadyrov was voted president of Chechnya by another suspiciously high majority. There were widespread reports of voter intimidation at both the presidential and parliamentary elections, and neither referendum was recognised by international intergovernmental bodies such as the Council of Europe or OSCE (Organization for Security and Co-operation in Europe).

On the TV, while local news anchors announced that Akhmad Kadyrov had become the first president of the Chechen Republic, I was confused. I may have been young, but I knew that Dzhokhar Dudayev was the first president of Chechnya. This new regime was becoming adept at erasing true history and replacing it with a version that the Kremlin deemed more palatable. They wanted to start with a clean slate, to wipe away the splattering of blood. In Russia, Vladimir Putin was more than halfway through his presidential term and his grip on power was rapidly turning into a chokehold. Following the horrific 2002 Moscow theatre hostage crisis, organised by Shamil Basayev – where 912 hostages were held at the Dubrovka Theatre, 132 of them dying in the rescue attempt – it was crucial for Putin to uphold his reputation as a ruthless and decisive leader. Appointing a puppet president in Chechnya, a president who would continue Putin's war against terrorists (which also meant war against civilians), was a major victory for the Kremlin.

It was a strange time to live in Chechnya. I noticed that more and more of the men in military uniforms carrying Kalashnikovs were Chechen speakers. The federals were still there, and the checkpoints were still in place, but law enforcement was diversifying. Since

Akhmad Kadyrov had become president there had been a push to pass the mantle of 'counterterrorism' to ethnic Chechens. In 2003 an amnesty programme was announced for rebels who fought against Russia, and many switched sides – sometimes under coercion, sometimes by choice. These were times of mass unemployment, and the prospect of joining the special forces was very appealing to some. Several Chechen clans – the Kadyrovs, the Yamadayevs, the Baysarovs – founded their own military squads, embarking on a vicious power struggle. Often, these warring clans were used as proxies for competing Russian federal agencies looking to settle their own scores. They proved as brutal at repressing the civilian population as their Russian masters. Akhmad Kadyrov's twenty-seven-year-old son, Ramzan, had been appointed the head of his father's security detail. In practice, this meant the younger Kadyrov was now in charge of his own ever-expanding private army, a force that would be commonly known as the kadyrovites, or *kadyrovtsy*.

But all that was happening off in the distance – on the TV screen, two streets down, outside the walls of our flat. In my little bubble it felt that Mum and I had finally found some stability. My grades were good. We got our first postwar cat, Lucky, and a pair of parakeets, Chiko and Tutti. Mum bought plants for the windowsills, and I developed a habit of planting fruit seeds, although I would abandon them the second they started to sprout. I've always been bad at finishing the things I've started.

Our house was filled with interesting guests – human rights activists, lawyers, journalists. Some of them appeared regularly; others would show up just once, to cover a story, and then disappear out of our lives again. Because it was dangerous coming to Chechnya, the safest option for visiting journalists was to stay with someone you knew and trusted, and our little flat fitted the bill. The 'price' that our guests had to pay was listening to my stories and letting me practise speaking English with them. I loved having people to stay and would pester my mother weeks in advance: 'When is Alik coming? When is Tanya coming? What about Lena? And Varya and Sasha?'

Mum's close friend and colleague, the journalist Anna Politkovskaya who wrote for *Novaya Gazeta* – we called her 'Anya' – was our most frequent house guest. No one could pinpoint exactly when or where

Mum had met Anya for the first time. Most likely, they had met in the Nazran Memorial office in 2001. In the following years, they'd become good friends. We often stayed at Anya's place in Moscow – a beautiful, spacious flat with large windows and book-lined shelves. The best part about her home was her giant chocolate-coloured Doberman called Martyn, who let me play with him for as long as I pleased. In the evenings, Anya would cook us strange foreign foods, such as turkey breast, and got terribly offended whenever I scrunched up my nose at it. She could be very stern, which made me a little scared of her. There was no slouching or incorrect grammar in front of Anya; she would always quietly correct me, never raising her voice, but managing to express a range of emotions, from joy to disdain, with just a single octave. She was tall and slim, with grey hair that contrasted with her youthful, angular face. I wanted to ask her why she didn't dye her hair like all women her age I knew – she was born in the same year as Mum, in 1958 – but tact held me back. She shared Mum's sense of humour, too, dismissing dangerous people and situations with ironic, withering comments. I loved her. Whatever fire burned inside my mother's soul, a fire that compelled her to move mountains to help others, Anya had it too. It's no wonder they worked so well together – a frantically busy and effective duo, with strong personalities that on occasion inevitably clashed.

'You know who Natasha was to Anya, right?' asked Sasha Cherkasov, one of Mum's Memorial colleagues, when we spoke about their friendship years later. 'She was her Virgil, taking her through all the circles of hell.'

This was an apt description of their partnership. Anya had been writing about the war between Russia and Chechnya since 1999. Just as Mum was more than just a human rights activist, Anya was more than just a journalist. When she wrote about the horrors that she came across – overcrowded refugee camps without basic necessities, secret prisons run by federals, bombings of Chechen civilians – her aim was to get through to the politicians and everyday Russians, to implore them: 'Do something. Help your countrymen. Don't ignore people's suffering because one day you might be the one who needs help.' Anya was often described as the voice of the voiceless, and Mum came to her again and again, asking her to cover one painful story after another, guiding her into the heart of darkness.

The number of official criminal investigations into human rights violations in Chechnya was appallingly low, which meant that torture and murder could be committed with near impunity. 'It gets drummed into their heads that you can do anything to a Chechen and nothing will happen to you,' Mum argued in one of her interviews. She and Anya wanted to see perpetrators punished according to the letter of the law. They sought justice, not revenge, and sometimes their hard work and persistence paid off.

There are many memorable cases, documented by Mum and Anya, in which Russian army officers were given prison sentences for war crimes committed in Chechnya. Even as a child, I was all too aware of the macabre details of these trials. But one case held a particular significance for us because the claimants, Rukiyat and Astemir Murdalov, became our close family friends. In the years that Mum worked with them, we visited their house several times, staying for a few hours to chat and drink tea. I remember being jealous whenever Anya stayed with them overnight, instead of us.

'You know that they have to work together on Astemir's case,' Mum would reassure me. 'That's why Anya's here. And besides, Stas is coming too and there is no way they would all fit in our flat.'

'Stas is coming too?!'

Stas, as we called Stanislav Markelov, was the best. He was a brilliant lawyer, but more importantly, he was incredibly funny, with an unlimited supply of quips and jokes. He always had me in stitches.

When Stas and Anya arrived in Grozny, we gathered at Astemir and Rukiyat Murdalov's large, immaculately kept house. It was the only inhabited house on the street: all the others still stood damaged and abandoned. In the front yard, right behind the gates, bloomed a beautiful rose garden that filled the air with sweet fragrance, green-fingered Astemir's pride and joy. There was something touching about seeing this slender, six-foot-two man, with a jaw so chiselled he might have stepped out of a black-and-white Hollywood movie, pottering about his garden, carefully planting and trimming his precious roses. We would return home with heavy bunches of flowers wrapped in old newspapers.

The moment the guests arrived, Rukiyat rushed to the kitchen to prepare some 'tea' – which in Chechnya always meant a full meal or at the very least a large spread with jams, sweets, bread, chopped-up vegetables and cheese. She was anxious that there wasn't enough food, although we repeatedly reassured her that everything was perfect. Whenever their youngest daughter, twenty-something Zalina, was home, she would sit with me and ask me a million questions and lightly tease me about my crushes. She was the image of both her parents, having inherited the symmetrical oval of her father's face and her mother's large, brown eyes framed by dark, arched eyebrows. The same was true of Zelimkhan, her older brother; they were more like twins than siblings. But of course, I only knew this from photographs of Zelimkhan. The Murdalov family was small by Chechen standards, but it was built on unconditional love and mutual respect. You could feel the closeness whenever you were near them. This made Zelimkhan's absence all the more noticeable. As a child, I used to sit out on their terrace with the lull of conversation in the background, listening to the occasional outbursts of laughter and – yes – the chirping of the birds drawn to the garden's small fruit trees. Inside the house, the temperature was about five degrees cooler. There is a special kind of silence that exists in the homes of the disappeared, a museum-like stillness where once-used objects become exhibits and photographs become shrines. Everything is kept in pristine order, as if the house itself is waiting for the missing person to walk in at any moment.

On 2 January 2001, Zelimkhan left the house to walk to his university and never returned. Witnesses saw the twenty-six-year-old student being abducted by the federals and taken to a nearby police station. The kidnappers were later identified as OMON – special police – officers from the Khanty-Mansiysk region of Siberia, a notoriously ruthless unit known as the Khanty. What happened to Zelimkhan that day came to light because his cellmates shared the information with his parents who, in turn, passed it on to my mother. For hours, Zelimkhan was beaten and tortured by an officer called Sergey Lapin, codenamed 'Kadet', and two soldiers under his command, all of them Khanty. They wanted Zelimkhan to become an informer, although he had zero connection to the rebels. When Zelimkhan was returned to his cell in the early hours of 3 January, he was a bloody mess. A bone was sticking out of his shoulder and his ribcage was completely crushed. His genitals were smashed to a pulp and his right ear was missing. As Zelimkhan began to convulse, his cellmates read prayers over him. Later that morning, his unconscious body was taken away and, after that, he disappeared. Zelimkhan's body was never found – a final blow to his parents, who couldn't give their beloved son a proper burial.

Rukiyat, Astemir and Zalina were prepared to take on the whole rotten army apparatus to get justice for their boy. Mum, Anya and, later, Stas would spend years on Zelimkhan's case, interviewing witnesses, piecing together events and finally identifying the perpetrators. The Khanty squad threatened and intimidated not only Zelimkhan's family but also the military-prosecution team that investigated the disappearance. Kadet, the torturer-in-chief, sent personal threats to Anya. Mum also feared for Stas's life, at one point asking him to stay away from Chechnya for a while. It didn't seem to cross her mind that she was the one permanently living in one of the most dangerous places in the world with her daughter. Thanks to the combined efforts of the super-trio and relentless campaigning from other human rights organisations, including Memorial and Amnesty International, Kadet would eventually be put on trial in 2005. 'This is a unique court case,' Mum said in an interview. 'For the first time, the trial of military personnel who committed crimes in Chechnya is taking place in the republic itself.' On 29 March 2005, Kadet would be sentenced in one of Grozny's courts to eleven years in a maximum-security prison.

After the trial, Mum showed me a stack of photographs, close-ups she had taken of Kadet at the trial. At one point, he had buried his head in his hands, hiding from the intrusive flash of Mum's cheap camera. 'Look,' she told me. 'Look closely. This is the face of a monster. He's sitting in a cage, where he belongs.'

I glanced at the photograph and was taken aback by his eyes – they were dull and vengeful, two dark pools burning with hate. It was a rare victory for a grieving family, but even this historic sentence was built on compromise – other criminals involved in Zelimkhan's torture and disappearance never faced their day in court.

Flawed as it was, the sentencing of Kadet represented a brief moment, early in Putin's climb towards authoritarian rule, when it seemed that the machine of state – the constitution, the judiciary, civil institutions – might still be bigger than him, that change might still be possible. That's why Mum and her colleagues from other civil rights organisations were willing to work with the government to propose structural changes. They participated in two-sided panel discussions and round tables with government commissions and councils with one goal in mind: to make people's lives better. To ensure that army officers didn't commit atrocities and that if they did, they would face punishment. To ensure that if soldiers obeyed criminal orders then they would be held responsible, and that inmates didn't get subjected to torture in prisons, even if they had committed crimes.

Mum was open to speaking with anyone, be it a slimy official or a colonel elbow-deep in blood, if it meant that lives could be saved. In doing so, she didn't betray her principles but rather demonstrated time and time again that for her, as for most of her colleagues, every human life was worth fighting for. Mum never fantasised about overthrowing the government; in fact, she rarely indulged in political debate. It was not her job. She simply wanted to live in a lawful society where everyone had a chance to live a peaceful, dignified life. In the end, the regime treated these aspirations as if they were the most dangerous, radical ideas imaginable. The only ammunition Mum and Anya had was the power of their words.

To be constantly surrounded by such an excruciating amount of pain at such a young age took a certain amount of stubborn obliviousness. I was determined to be light and carefree. Sometimes, when cleaning our flat, I would stumble across a handwritten missing person report or a witness testimony that included graphic details. Occasionally, I came across photographic evidence: a pale male body with watercolour-like bruising, lilac fading into yellowish-purple. I arranged these discoveries into tidy piles, tucking the photographs away so that Mum could easily find them. At night, when these images swam in my mind, I shooed them away.

To visitors from outside Chechnya, our way of life – with buckets of water and holes in the wall – seemed exotic and edgy. They would *ooh!* and *aah!* at it. Sometimes this irritated me – it was as if we were museum exhibits. But Mum had put a lot of effort into making our rented place look cosy, while fixing up our studio flat in her free time. I was responsible for keeping everything tidy. In Chechnya, having a dirty home is considered entirely unacceptable. Cooking and laundry were my mother's jobs, but everything else – the dishes, dusting, sweeping and mopping – had been my responsibility since the age of seven. Friends and visitors considered our flat a glowing oasis among the ruins and destruction.

But, while building a home was important to us both, I also knew how crucial Mum's job was. I felt a mixture of pride and sympathy whenever I walked past a line of women outside the Memorial office, their weathered, lined faces suddenly lighting up, faint smiles appearing at the sight of a child. 'Where is Natasha? When will she come?' they asked. Her colleagues didn't cut it – Shamil, Shakhman, Lida – they only wanted Mum. Eventually, she would convince them that the rest of the team was just as dedicated and trustworthy as she was, that she couldn't take on every single case.

By late 2003, Mum and I had established something resembling a routine, dividing our time between work, school and flat renovations, until one day it was interrupted by an impatient drumming on the door. I opened it to find two neighbourhood girls, red-faced and out of breath, their short black fringes glued to their foreheads with sweat.

'There were two women . . .' they began, speaking over each other.

'They were asking who the ground-floor flat belongs to . . .'

'. . . so mean-looking!'

'They said that they'll be paying you a visit . . .'

'One of them was like, "This is our brother's flat. You better tell your friend to clear out!"'

'They're going to come back, for sure!'

'Razet was passing and she told them where you and your mum live!'

I stood frozen in the doorway, unsure of what to do. I was alone in the flat. Barely anyone in Chechnya had a phone in 2003, either a landline or a mobile, so calling Mum was out of the question. Why did that stupid neighbour Razet tell them where we lived? In the end I just locked the door and decided to sit still and wait for Mum to come back. Not long after, there was a loud banging. I stayed quiet, not moving a muscle as the noise persisted.

'Open up, we know you're in there!' yelled one of two angry voices. I didn't move.

'You tell your mum to get the hell out of that flat, understand?'

I hardly dared to breathe. Finally, the two witches left. That was how they appeared to me – intimidating and impertinent, and, I imagined, with large crooked noses and warts all over their faces.

Mum's face went white with fury when I told her. 'Well done for not opening the door to them, Lanuska,' she said, hugging me. 'Don't worry, I'll make sure that they never come back.' And as far as I'm aware, they never did. Instead, their brother, the supposed original 'owner' of the flat, turned up at Mum's work and threatened her with a lawsuit.

This was a common story in the chaos of post-war Chechnya. Tens of thousands of people had fled, leaving homes to which they hoped to return as soon as it was safe. But often, while they were away, crooks and opportunists would move in there, grabbing their land and bribing officials to provide them with fake documents, making them the 'legal' owners. Upon their return, the refugees found strangers living in their homes, resulting in conflict and court battles.

The scam artist Mum and I fell victim to was of a different type: one who preyed upon 'weak' and 'unprotected' families, who were easy to destroy. A half-Russian single mother with no family in the local area, Mum appeared to be the perfect target. That's how our lives were upended by a man whom we only ever knew by the pseudonym 'Takhtarov'.

Takhtarov summoned Mum to court, claiming that *we* had occupied *his* property while he lived abroad as a refugee. That Mum and I had lived in the flat during the nineties, and that she had ownership documents, including the title deed, was irrelevant. According to Takhtarov, we had lied and forged all the papers. Nonetheless, Mum called numerous witnesses – old neighbours, friends, colleagues – frustrating Takhtarov's plan to get rid of us. Only half aware of what was going on, I eavesdropped anxiously, piecing information together as the legal process stretched on for months.

To make matters worse, Mum told me that she would have to miss my tenth birthday. She would be at a conference in Barcelona until

4 March and my birthday was on the 3rd. No amount of promised cake and presents could make up for it. I never asked for anything fancy anyway, knowing that Mum couldn't afford much. But my birthday meant everything to me, and Mum not being there would strip it of all its magic. She always found a way to make the day special. Every year there was a cake – bought from the market – a variety of sweets and juices, a pretty dress for me to wear and an open invitation to all the neighbourhood kids. Not every child in Chechnya had the privilege of hosting their own little birthday party.

I didn't throw a tantrum – that never worked with Mum – but I sulked in the corner, going through a list of resentments in my head. *The other day, Mum yelled at me for no reason! And she never thanks me for keeping the house clean, she only tells me off when it's dirty. And what did she give me for the last two birthdays? Jeans, both years! You can't give someone a present that they need anyway. And what does she do with the things I've given her, like that blue satin needle cushion that I hand-sewed? She keeps it in a desk drawer in Memorial, rather than displaying it.* I spent an entire evening revelling in self-pity.

While Mum was away in Barcelona, I stayed with the same relatives who used to live in the Karabulak refugee camp. They had moved back to the outskirts of Grozny, where they had set up a car-repair business. Their newly restored home was quite a departure from the tent they used to share. In typical Chechen fashion, it consisted of several small buildings with one or two rooms that all faced a large courtyard. At the back there was a small allotment for produce and an outhouse – indoor plumbing was the norm in apartment blocks, but not yet in detached homes.

Because my Auntie Tabarik had eight children and very little money, her family didn't tend to make a big fuss of birthdays. Nevertheless, when mine arrived, I expected *a little bit* of fuss – I was turning ten after all. But despite the heavy hints I dropped, nobody remembered – each member of the family went about their usual morning routine. I wasn't even taken to school because it was too inconvenient for my cousins to drive me into the centre of Grozny. At first, I couldn't believe it. I thought it was some sort of prank. Surely someone would say something soon. But as the hours went by, I accepted the harsh truth – no one cared about my birthday here – and I hid behind the garden swing for another sulk. The most important day of the year, the celebration of *me*, was for them just an ordinary day. I sat down to process this. *Does my existence even matter? If, for so many people, 3 March is just another day, am I irrelevant in the great scheme of things?* This event, or rather non-event, led to me spending most of the day alone, feeling as though there was a heavy cloud full of tears floating above me. Now I really understood how Harry felt when the Dursleys ignored his birthday year after year.

The next day, my happy shining Mum came to pick me up. 'Happy birthday, Lanusya!' she cried out, giving me a big hug. 'Oh, it was your birthday, of course!' said Tabarik with a sweet smile. But I didn't care, or hold a grudge, not now Mum was back.

'Lanka, there's a huge surprise waiting for you at home, but I have to warn you, not all of it is for you.' When we reached the flat, I found two gigantic suitcases in the hallway. 'You can open them,' said Mum. And so I did.

A colourful stream of toys burst out of the unzipped cases. There were too many Barbie dolls to count. There were stuffed toys that didn't look like anything I'd ever owned; they were *European*, made of good-quality material, resembling real animals, and missing the crazy sideways-looking eyes of my own soft toys. There were tiny doll-sized kitchens, clothes, shoes, telephones, furniture and accessories. There was Lego, there were toy cars, pens, pencils, puzzles and strange colourful blocks, the purpose of which I could not discern. While I was rooting around in my heap of treasures, Mum was telling me about her trip, but I was surrounded by an impenetrable bubble of joy, so was barely capable of hearing anything.

'Oranges, Lanka!' she exclaimed. 'Can you imagine, there were oranges growing on trees in February!'

The next day we had the best birthday party of my life. First, Kameta and her sisters, who lived in the flat directly above, put on a little theatre performance. Having been instructed to stand on our balcony, I saw several dolls, with strings attached to their waists, descend from the window above. The puppets exchanged insults then broke out into a fight, plastic Barbie dolls swinging and smashing into each other. I was laughing so hard I had tears streaming down my face. I reached out my hands to catch the dolls, but they were swiftly pulled away.

'Wait!' shouted Kameta. 'We have another surprise!'

They fumbled for a few minutes and then I saw a sack being lowered on a string. It hung close to my balcony, and suddenly I heard a mewing coming out of it. 'It's a cat in a sack!' yelled Kameta. 'You get it? A cat in a sack!' I thought I would die from laughter. I carefully caught hold of the sack and put it on the floor, releasing a dishevelled grey-and-white cat called Johnny, who belonged to our neighbours. After a hefty amount of fuss, I released him and he shot back to the fifth floor, this time taking the stairs.

Several hours later my friends gathered in our flat, awed by the sight of the toys covering every inch of the living room floor. We refused to stop playing even for a second, even to eat birthday cake, so Mum brought the cake to us. I blew out the candles in a hurry: nothing could distract me from that magical toy mountain.

What made that evening so special was knowing that tomorrow most of the toys would be gone; they were being given to an orphanage in Grozny. I was allowed to keep a couple of Barbie dolls and some accessories, but everything else had to go. The next morning, I had to make one of the toughest decisions of my life: I had to pick a perfect Barbie. I lined them all up and eliminated dolls one by one, selecting a shortlist first and then finally making my choice. I settled on a white-haired doll with blue eyes. She wasn't the prettiest one, and her hair colour was not ideal, but she had hinges in her elbows and knees, which made her super-flexible. This tipped the scales in her favour, and it was decided that she would be called Elizabeth, the circus acrobat. I also picked a Ken doll, Peter, who was to become a notorious womaniser, and a severe-looking Action Man, Jonathan, who had a missing leg and the most meticulously sculpted muscles I had ever seen on a doll. Jonathan was the husband of Jessica (my other Barbie doll) – miraculously returned after being lost in the mountains for years and suffering from amnesia. His leg had been eaten by a bear.

I parted with the rest of the toys with a light heart. Mum had instilled in me the importance of sharing with those who were less fortunate. This was so ingrained that I even censored my own fantasies, never letting myself want too much. We carefully stuffed the toys back into the suitcases, and I let my mother take them to the orphanage.

As much as Mum tried to shield me from it, in spring 2004 I became aware that we might lose our ongoing case to keep our flat. The judge was a distant relative of Takhtarov's, and Mum had tried but failed to get the case reassigned to another judge. Such were our crippled and corrupt courts. Besides, she was preoccupied with her own important work, leaving her with little time or energy to look after her private affairs. One day, we found ourselves unable to get into the flat – Takhtarov had changed the locks on *our* front door, the beautiful, expensive new metal door Mum had paid for. Throughout my childhood, I had seen and experienced many instances of injustice and humiliation, but this stood out. The sheer impertinence – what we call *naglost* – made me shake with rage. 'How dare he!' I yelled at Mum. 'I hate him! He's a pathetic, disgusting coward and a liar! I hope he burns in hell!'

I hated Takhtarov with a passion. I imagined dozens of ways we could defeat him – most of them ending with him humiliated and exposed in front of a laughing crowd. I wanted to meet him, to give him a piece of my mind. I dreamt about seeing him behind bars, while Mum and I walked by, throwing him contemptuous looks. One of us would say something like, 'Enjoy your new home!' I trialled different lines we could aim at him, debating which would be the most cutting.

The next day, I took a piece of pink chalk and, in large uneven letters, I wrote *Takhtarov! This flat will never be yours!* across the walls of the ground-floor balcony. Standing on tiptoes, I could reach it with ease. I stepped back to admire my handiwork; the pink words looked bright and fierce against the cheese-grater holes of the balcony wall. Several days later, Mum came home with news. 'Lanusya,' she snorted. 'You'll never believe it, but Takhtarov has made an official complaint that we're threatening his life! He's using your sign as evidence!' We burst out laughing.

'So, Lana is a criminal now.' Mum finished what must have been the tenth retelling of the story to friends. 'Pure Kafka,' someone replied.

I drew over the chalk words again and again, even after we lost the case. The relative-judge ruled that the flat belonged to Takhtarov and that we had to leave immediately (although in fact Takhtarov had already locked us out). The letters remained bright, even after the holes of the balcony were filled with cement. Mum later learnt that we were not Takhtarov's first victims: a con-artist, he had stolen large sums of money from other people and was on the run from the law in several European jurisdictions. Of course, he had never intended to live in the flat himself, quickly finding tenants and disappearing, as all good fraudsters do, in a cloud of legal smoke. One day, I walked past the flat that should have been our home, watching in anger as a young couple moved their belongings in.

'Welcome to our flat!' I yelled at a puzzled woman. 'I hope that you'll be very unhappy here and I curse both of you!' Triumphant, I walked away, constructing a powerful and unbreakable curse in my head.

Mum seemed strangely unfazed when I told her. 'Lanka, I have sad news,' she said quietly. 'Come, sit. I managed to look inside the flat the other day. The new tenants opened the door for me. Well, it turns out that there was a flood in the flat and Takhtarov, bastard that he is, did nothing about it . . . Your piano didn't survive the flooding. I'm so sorry.'

I didn't know what to say. I thought of my piano teacher, Larisa Sergeyevna, remembering the sadness on her face when, with no means of transporting it to Russia, she sold the piano to us. She had owned the instrument for decades. How would she feel if she found out it had been damaged beyond repair? Why did I suddenly feel so guilty? I buried my head in Mum's lap and sobbed, as she gently stroked my hair.

The next day, heading to the dumpster, I noticed a group of boys hitting something with iron bars. When I looked closer, my heart sank. It was my piano – a beautiful noble animal – being wrecked by the little vandals. It cried too, in a hundred different ways, producing a new sound each time the iron bars smashed into it. As the dark, polished wood cracked, little pieces flew up in the air, and it was rapidly reduced to splinters. I just stood there, rubbish bin in my hands, feet glued to the ground, watching as one of the boys took a lighter out of his pocket. Minutes later, the piano's carcass was consumed in red-orange flames. The bonfire danced and grew, as the hypnotised boys fed it wood. Soon, my left arm was aching from the weight of the bin. I chucked its contents and walked away, looking back after every other step.

'At least we don't have to look at it every time one of us empties the bin,' Mum tried to console me that evening. Then we sat at the table in silence, not knowing what to say. I never went back to playing the piano.

You would think that living through a war – or under the 'counter-terrorist regime', as they called it in the Kremlin – all of our problems would be caused by the federals. And, indirectly, this was true: you could probably trace our series of misfortunes back to the outbreak of the first war. But the fact was that we were running out of luck. Our cat, Lucky, died in mysterious circumstances; her body was found near the same dumpster where our piano was burned. Both our parakeets fled, one after the other; the first time it was my mum's fault, the second time it was mine. And just as Mum was trying to figure out where we should live, there was another knock on the door. Our landlady had come back to Grozny with her sons and wanted to move in immediately. She gave us two days in which to leave. Mum sent me away to Deshi-Yurt while she packed up our belongings, before dragging them to the fifth floor, to leave with the neighbours. She told me we'd go to the Urals for a couple of weeks and after that she'd make a plan. I chose to focus on the fact that I'd see my beloved Baba and my cousins again, rather than on the uncertainty that would await us on our return.

Unlike all the previous summers, this one seemed to have flown by. We stayed with Auntie Sveta and Baba in July. My older cousins – all boys – let me hang out with them. We rode bikes to the river and dived in from crumbling clay banks, swimming for hours in muddy water. When the sun went down we made fires and baked potatoes, shooing away bloodthirsty mosquitos. When the weather turned, as it often did during the temperamental Ural summers, we used Sasha's present – a small Sony camcorder – to shoot a complicated crime drama titled 'Murderous Murders'.

In August, I was back in Chechnya, unsure where we'd be at the start of the school year. Our few possessions were still with Kameta's parents and I was spending time at Deshi-Yurt. But in the final days of August, Mum came to collect me, with a huge smile that wouldn't leave her face.

'Lanka, we have a flat!' she beamed. 'It's a mess and needs a lot of work and it's in Ippodromny, but it's ours. And you will have your own room and you can decorate it however you want!'

I couldn't believe my ears. We were moving to Ippodromny, miles away from our old neighbourhood? But what about my school? 'It's a half-hour walk, I checked,' Mum reassured me. 'You can still go to your old school.'

Memorial had helped her with the purchase. Her colleagues had decided to use some grant money to buy us a home; they couldn't have their most valuable employee living on the streets. So, after all that Mum had done for others, never asking anything for herself, a little of it was returned to her with the sound of clinking keys.

Days later, in the final days of summer 2004, we moved into the flat that would become our home for the next five years. This time, we would not let anyone take it away from us.

How People Conquered Fear
by Natalia Estemirova

Once upon a time there was an evil, treacherous being called Fear. He loved nobody and wanted everyone to obey him. But people grew tired of the sound of his voice and having to lower their eyes under his wicked glare, and so they exiled him, sending him as far away as possible. Fear screamed and stamped his feet, but the people only laughed at him. Fear's anger made him shrunken and hunched, and he finally decided to retreat to the secluded woods of the mountains. He found himself a tree hollow and lived there with the owls and the spiders.

Some people enjoyed hiking in the mountains. They gathered forest nuts and wild raspberries and chatted with one another. Their voices filled the forest and Fear was furious. Concealing himself, he tripped people who passed by, or laced them with cobwebs, or screamed in their ears. This frightened the people who came to the woods, but then they would laugh again, and Fear would crawl back into his hollow, looking out with his tiny evil eyes.

But then some people moved too close to Fear's lair. Nearby there was a green valley with a wide stream that ran through it, irrigating the land. People began to build huts to live there, and very soon children were running up and down the slopes and women were washing laundry in the stream. The village grew larger and larger. The residents painted their houses bright colours and threw loud parties. They even built a palace from glass and pink limestone, and every evening they sang cheerful songs. They called it the Palace of Joy.

Fear flew into a rage and decided he would get rid of the people at any cost. He howled at night and blocked forest paths. But each night the people slept soundly and didn't hear a thing. The next morning they cleared the rocks, exchanging jokes as they worked. Then Fear blocked the mountain stream. The grass started to wilt, but the people dug wells and their gardens turned green again. Then Fear unblocked the stream. Water rushed down and swept away everything that was planted. 'Well, well, now you're going to starve to death!' Fear gloated. But the people began to make colourful toys and dishes out of the clay the flood had left behind, which helped them survive.

'It's all because of the sun,' Fear decided. 'It shines over the valley so brightly!' So he gathered all his powers and blew dark clouds into the sky, all close to one another, so that only a few rays managed to break through. But the people made mirrors and set them up on rooftops and walls. The sun's light hit the mirrors and multiplied, and soon the valley sparkled again.

Fear had to reconsider his schemes. What are the people's strengths and what are their weaknesses? He thought for a whole year and concluded: laughter is their strength and curiosity is their weakness. And, indeed, the people, especially the children, loved to stick their noses anywhere mysterious.

So Fear put on a bright-green trench coat in order to blend in with the locals, and went into the village. He held in his hands a small grey box. A young boy he met along the way stopped jumping around upon seeing the box and asked Fear, 'Sir, what's in that box?'

'Do you want to have a look?' asked Fear.

'Of course!' exclaimed the boy.

'Well then, lean over.'

The boy leaned over the box and Fear pressed a button. The lid suddenly opened and out jumped a scary demon on a spring. His face was so terrifying that the boy froze and his little heart sank. The lid closed, but the boy didn't smile anymore. He went home in gloom and went straight to bed. His mother was worried and the usual smile disappeared from her face too.

Fear continued to walk around the town, luring children in and stealing their smiles. The parents were frightened by their children's dead eyes and became sad themselves. They rushed to find doctors, but there were none because no one ever was ill in that town. And then Fear reappeared. This time he was wearing a charcoal gown. He looked much bigger now.

'Are you looking for a doctor?' he enquired.

'Yes,' the townspeople responded.

'I'm Doctor Reaf. I can cure any illness, but I have conditions.'

'Oh, tell us, we'll do anything!'

'You must obey me and do whatever I say without question.'

'Just tell us what to do. Please save our children.'

As he spoke, Fear grew until he towered above the crowds and the townspeople had to raise their heads to see him. Fear realised that he had everyone in his pocket and they would do whatever he ordered.

'Stop singing,' Fear commanded. 'Stop dancing. The children followed your example and it exhausted their strength.'

'Well,' everyone thought, 'he's a doctor, he knows best.'

The songs were gone. Silence hung over the town. Boredom climbed into households. Every day the townspeople laboured without any joy. Vermin devoured the harvest. They stopped baking pies; many people didn't even have enough bread to eat. More and more people became ill.

'It's the mirrors. They sparkle and irritate the eyes – that's why many people keep getting headaches,' declared Doctor Reaf, standing on the balcony of what used to be the Palace of Joy. Now all the windows were draped in thick, dark curtains, so the sun couldn't penetrate the rooms.

After taking down the mirrors, the townspeople painted their houses dark grey, put on plain clothes and destroyed all the toys (according to Doctor Reaf, they too drained children's energy).

Following the sickness came death. The people were rarely seen in the fields or on streets, except for funeral processions. After a while there were more graves than living people in the valley. The silence was broken only by sobs. No one smiled anymore. No one, apart from Doctor Reaf.

His scowl was scarier that the scariest grimace. He counted the remaining citizens and imagined the day when there would be not a single soul left. In order to bring that day closer, he recruited spies. They hung around doorways and windows in the evenings, and if they heard music and laughter they reported it to Doctor Reaf. In the mornings, he gathered the townspeople in the square and called out the names of the rule breakers, and the wrath of the crowd fell upon those miserable souls.

Doctor Reaf hadn't cured a single person, and, paralysed by fear, the people stopped thinking clearly. They couldn't understand where the evil was coming from.

In one of the houses, a girl was lying on a large wooden bed. Her eyes were shut, her thin hands rested lifelessly on her chest, and it seemed that she was about to stop breathing. Next to her kneeled an older boy. He held a glass of milk to her lips and begged, 'Tammy, please, just one sip. Our neighbour brought it and said that it ought to help you.'

'No need, Ader . . . Drink it yourself, nothing can help me now. Please, don't distract me, I want to remember the song that our mother used to sing and then I shall die.'

'Just tell me what you want. I'll get you anything!'

'It's the only thing I want. I used to play with my doll while she sang. I think if I saw that doll, I would remember the song. I'm too weak to talk, please leave me.'

Ader left. He could barely see the path because tears burned his eyes. When he reached the bank of the stream he looked around.

'What am I to do?' Ader asked himself. 'When our parents died, I knew I had to take care of my sister. But now she's dying too and I can't save her.' His hands sank into the moist soil of the bank and he began to knead it. Suddenly he realised that the soil he was kneading didn't fall apart but kept its shape. This was the same white clay they had used to make toys and dishes. He took a lump of it in his hands and made a ball. Then, with the help of some green grass, he drew a pair of eyes and, with the juice of some red berries, cheeks and lips.

Ader went quietly into the house, so as not to wake Tammy up. She didn't stir. At the bottom of a trunk he found shreds of colourful fabric. Ader arranged them on the doll's head and called his sister. Tammy opened her eyes. At the sight of such a colourful miracle, she opened her eyes wide and whispered, 'A doll!'

Her weak hands stretched towards Ader's wonderful, funny creation. The boy couldn't believe his eyes. His sister was asking him to help her sit up and open the curtains, so that she could look at her present properly. He tore the dark rags from the window and the sun burst into the room. Suddenly he heard a strange sound behind him. Tammy was singing their mother's song while admiring the doll. For a minute Ader was scared because Tammy had said she wanted to sing it before she died. But she was already lifting her legs off the bed. Then Ader remembered that he was carrying something secret in his pocket. It was a stick with little holes in it. If you blew into it and pressed on the different holes, beautiful sounds came out of it. He started to play along to Tammy's song. Soon she was spinning across the room. Their astonished neighbour stood at the door. Thinking that Tammy had died, she had come over to help Ader bury her, but Tammy was smiling and dancing, only pausing to drink the milk and eat a piece of bread. The neighbour laughed, looking at the happy sight, and forgot about her own troubles. Then she went back to her house, bringing a bouquet of smiles back with her. She shared the news with everyone and encouraged them to join in. For the first time a sick child was cured and Death was left with nothing.

People answered the neighbour's call, bringing their children with them. They dug out old toys, put on their colourful clothes and sang half-forgotten old tunes. The townspeople smiled, danced, laughed. Someone started to reflect the sun's rays in a mirror, and then everyone rushed to look for their own mirrors. They cleaned them and the light jumped along the walls and windows, lighting up happy faces. Everybody sang Tammy's song, playing along on recorders, guitars and harmonicas.

The large crowd moved towards Doctor Reaf's dingy palace home. For a while he couldn't hear anything because of his thick curtains. Then he thought that the forest was making too much noise. 'Is there going to be thunder? I must check.' He opened the curtains slightly and jumped back, blinded by the light. People were reflecting all the sun they could catch in through his windows. Fear fell backwards in shock, and as he fell he broke the window and a joyful wind swept into the palace. It tossed the curtains aside and let in a stream of sunshine. Meanwhile, the people entered the palace. They walked through its chambers, tearing down curtains and cobwebs, and called for Doctor Reaf, but he was nowhere to be seen.

'Whom did we fear so much,' asked the puzzled people. 'Whom did we obey so completely?'

They didn't notice that something dark and tiny, like a spider, scuttled past them. It was Fear, small again, running away to the woods, far away from the people who had liberated themselves from him. Fear lived in the forest again, scaring children who had strayed too far from home, and the townspeople taught their children never to poke their noses where they didn't belong, and never to part from each other without a song and a smile – even when times are difficult and scary.

6

Three Villages
2000–4

It usually started with an offhand, matter-of-fact statement from Mum: 'Lanka, for your spring school break, you're going to the village.'

Everyone in Chechnya comes from a village. A young city, Grozny was founded in 1818 by the Russian general Alexey Yermolov as a fortress on the banks of the Sunzha river. The original name, Groznaya – meaning 'menacing' and 'formidable' – was supposed to inspire fear. But even if you were born and bred in Grozny or one of the other seven larger towns and cities, 'home' was the village where your father's family came from.

Chechnya's most ancient villages, the cradle of the Vainakh people, are nestled in the steep Caucasian mountains, but the flatlands on the north side of the Terek river are also home to dozens of rural settlements. Mum's job sometimes took her to the most awe-inspiring parts of Chechnya, though not for very cheerful reasons. She and her colleagues would follow the trails left by Russian soldiers after late-night *zachistkas*. They would arrive discreetly and examine the houses of men who'd been kidnapped and disappeared. Hours were spent documenting every detail of what had happened, sometimes even in the middle of a funeral for a murdered victim. Villagers trusted Mum because she treated them with compassion and respect. Even after sharing the most horrific details of what had been done to their loved one, they would be eager to show off their beautiful village. Mum took her small digital camera with her and took snapshots of her surroundings. Whenever she showed me photos from her work trips, I would gasp with envy. I remember one in particular: Mum is standing next to a woman against the backdrop of a spectacular mountain range topped with feather-white snow. It looked like one of those artificial sets from a photography studio. I was instinctively drawn to those enchanted landscapes despite having seen them only a handful of times. And horses! Ever since I was little, I'd dreamed of elegantly swinging into the saddle and galloping off at full speed through some meadow. As a Chechen, I was supposedly born in the saddle, but so far I'd only ever circled around on a lunge while somebody held the pony or donkey's bridle.

'When are you going to take me with you to the mountain villages?' I nagged Mum. 'You always tell me about how beautiful Vedeno is.'

'Someday I'll take you,' she promised. 'It's not like I'm going there for a holiday. Speaking of which, there's so much wasted tourism potential in these spots! They could open ski resorts in the mountains, there's always snow . . .'

'But aren't there mines everywhere?'

'Yes, and nothing is being done about getting rid of them. Every *cheremsha* season, some unfortunate lads get blown up.'

The craze for *cheremsha* or *honk* overtook the Caucasus at the start of every spring. A type of wild garlic that looked like lily of the valley but smelled like vampire repellent, it was most commonly eaten cooked, fried in sunflower oil and salt. I couldn't stand the taste or texture of it, but Mum would often return from her trips with plastic bags full of *honk* – the only 'payment' she was ever willing to accept in return for her help, apart from the occasional jar of homemade jam or chunk of beef. It would be considered an insult to have refused them. Hospitality and generosity are two traits that Chechens take serious pride in, even when they don't have much to offer. 'Please, have some tea first,' villagers would say to Mum and her colleagues before sharing their tragic testimonies. By 'tea', they usually meant a full spread with hot dishes, vegetables and cheese, often requested last-minute from their neighbours. And if Mum visited another house, she was again obliged to take a bite, to respond with politeness to this generosity.

Mum wanted me to be close to that part of my culture, to breathe the fresh country air. She wanted me to be independent but it was important to her that I belonged, and also that I was safe when she was away on work trips. While her immediate family were Russian and lived in the Urals, I spent some of the happiest times of my childhood surrounded by her Chechen cousins and their children. Our relatives were scattered across three flatland villages that lacked the drama of the mountains but made up for it with their own soft, countryside charm. Each village had its own merits, and depending on which one – and which family – Mum sent me to, I'd find games to play and stories to create. My most frequent visits were to Deshi-Yurt,* the prosperous village of red-brick houses where I'd completed my first grade. Malkhoy's landscapes were unquestionably the plainest, but it was home to my beloved Auntie Zina who was the best cook and who always saved the warmest hugs for me. Alkhazur was the prettiest of the villages, with well-paved roads lined with lush walnut trees.

We would arrive at a relative's home in the early evening, to be greeted at the gate. Often, Mum would stay the night and catch up with her cousins and aunts, but sometimes she would only have enough time for a cup of tea before heading back to Grozny. 'Don't forget to study,' she'd tell me each time, tucking a fifty-rouble note into the pocket of my duffel bag. I soon found my way around with ease, learning exactly where the secret stash of boiled sweets was hidden and which towel I should use.

The way Chechen homes are built reflects the Chechen character. Usually, only one side of a house is visible from the street; the rest is hidden behind a gated fence, the height and material depending on the financial circumstances of the inhabitants. Houses are arranged like mini-fortresses, concealed from prying eyes. Sometimes, this impulse for privacy leads to absurd displays – ornate iron gates erected before a fence has been put up. The heart of the Chechen home is meant to be revealed only to family, neighbours and guests. Rarely is there a single house; usually a cluster of two, three or more small buildings are arranged around a courtyard with an open terrace where in the summer most meals are taken. Some courtyards are adorned with trimmed rosebushes and seasonal flowers such as daffodils and irises. Kitchen gardens and allotments stretch out at the back, and can

---

*For the sake of my relatives' safety, I have invented names for all three villages described here.

sustain a household for an entire year. Without their own produce, many Chechens would not have survived two wars on their meagre salaries and pensions. None of my relatives owned cattle but our neighbours did, and we were often sent over with a glass jar to collect milk. I tried milking a cow a few times, but was put off by the whole process; I much preferred stroking the silky fur of a calf as it nuzzled my free hand with its leathery nose.

In the evening, whichever village it was, the whole family gathered for dinner. My favourite meal was *chepalgash* – the thinnest flatbread stuffed with Chechen cottage cheese, and sometimes spring onion, and soaked in melted butter. We'd pick the slices up with our greasy hands and I'd inevitably be teased for using a napkin (*city girl!*). I'd eat until I struggled to move. After dinner, it was time for *Clone*, a Brazilian telenovela that told the story of an impossible love affair between a young Muslim woman from Morocco and a rich and sensitive Brazilian boy. Inevitably, the path of love did not run smooth, and they were each forced to marry people they didn't love. This show had all of Chechnya glued to their television screens; even men gossiped about the characters' latest antics. 'What a preposterous thing for a Muslim girl to run around with an outsider who doesn't share her faith. That sort of thing would never happen in Chechnya!'

Deshi-Yurt was especially dear to me, although I'd never have admitted that to relatives elsewhere. I was always eager to return because of Diana and Selima. Technically, they were my nieces, but our relationship was so complicated that it was easier to call them cousins, especially because Diana and I were born in the same year and Selima was only a year younger. Although both had light-brown hair that matched their eye colour almost exactly, as sisters they couldn't have been more different. Each time the three of us were reunited, the atmosphere was cordial for a few hours and then we would become like three rival countries existing in an anarchic state with perpetually shifting alliances and grudges. In the early days, when we were too young to help with cleaning, wear skirts or care about boys, we played outside from morning to night. My aunts would only allow us back in the house briefly, to grab a snack, before yelling, 'I'm trying to clean, stop bringing all the dirt inside!' We happily obeyed and spent our days playing hopscotch, hide-and-seek and tag. We climbed trees, ate unripe fruit that gave us stomach aches, were bullied by the local children and bullied them back, and got chased by packs of stray dogs and, on one unfortunate occasion, a calf with small horns.

On one occasion, we were so preoccupied with one of our schemes that we disappeared off the streets for a couple of weeks. I was about eight or nine, and my relatives were renovating a roofless room attached to their house; we, the children, were tasked with clearing away the weeds and bits of old slate. At first we stuck to the task at hand, but once we'd removed all the rubbish we realised that this space was the perfect playground. Little by little, we fished out the necessary materials – wooden beams, plastic liner, slates – and set about building our own house. Pieces of Styrofoam and half-rotten fibreboard with peeling paint showed up out of nowhere. With a couple of hammers and some nails from a parent's toolbox, we proceeded to knock everything together. Selima even used a saw to cut windows in a large piece of fibreboard that was to be a wall. What we produced looked like a shabby shed, something that the Big Bad Wolf could blow down with a single puff. But to us, once we added a colourful rug (an old prayer mat) and had sourced some leftover squares of fabric for curtains, the house was perfect.

During the entire building process, we didn't fight with each other. Only one dilemma had caused a rift in our otherwise peaceful cooperative – we couldn't decide whether we should build a second floor. We hastily put some more cardboard on the roof and decided to test it by making Sulim from next door stand on it. He climbed up on the roof, stood there for a moment and proclaimed that it was safe to build on, then promptly fell through the cardboard and got stuck halfway. He put on a brave face as we helped him down, but after that we abandoned the idea of a second floor.

Our absence was noticed. 'What are you doing up there all day long?' enquired Kokka, Diana and Selima's grandma. She was short and stocky with a broad face that somehow always made her look as if she was smiling – and she was right now, because we three weren't bothering her and the house was spotless.

With the structure in place we threw ourselves into decorating, bringing in old blankets and even installing a little kitchen next to the house. We made a stove with bricks that we'd found and placed a grill on top. Now we had no reason whatsoever to return to the outside world; we fried eggs for lunch and baked potatoes for dinner. From time to time we accepted meat and canned goods from Auntie – she wanted us to eat properly.

When the house was eventually finished, it was time for the games to begin. Thanks to my scripts, once roles in our imaginary family were assigned they were stuck to, and the agreed story never changed once we began playing. The neighbourhood kids were fascinated, and from time to time they joined our contemporary theatre group, assuming various roles – but the moment they broke character they were out. We acted out kidnappings, treasure hunts, monster attacks and, on one occasion, the delivery of a baby – a full-size cat that ran away the minute she was 'born'. But it never occurred to us to include war in our play – it didn't seem interesting enough.

It was decided that Diana should be the mother, I would play the elder sister, and Selima would be the younger. At first, we wanted to enlist Sulim to play the father, but Diana said that she didn't want to marry him, so he was recruited as our brother. Sulim was no stranger to our role-playing games; because of the scarcity of other boys (they didn't want to mingle with us girls), he had to perform a whole range of roles, from a bus driver to a thief who was out for our gold. Diana's character was the main breadwinner, strict but fair. Selima played a spoilt troublemaker who had to be taught a'lesson at the end of each day, and I was a university student with a part-time job who suffered from constant headaches. I was so dedicated to the role that I stole some of Auntie's yellow pills to soothe the pain, and after a while convinced myself that I was actually feeling poorly. The little pills that I swallowed like sweets turned out to be valerian root, something that calms you down and can help you sleep. When Auntie discovered that her pills were missing, I'd already taken half the bottle. I must have experienced a supreme state of serenity and no doubt mild indigestion, but it put an end to our house experiment, and we broke down our stage to make way for the builders. Then, Diana and I had our first squabble in days.

Diana terrified me at times, as much as I hated to admit it. She had a hold on everyone, even her no-nonsense grandmother, Kokka.

Whenever my cousin's toffee-coloured eyes lit up with that devilish fire and her mouth distorted into a mischievous curve, I knew it spelt trouble. There was no way to reason with her after that. She would do everything possible to annoy and upset those around her. She stood in front of the TV while we watched it, and whenever we asked her to move, she would yell, 'Make me!' and start giggling. She would throw wet paper balls at her sister, shout insults at the neighbours, break precious things and decapitate Barbie dolls. And yet, I had never felt more respect towards a person my age. Diana's confidence and complete disregard for others' opinions was enthralling: she was chaotic, unpredictable and fearless. She cheated in every game, invented rumours that tore friendships apart, bossed others around and got her way each and every time. The girl was a natural-born leader who would have been a CEO – or perhaps a dictator – had she not been born in a small village where women were expected to contain any sign of rebelliousness.

Diana and I considered Selima a baby, despite her being only a year younger. Quieter and calmer, she too had a fierce personality. She was usually good-natured and affable but, when provoked, could throw disturbingly loud fits. One time she coloured in my Ken doll's eyes and mouth with a blue pen. I was shocked and rushed to rescue him with soap and warm water before attacking Selima.

'Why did you do it?' I yelled. 'What did I even do to you?' She quietly watched my attempts to clean the doll without saying a word. In the end, she confessed that it was revenge for an insult I had made about her doll the week before; she hadn't forgotten it.

Selima's attempts to stand up to me and Diana often ended in her bursting into tears, but she never backed down. And when they faced a common enemy, the two sisters always had each other's backs. Sometimes we ended up having spectacular brawls. Whenever Diana used her dirty tricks – clawing my face, for example, or tugging my hair – I would punch her in the stomach until we both ended up rolling on the floor like a pair of cats. Sometimes, adults broke us apart, but as we were pulled away we resorted to spitting.

'You're a stupid sheep!' I yelled at Selima in Russian.

'MAAA! Lana just said something bad about my father,' Selima, who didn't speak much Russian, would lie.

Diana was never afraid to take fights to a whole other level. Once, when I told her that I would tidy the house with Selima before helping her, she threw a terrible tantrum. The fact that this arrangement was agreed between the three of us the night before didn't deter Diana – she demanded I split the chores with her first. When I refused (and Selima backed me), the argument quickly became heated.

'TRAITOR!' she screamed at her little sister. 'You're supposed to side with me, I'm the eldest!'

'But you're not on my side right now!'

'I'm not even refusing to help you. I'm just saying I'll do the patio with Selima and then I'll help you with inside,' I butted in.

'No, you're not helping me anymore' – Diana grew red in the face – 'because . . . I'M KICKING YOU OUT OF MY HOUSE!' She followed through immediately by tossing my holdall into the yard.

'Are you crazy?' I ran outside but already I was getting hit on the back with the rest of my possessions.

'Here are your stupid dolls! And here are your shoes! Get your stuff and get lost forever!'

In a fit of fury, Diana continued to toss out my stuff while I ran around, gathering things into the bag. 'You will regret this!' I screamed. 'You will come crawling back to me!'

'Never! You got everything? Now get out before I hose you down.'

Indignant, I marched towards the gate swearing never to return. Thankfully, there were plenty of other relatives I could stay with in the village until Mum came to pick me up. I knocked on the door of Kokka's sister and waited at her house until, several hours later, Kokka appeared with her two granddaughters behind her. My cousins looked rather defeated.

'Stop with the drama, get your bag and come back home,' Kokka told me.

'Not until I hear Diana's apology.'

'From what she was telling me, it was your fault too.'

'How dare she! I was going to help her anyway!'

In the end, we reached a compromise and all three of us said sorry. I was fuming, because this time it was not my fault, not even a tiny bit. Diana always got her way.

At home, we sat and sulked for a while until one of us made an awkward attempt at reconciliation. That's how it always went after our fights. We would treat each other with exaggerated care and respect – 'No, YOU have the last chocolate . . . Would you like to play with my doll?' – until the cycle would be repeated again. At night, after making up, we were too excited to fall asleep. Sometimes my cousins asked me to sing them a sad song or tell them a fairy tale. No matter how hard I tried to get them into reading, I never succeeded, but they loved listening to my stories. I even managed to retell in detail the first three *Harry Potter* books. Before falling asleep, Diana, Selima and I shared our deepest secrets and swore always to be there for each other.

'Are we your favourite cousins?'

'Yes.'

'More than your Russian ones?'

'You two are my favourite girl cousins and Sasha is my favourite boy cousin.'

'Swear to Allah.'

'I swear.'

All was resolved and they would fall asleep, but I couldn't because my heart was too heavy with the love that I felt for these two girls breathing beside me. The world of children is both exhilarating and belligerent, but my personality was forged in those games, fights and truces. The role of ringleader never appealed to me but I also had too strong a personality to comply with anything I didn't like. At night, unable to sleep, I would flick through favourite memories from the day and let another episode of my imaginary fantasy tales play out inside my head like a TV series.

A sole mosquito buzzed in the dark, looking for victims. That sound always puts me in a melancholy mood; it's always the lonely ones that fall asleep last.

Malkhoy was a sleepy place that could be painted with just a few brushstrokes of ochre, beige and brown. It was only remarkable as the home of my favourite aunt, Zina, my mum's cousin, who lived on the outskirts of the village with her two daughters, Madina and Makka, and her husband, Salman. Their modest house was built of traditional handmade clay bricks, covered in white limewash. Inside, the rooms were always sparkling clean. On the table a loaf of freshly baked bread would sit waiting to be eaten with *to-beram*, made of thick sour cream mixed with local salty cheese called *kald*. 'Tell your *detsi* [auntie] what would you like me to cook for you,' Zina would suggest each time I sat at her kitchen table.

Everything about Zina was soft and tender – her tiny, warm hands, her round face framed by a patterned headscarf and even her voice, which she never raised. Her daughters took after her; both good-natured and calm, they were like the older sisters I never had. Unlike Diana and Selima, Madina and Makka were twelve and ten years older than me, but we still had loads of fun together. Salman was quite the opposite. Standing six foot four, with skin often blackened from the soot he handled at work, a hooked nose and steel-blue eyes, he was how I imagined Captain Blackbeard might look. When he was around, the low bass of his voice rumbled like thunder, shaking the china inside Auntie Zina's cupboards and crashing through the gentle atmosphere of our feminine world. I was scared of Uncle Salman, but there was no need to be – whenever he saw me, his mouth softened into a big smile. He would scoop me up in his arms as if I weighed nothing. He sat me in the front seat of his Soviet-era lorry that smelled of stale tobacco and took me on drives around the village. When I was seven or eight, he let me look at the most dangerous thing – a solar eclipse – through the square glass of his welding helmet. From inside his helmet, the sky looked green and the platinum sun was tiny like a coin.

Life in Malkhoy moved at a slower pace than in Grozny, but it was never still. Women ran the house while the men went to work – or simply pretended to, as there was so little to be done during the war years. In Zina's household everyone was employed. She was a kindergarten teacher, which suited her perfectly; Salman was doing whatever jobs a man with a pair of strong hands could do – construction, welding, driving a lorry. Madina, the younger, was a trained pharmacist; and Makka ran a one-woman atelier from her living room. While Makka worked, I sat on the floor and sewed dresses for my Barbies using offcuts of fabric, and it was there, to the pleasant hum of an electric sewing machine, in a patterned jungle of colourful fabrics, threads, old magazines and hand-drawn designs, that my love for fashion and 'girly stuff' was born. It might seem unlikely for a tomboy like me – always up in the trees with scraped knees and dirty hands – to love fashion, but I was fascinated by my beautiful grown-up cousins and the way they applied a touch of mascara and eyeshadow, the way they walked through the ruins in stilettos, mud never seeming to touch the bottom of their ankle-length coats. There was an unspoken but nonetheless strict dress code in Chechnya – no shorts for men, no trousers for women. Skirts and dresses had to be knee length at least and shoulders had to be covered. When I was thirteen, I would be shouted at on the streets for still wearing jeans, and it was to Makka that I would go for an appropriate, knee-length black skirt with a frilled hem. It wasn't me at all, but it stopped men from harassing me on the street. That wouldn't happen for another few years, though – back then, in the village, I was free from skirts, chores and expectations.

Zina let me roam around the neighbourhood and make friends with local kids. And when there was no one around, I embraced the spectacular boredom of endless summer days. As an only child with a boundless imagination, sometimes what I wanted most was to be left alone in my fantasy world. Some days I would go to the poppy field behind the house and spend hours there. I loved the crunchy sound of the dry grass under my feet, but most of all I was mesmerised by the silky crimson poppies that looked like drops of blood. I barely ever touched them, knowing that the petals would instantly fall. Leaning against a rock, I would watch the poppy heads sway in the tiniest breath of wind; this landscape – the blue cloudless sky, the huge field with its yellowed grass and blood-red flowers – spoke to me. Little by little, in the village silence, I would enter a sort of trance and almost melt into the sun-heated rock burning my elbows. No one bothered me in that field; no one called me in to eat – it was as though I was the only creature on the planet. It was Mum who cultivated that love for nature in me. So little beauty remained in Grozny that nature's every manifestation became precious. 'Look, Lanuska,' she would say, pointing at a rose in someone's garden or a flock of birds rising in the sky.

Emerging from my trance, I would leave the field, heading back, still stunned, sated by the sun. Auntie Zina never asked where I'd been; she simply hugged me with a smile and kissed me on both cheeks. That's why I wanted to keep going back to Malkhoy – for that sweet, warm love from my aunt and her daughters, which nourished my soul. I returned it in full. They spoilt me, cooked my favourite dishes and listened carefully to all my stories. I loved being loved. I grew up in a women's world and only trusted women. Men bore guns, they killed and maimed and looted and drank and beat their wives and forbade their daughters from studying at universities. Women created life and maintained it, made money and fed everyone, rescued their loved ones and made everything cosy and beautiful. That was what I saw growing up, and it would take a long time for that impression to change.

Sometimes, in a crossover episode, Auntie Zina would take me to Alkhazur – the third village of my childhood – to visit her mother Chovka, my grandfather Hussein's older sister. You entered Alkhazur through the gates of an arch that led on to a long gravel road lined with tall walnut trees which cast much-needed summer shade. I felt at home as soon as I smelled the familiar scent of fresh dung. There were cows everywhere, and most of the streets were bordered by little drainage ditches. Sometimes they would dry up, but usually they ran with brown-coloured water, sweeping away any rubbish. My great-aunt's house was just off the main road, on a leafy street tucked away behind a shop.

Detsi Chovka was a formidable matriarch who kept everyone in line. During the deportation of 1944, she lost her younger brother Hussein, buried her parents and had only her two sisters to rely on. The Detsi that I remember spent most of her day sitting or lying on her bed with a string of beads in her hands, whispering prayers or feeding her magnificent white chicken from the porch. Detsi survived against all odds, married and had six children, who in turn all married and had more children until the family tree blossomed again. Detsi was very large and her thick calves were always swollen because of numerous illnesses. Weak health, however, didn't prevent her from giving detailed instructions to whichever family member was nearby, nor from gossiping with her neighbours.

One particular summer, when I was about eight or nine, my mother left me with Detsi for several weeks. Most of the time it was just the two of us, and so to kill time I would explore every nook and cranny of the house, playing outside with stray dogs and plucking hazelnuts off the bushes. In the afternoons I would climb the tall cherry tree that grew at the back of the house, nestling in its crown. Under the blue dome of the sky, the world looked like the inside of a snow-globe – a flat sea of green and brown, the humble houses of our neighbours, colourful allotments. I spent hours up there, reading, daydreaming, coming up with stories in my head while eating the delicious juicy cherries I had picked.

I had a very spiritual, but also practical relationship with trees and rated them according to climbability. If I could jump from branch to branch of a tree until I reached the top, then I admired it straight away. Unclimbable trees didn't excite me so much, with the exception of walnut trees; most of the ones I came across had a smooth trunk with crown and branches out of reach.

'Get off that tree! Stop eating cherries!' Detsi yelled from the veranda.

'I'm not going to fall.'

'You will! I'll tell your mum, you little rascal.'

'Tell her all you want. She lets me climb trees!'

It was true. No matter how high up in the branches I went, Mum never told me off. If she bumped into an acquaintance on the street and the conversation became boring and adult, I would look around for the nearest tree. To the horror of Mum's company, I would climb higher and higher and swing from the top. Mum was unfazed.

'Natasha, how can you allow her to climb so high? Aren't you scared she'll fall?'

'She hasn't fallen so far – she is a monkey.'

Mum rarely let anyone interfere with her parenting techniques. And in return, I refrained from telling her about my most dangerous exploits.

In Alkhazur, Detsi Chovka and I continued to clash.

'Stop reading so much or you'll strain your eyes,' she reprimanded me whenever I disappeared inside the cold, cave-like bedroom with a book. A compassionate neighbour, who'd been watching me wilt with boredom for days, had brought a couple of volumes from her house (I had already read every book I could find at Detsi Chovka's).

One of them was *The Count of Monte Cristo* by Alexandre Dumas and the other was a selection of rather explicit novels by Émile Zola. I was slightly disgusted by the misadventures of the Parisian courtesan Nana and was confused about the disease that vanquished her at the end (it was syphilis). *Monte Cristo* was a different story – I couldn't put it down. This dark and twisted novel had everything I loved – adventure, an unlawfully convicted prisoner, secret treasures, murders, revenge and even hashish-induced hallucinations.

Beyond the world of books, time in the village seemed to flow differently to how it did in the city. Days blended one into the other. Nights, hot and sticky, were accompanied by an orchestra of crickets while Detsi, sitting on her bed, whispered prayers as she moved beads along the string.

In the village, my faith hardened because it was all around me. Back then, for most Chechens, having faith was as natural as breathing or eating – something that was essential for sustenance but did not require close attention. As a child, I believed in God – *Dela* – with feverish sincerity.

'I pray to Dela every night,' I boasted to Detsi Chovka, interrupting her bead count. 'I pray for Mum and for peace. And I talk to him too, as if he were my friend.'

'Allah is not your friend. Don't say such blasphemous things!' she replied, outraged. 'He is your creator; we are all mere slaves to him. Our lives are just a flash before eternity, so we must lead them with devotion, in good faith.' I was dismayed. 'But it's a good thing that you pray,' she added. 'Do you know *Bismillah*?'

'I know the beginning,' I replied, and began repeating the first lines of the most basic Muslim prayer: '*Bismillah er Rahman er Rahim, Alhamdulillahi Rabbil Alamin, Er Rahman er Rahim . . .*'*

'*Maliki Yaumid Din*,' she continued. 'Repeat after me.'

Iyaka na' budu wa iyaka nasta'in
Ihdinas siratul mustaqim
Siratallazina an amta alayhim ghayril magdubi alayhim walad daalin.
   Amin.

---

*In the name of Allah, the Most Gracious, the Most Merciful.

She patiently recited the prayer again and again until I had memorised it and could clearly say it without any prompts.

'Good girl! When you're older, I'll teach you how to do *lamaz*. You'll have to do it five times a day in order to be a good Muslim. But keep praying to Allah and he will give you anything you ask him.'

'Anything? Absolutely anything?'

'Anything, if you pray hard enough and strengthen your faith, your *iman*. When the time comes, you'll fast during Ramadan too. It's one of the foundations of Islam.'

'Yes, I know that.'

For us kids, it was, of course, all about Eid al-Fitr – the final day of Ramadan. And it wasn't because this day marked the end of a period of fasting – we didn't have to do that yet – but because Eid was the closest thing we had to trick-or-treating. Kids went around their villages in their best outfits, knocked on every door, and, in return for a small prayer, were given sweets and biscuits. At the end of the day and with hands sore from the heavy bags, they headed home to tables overflowing with mouth-watering food – *chepalgash*, *galnash*, *plov* (rice with meat and vegetables cooked in a giant *kazan*, a deep castiron pan), fruit and salads. But while hungry and excited adults were saying their prayers and laying the table, we were busy counting our sweets and seeing who had the highest number. Unsurprisingly, back in Deshi-Yurt, Diana won every single year.

The day after my conversation with Detsi Chovka, I decided to test my upgraded faith. Outside the front gates of Detsi's house, I had found a litter of cheerful stray puppies and had been secretly saving scraps of food for them. I was always being reprimanded for my love of dogs. They are considered unclean animals in the Quran, but how can something so adorable be considered unclean? I fed them, rubbed their bellies and let them gnaw on my hand. Then an idea occurred to me. I focused hard on the puppies, looked up at the sky, recited *Bismillah* and asked: 'Dela, you are almighty and we are all just worms compared to you. This human life is just a flash before eternity. If you are real . . . make these puppies talk!'

Then I listened for a sign. Nothing. There was no response, though I strained my ears just in case. The puppies continued to squeal and bark for attention. After a couple of further attempts, I gave up and ran back to Detsi Chovka with my alarming findings.

'Detsi, are you sure that Allah really does whatever you ask of him?'

'If you pray hard enough, yes. What did you ask of him?'

'I asked him to make the puppies talk.'

'What on earth . . .? Are you crazy? You fool!'

She berated me for a good quarter of an hour for doubting Allah, and told me never to do such a thing again. I felt deeply embarrassed because it was not that I really wanted the puppies to talk that much anyway. My *iman* was very weak that day. Nonetheless, from then on I decided never to involve anyone in my relationship with God.

Detsi Chovka was undoubtedly a devout Muslim, but nothing could erase magic from the dark corners of the village – neither modernity nor Islam. There were witches and fortune tellers, healers and fraudsters. There were tales of jinns that inhabit your body and make you do crazy things. And of Dajjaal, the false messiah who appears before the believer and commands him to denounce Allah. Those who refuse to do so he decapitates with a swift motion of his sword, but that person goes to heaven right away. Religion mixed with superstition and old pagan tradition morphed into other things. 'Stop sitting with your legs crossed, you will attract Shaitan the evil spirit,' I was told. My relatives' attempts to tell me off for being left-handed (I was feeding all the food to Shaitan) ceased after I smashed a plate and refused to share a table with them until they left me alone. It is no wonder that Chechnya existed in a mystical, magical plane. In times of war, when life and death are so near each other, the gates between the two worlds are never shut, and all sorts of things come to the surface. Ghosts and ghouls slipped in and out, making their presence known in strange unexplained sounds, in the play of the light at dusk, in the wailing of an unfamiliar bird.

Detsi Chovka practised healing and knew how to cure Mum's migraines better than any doctor. When Mum complained of headaches, Detsi would take out a special kerchief from her cupboard and sit Mum down on a stool. Then she would fold the kerchief and gently wrap it around Mum's head, whispering inaudible prayers. The thin worry line between my mother's eyebrows would slowly disappear and her shoulders relax. 'It's gone, Chovka,' she would declare with a smile of relief. 'Shall I tell you your fortune too?' her aunt would ask, but Mum would politely decline. This service was more popular with a gaggle of Chovka's many granddaughters, though, including Makka and Madina. They would surround her like a flock of birds while she patiently moved little stones around, a calm, self-assured expression on her face. After some manipulations, she unfailingly pronounced that the objects of her granddaughters' affections reciprocated their feelings.

I loved it when all my second cousins came to stay at the same time. All the mattresses would be dragged into one bedroom and laid in a row, and we would have a super sleepover, giggling and chatting until midnight. Most of my cousins were older than me, in their late teens and early twenties. When their conversations turned to boyfriends and fiancés, I buried my head under the pillow. Why couldn't we just stay in this moment forever? Why did they have to grow up so fast, leaving me behind?

Dating in Chechnya was an even more modest and strict affair than in a Jane Austen novel. Even after months of seeing each other, couples could not get close enough for even an accidental brush of hands. Meetings were usually chaperoned by a younger female relative or friend. Many a time I was dragged along by my cousins, to jealously observe the young, awkward men who would take the girls out. Whether it was Detsi Chovka's clairvoyance or the fact that her granddaughters were young and pretty, one after the other they left the perfumed innocence of girlhood and entered married life. After that, everything changed: there were no more sleepovers, gossip marathons, or dance parties. From then on a woman would become part of her husband's household and only come home for short visits. She would carry herself differently, her mannerisms would change and only a few strands of her hair would show under her headscarf.

Children were always welcome at weddings, along with anyone who happened to be in the neighbourhood. At Chechen weddings – *lovzar* – the bride and groom are kept in separate houses and the bride is not permitted to talk for the whole day. She stands quietly in the corner, her face covered by a veil, while everyone else eats and dances. Only as the wedding winds down is she taken by her female relatives into a back room so that she can finally have a snack. The bride's silence is part of a ritual called 'tongue opening' in which – at the end of the wedding – the groom's friends and younger male family members shower her with jokes and anecdotes, trying to get a reaction. The men also give her banknotes until finally she utters her first words. Then she is officially a part of the household.

A bride's parents are not allowed to be at the wedding since they've already given their daughter away. When they hand the bride to her new family, she is supposed to cry, mourning her final moments of girlhood and her parents' house. When one of my cousins was getting married and we were all shoved in the back of the car, she failed to produce a single tear because she was so giddy with excitement. 'Fatima, you have to cry!' her female relatives scolded her. Fatima rubbed her eyes and pinched her cheeks in between explosions of laughter. But when we arrived at her new home and were greeted by her husband's family, she burst into tears. At the moment the bride appeared, young men with Kalashnikovs started shooting in the air – another tradition; it is supposed to ward off evil spirits. The highlight of any wedding was the traditional *lezginka* dance where people stand in a circle and couples take turns dancing in pairs, always without touching. In the countryside weddings are considered important social occasions for young people, where they might find a potential match, since there were so few opportunities for them to meet. But, as a child, I couldn't have cared less about boys or dancing, and the best part of *lovzar* was that you could eat industrial quantities of *plov*.

'When I have my wedding, I will have Mum by my side,' I used to tell Auntie Zina. 'And my husband is going to pick me up on a horse, like in olden times. But I will be riding my own horse and it will be brown, not white.'

'You can't bring your parents to your wedding, that is not our tradition,' she'd laugh.

Mothers who couldn't attend their daughters' weddings would greedily ask female relatives for every detail – who wore what, what was the mother-in-law like, how many presents did the couple receive. After sending off their daughters, on the morning of the wedding, their only glimpses of the day would be from wedding photos.

As much as it broke my heart seeing my cousins leave their parents' homes, something good did come of it eventually: sweet and chubby babies that turned into funny toddlers and then into proper children that you could play with. I loved kids. And I couldn't have been happier when, a year after Makka's marriage, I met a small pink bundle with a cute, olive-skinned face called Zalina. There was a never-ending stream of nephews and nieces in every village, but Zalina was the most special. When she was a baby I was about ten years old, and I would rock her to sleep, play with her and change her nappies. It was as if I had my own living baby doll. Under Makka's and Zina's supervision I bathed her in a plastic tub, carefully supporting the back of her neck. With every visit to Malkhoy, I watched my baby niece grow. We were inseparable. When I held Zalina close to me and squeezed her tiny hands with my fingers and whispered fairy tales in her ears, I knew, even as a ten-year-old, that one day nothing would make me happier than being a mother.

During childhood visits to the three villages, I watched several of my cousins being given away, but the wedding I remember most vividly was that of a complete stranger. On one of my visits to Diana and Selima's house, we were taken to another village for the wedding of a distant family member. I'd never been there before. Hours of celebration passed and, after all the *plov* was eaten and the dancing had finished, Diana, Selima and I didn't know what to do with ourselves. We'd already explored every bit of the street and so ventured to the next one, until we ran out of road and found ourselves on the edge of the village. Before us stretched cornfields and beyond that there was an inviting, vivid-green meadow that seemed to have been perfectly designed for frolicking. As we got closer, we noticed that it was cordoned off by rusty barbed wire.

'We're not allowed to go any further,' one of our new friends from the village told us, her voice full of anxiety. Her companion nodded. 'You really shouldn't be going there.' Diana, Selima and I ignored them both and confidently sneaked into the meadow through a small gap in the barbed wire. The meadow wasn't as idyllic as it had appeared. Yes, there were cheerful clusters of summer flowers and the coarse grass felt nice to touch, but on the ground lay scraps of metal and bits of rotten rubbish. The three of us scattered, all heading in different directions, until we heard someone shouting, 'Stay where you are! Don't move!'

Surprised, I turned around and saw a man on the other side of the field waving frantically. At first, I thought, or rather hoped, he was shouting at someone else, but there was no mistake – we were the only ones in that meadow. My attention fixed on his tanned, thin arms, which gesticulated in an almost comical way as he yelled, 'Mines! There are mines in the field!'

Instantly, I felt my body temperature drop to zero and my stomach spasmed. At the same time I heard a familiar, high-pitched cry coming from Selima, who was standing several metres behind me – closest to the barbed wire. I can't remember whether Diana and I cried – perhaps we were trying to save face in front of Selima, or perhaps I have erased my embarrassing reaction from my memory.

'Why did you go in there, you fools?' the man continued. 'There's barbed wire and a sign right there!'

From where I was standing, I couldn't see the sign.

'We're not from here!' shouted Diana. 'We didn't know!' Even when faced with potential death or a lost limb, she talked back.

'Just don't move! There's a guy in the village who will get you out of there. But you can't take a step or sit down.'

Selima continued to cry. I was worried that, in a panic, she would collapse or run, so I did my best to console her. Her wailing confused me and somehow it felt as if it could activate the mines. My heart was pounding so loudly it seemed as if it had become the whole of me; small and scared, I was the size of my heart. So many times on my walk to school in Grozny, I had been anxious about sappers blowing up a mine; now I was closer to one than I had ever been.

Nature, meanwhile, was oblivious to our turmoil, the sun standing high in the sky, wind gently caressing the tall grass.

The news must have spread because more and more villagers were gathering by the meadow. In the small crowd I spotted the two girls who had warned us to turn back. If only we'd listened! 'Don't you worry, girls!' we heard the women shout. 'Badruddi will get you out. He knows this meadow. He's a professional.' (Frankly, the name of our hero has slipped my mind all these years later, but Badruddi seems fitting enough.) While we stood the onlookers cheered us on – young men cracked jokes to make us smile and women promised to feed us delicious *khingalash* (flatbread stuffed with pumpkin puree). Some time later – it could have been fifteen minutes or half an hour – a white Volga stopped in the middle of a farmer's field and we saw tiny Kokka emerge from it and run towards the barbed wire holding on to her headscarf. That's when I felt scared again, seeing her terror.

'ARE YOU OKAY, GIRLS?! Are you injured? Why did you go there? My heart can't take it!' Kokka exclaimed, the questions one after the other, wiping her tears with a borrowed kerchief. We tried to reassure her, worrying about her heart, which was indeed very weak. I kept wondering why Badruddi hadn't arrived. What if he was in another village? Would we spend the night here? What if we got so tired we fell down? In my head, I kept replaying the poem:

> *Mines are not toys,*
>   *Tripwire mines and missiles*
> *Are dangerous traps,*
> *And . . .*

And? What was the next line? I had memorised this poem in second grade, in mine-awareness lessons. We had been given brochures with a visual description of each mine and stories of children who had stepped on them. The worst, most insidious kinds were booby-trap mines disguised as toys or lighters. Although these types of mine are prohibited by most states (as I learnt years later), during both Chechen wars they maimed over 700 Chechen children and killed 114. Years later, I would meet one of the survivors, who picked up a mine shaped like a lighter – a girl named Asya, who lost an eye and the palms of her hands.

Time passed, and with no sign of our saviour, I was nearing breaking point, trapped and desperate. How long had it been? Diana and Selima were both silent, their backs turned to me, waiting. At least their grandmother was there; my mother was far away, and now I needed her more than ever. But I vowed not to let her find out about what had happened, in case she refused to send me to the village again. I was so thirsty I could hardly swallow. Yet, the fear had faded –

being scared took too much energy – and a numbing sense of paralysis had overtaken my body, enveloping me like an anaconda.

'How are you holding up, girls?' a man's voice asked. 'Shall we get you home?'

No matter how hard I try, I cannot remember the face of the man who came to our rescue, the mysterious Badruddi. How did he know his way around this field so well? Had he lost his cattle here? (Animals, sadly, are the victims of war too.) Or was he an ex-fighter, a local legend? He could have been forty or sixty for all I knew, but his voice – kind, softly spoken with a faint note of mischief – has stayed with me. He calmed us down and instructed us to stand with our hands stretched at our sides. Kokka was looking at her grandchildren, still holding a kerchief to her mouth.

'You are not in danger from what I can see,' Badruddi reassured us. 'There was a mine where you are standing,' he pointed at Diana, 'but it was detonated years ago.' My heart flipped again as I remembered how far I had run before stopping.

'I will get you out, one by one. Just be patient and keep your hands and feet where they are.' Now that someone was in charge, the sense of dread was gone, and instead I became impatient. Badruddi carefully made his way towards Selima, slowly putting one foot in front of the other while keeping his gaze firmly on the ground. Because Selima was on the edge of the meadow, it wasn't long before she was lifted up and carefully taken back to safety. When her feet touched the ground again, she disappeared in her grandmother's embrace. No one clapped but the women formed a circle around Selima, patting her head and shoulders. Badruddi was already making his way to Diana, who was standing further away. I watched jealously as she too stretched her hands towards our hero and was carried away from the deadly land. He walked slowly, handling his precious cargo with care, and even stopped for a second, hesitating. Women and a handful of men held their breath. Afterwards, there were jokes and outbursts of laughter, but not until Diana was next to her sister. Then it was my turn.

Badruddi cut through the path freshly forged by our feet just an hour earlier – or was it three hours? Time didn't make sense anymore. Not even for a second did he change his pace, walking with the same measured tread, keeping his eyes down. It felt like an eternity before he was next to me. 'Hold on to my neck,' he instructed as he lifted me up. We were about the same height, the three of us, and I was perhaps smaller than Diana and Selima, but I was still worried that I was the heaviest, the most inconvenient to carry. What if he's so tired that he drops me? The barbed wire fence slowly got closer and closer, a row of people waiting beyond it. Three, two, one . . . I was safe.

After that all was a blur – heartfelt thank-yous to our saviour, kisses, squeals, laughter, reprimands: 'What were you two thinking, you the eldest?' and a back-stab from our former friends, 'We TOLD them not to go to that field!'

It's incredible how eager we were to turn this most terrifying of moments into something to laugh at. Hours later, back in Deshi-Yurt, we retold the story to the neighbours, interrupting each other and artfully embellishing it.

'Come to think of it, I might have *seen* a mine on the ground and almost stepped on it,' declared Diana.

'You're such a liar,' retorted Selima.

'I swear I'm not.'

'Swear on Allah.'

'I will not use Allah's name in vain for such nonsense. But it's true!'

By the time Mum came for me, the story of the minefield had been reduced to an anecdote. The anxiousness, the excruciating wait and all the horror had faded, freeing space for more pleasant things – water fights; drives in the back seat of the old Volga; tiny, warm baby chicks cupped in my palms.

The minefield was a reminder that nowhere else was the ever-changing cycle of life and death as pronounced and honest in its simplicity as it was in the village. War had ripped through the social fabric, leaving a bloody trail, filling cemeteries with fresh graves. But it didn't fundamentally change the way villagers lived, the way they married and how they buried the dead. Traditions and faith guided Chechens through every disaster. In times of need, the people always looked after each other, united as one. What I didn't know then was that it would take less than a decade for that unity to wither and corrode. During my years in the three villages, that feeling of solidarity was an absolute, something I always regarded as a given. When I attended a funeral for the first time in my life, aged eleven, this culture was revealed in a new light, in all its power and raw beauty.

In Chechnya, a funeral is not just a religious ceremony but an important social event. According to tradition, the deceased must be buried on the same day they die, and so a grieving family begins preparations in haste, calling relatives and friends and opening their gates so that everyone can pay their respects. I thought of funerals as old people's affairs, as children were only invited if they knew the deceased, and had never been to one. In the villages, I found out about death when my sturdy, middle-aged aunts hastily pulled on plain headscarves and left younger family members lists of chores that had to be completed during their unplanned absence.

This funeral was especially tragic because it shouldn't have happened. Only three days after her wedding, my beautiful twenty-year-old cousin Zarema, one of Kokka's nieces, was killed in a car crash, along with her husband and his pregnant sister. Having missed the wedding because of work and school, Mum and I now found ourselves heading to the funeral in gloomy silence, not knowing what to say. There would be no playtime with Diana and Selima on this trip.

When we arrived at Deshi-Yurt, the gates of my uncle's red-brick house were already blocked by cars, and we entered to a chorus of wails. Mum hastily fetched a small headscarf from her bag and tied it around her head. At the gate, women were separated from the men and joined a circle of mourners in the front yard. Half-crazed from bereavement, Zarema's mother couldn't lift her gaze from the ground when she greeted us, but I noticed that the whites of her eyes were pink from all the crying. She sat in a large circle of weeping women and anytime someone new arrived the howls grew louder. My mother never cried, but when I awkwardly glanced at her, not knowing what to do with myself, tears were streaming down her face. She gave her cousin's wife a huge hug. It was customary that every woman entering the circle had to cry, even if she hadn't known the deceased, and other mourners mirrored her. That was the way it was done – you paid your respects by sharing grief with others, by taking a sliver of their pain away. After the round of weeping, you composed yourself and talked about trivial matters – family news, weather, new purchases. The hushed chatter went on until another woman entered the circle, then the weeping would start again.

Magomed, Zarema's father, was in their neighbour's house, where the funeral would take place. I peered inside the black iron gate and saw a large group of men, young and old, wearing *pyas* – traditional Chechen skullcaps. Standing in a circle, they stomped their feet on the ground, raising small clouds of dust, clapped their hands and in unison chanted the first part of the *shahada*, a declaration of faith: '*Ash-hadu an la ilaha illa Allah*' ('There is no God but Allah'). This was *zikr*, a mystical religious dance rooted in Sufi Islam. They swayed from side to side in perfect symmetry, never interrupting their prayers. Then they started rotating in one direction, as if tied to an invisible wheel. The collective repetition of movement and prayers put participants in a religious trance. I'd seen *zikr* performed before, but watching men that I knew take part in the haunting, transcendental ceremony was like lifting a curtain on some ancient magic. I admired these communal rituals, although I found them scary too. It seemed that people knew what to do instinctively, as if their ancestors were whispering in their ears. For Mum, raised elsewhere, it was harder to settle into these time-worn Chechen rituals; this was why she made me spend so much time in the villages. The grip of this culture could be as suffocating as it was comforting, but you were never left alone with your grief. There was always someone willing to share your pain.

Lack of childcare was probably the reason why, in early May 2004, I found myself piled in the back of the car with Mum and her colleague Tanya Lokshina, heading to the mountains. Mum fulfilled her promise. I sat in the middle seat nursing motion sickness, feeling every bump of the dirt track. As we drove up the treacherous windy roads, the view became more and more picturesque. Endless nauseous bends later, we drove into the most spectacular high valley. The first thing I noticed was the sky – it seemed vast. The sun was generously dispersing its rays among the forested mountains, which were too tall and grand for me to take in. I embraced my own insignificance in the face of these sharp cliffs and ancient snow-covered peaks, marvelling at the contrast of light and shadow against a backdrop of azure and luscious green. This was a stunning, half-wild land, with no safety barriers, information or warning signs. The beauty of the landscape was so overwhelming that, for a moment, it gave me a confusing, anxious feeling, as if I was somehow not entitled to look at this beauty for too long. When we stopped by a small waterfall for a drink and some fresh air, I cupped my hands and drank greedily, burning my throat with ice-cold mountain water.

Arriving at a small village sometime later, we were greeted by a local family Mum knew. Their house sat on a green platform with a gentle descent towards a mountain river. Mum left me with the family and I instantly made friends with Seda and Khava – two sisters about my age. Meanwhile, Mum and her colleague carried on to a village further on. I knew their trip's grim purpose but chose not to dampen my excitement about being in the mountains.

The sisters showed me around. We started off by petting a recently born baby calf. Then, we decided to roll down the hill. I stretched my arms along my body, straightened out like a stick and rolled and rolled, dizzy from the rapidly changing kaleidoscope of sensations. Afterwards, we chatted and played games, telling each other the names of our crushes, knowing that we might not see each other again. Then, we carefully made our way down to the narrow river filled with grey rocks. I rolled up my jeans and stepped into the freezing water, testing how long I could withstand the cold. The girls were used to the temperature, so they just laughed when I jumped out, squealing. There was, of course, an obligatory splashing, until we were all drenched. Cooled, we climbed back up the hill and went home to have lunch.

The fun continued in the afternoon when the girls' older brother, Yusup, returned from school and began his shepherding duties. The family had several horses grazing nearby, and I was very eager to see them. We walked up a wide gravel road until we reached a large meadow, and there I saw them – tall, handsome horses in every colour imaginable.

'That one is young,' said Khava, pointing at a tiny brown horse on the horizon. 'He's really wild, only Yusup can ride him.'

'Do you think I could touch one of them?' I asked.

'Ha-ha, you can ride them, if you want!'

I couldn't believe it. Something I had dreamed of my entire life was about to come true! Overwhelmed, I squealed and jumped up and down. The girls brought two horses to the road. Yusup went ahead to catch the brown stallion, and a minute later he had mounted it – a little figure sat astride a giant horse. He was a fantastic rider, and I watched in awe as he pranced in the distance. Then it was my turn. I was given an old white mare, known for her gentle, obedient disposition. The others laughed, watching my awkward attempts to mount the horse, and finally Yusup gave me a much-needed push. After brief instructions, the bridle firmly in my hands, I set off down the road. We slowly trotted along, moving into the twilight of the woods, me at the back, the others at the front turning around every now and again to check I was okay. A happy grin was permanently fixed on my face until we approached a narrow path that hugged the mountainside. Nervousness washed over me, and my first thought was to get off the horse, but she had a mind of her own. Unfazed and with implacable determination, she slowly trotted towards the edge of the cliff with apparently no inclination to stop. I panicked. The horse seemed to have suicidal tendencies!

'HEEEEEEEEEY!' I yelled in desperation. At this the three siblings stopped and quickly turned around.

'What is it doing? It's going to kill me. It's going to jump down!'

Yusup turned his horse around and in a flash he was beside me, grabbing the old white horse by the bridle and giving it a strong yank. Her back leg slipped and I could feel her leaning precipitously backwards. She sent several small stones tumbling down the mountainside. For a second, I felt as if someone had removed my insides. I couldn't breathe. But before I even managed to scream, the horse was back on the path, guided confidently by the young shepherd. He held her reins as we slowly rode back to the house.

The sky was now completely dark and there were car lights flashing in the distance; it meant that Mum was back. I was still shaken by what had happened and the siblings seemed rather quiet, but we didn't talk about it. 'She's an old horse,' Yusup said. 'Probably losing her mind.' Still, despite the near fall, it had been one of the most special days of my life.

Mum's day had been very different, however. After dropping me off, she and Tanya had continued their journey up the mountain. They soon reached Rigakhoy, a settlement so remote that it might as well have been on the edge of the earth. Perhaps that's why the federals assumed they would get away with what they did – that they could write it off as another successful counterterrorist operation. But after Mum heard about what had happened in Rigakhoy, she became obsessed with bringing the perpetrators to justice. It was one of the defining cases of her career.

On the morning of 8 April 2004, Imar-Ali Damayev had six children and a wife. His wife's name was Maydat Tsinstayeva, and his children were seven-year-old Umar, five-year-old Djanasi, four-year-old Zharadat, two-year-old Umar-Haji and the twins, Zara and Zura, who were not yet one. A family of farmers, they lived in a small homestead with cattle and poultry. Umar was the only sibling old enough to attend school, which saved his life. At approximately 13:30 that day, while Imar-Ali was visiting a cemetery at the side of the village, he watched as two Russian fighter jets flew above the houses and launched several bombs. One was dropped directly on his house. He ran as fast as he could, but by the time he was close, his home had been reduced to a pile of rubble and a crater. In front of it lay the prostrate body of his horse, covered in blood. The roof of his house had collapsed and his wife and children were nowhere to be seen. He called out their names, hoping that they were hiding somewhere, but no one responded. Then, with the help of neighbours, he cleared away the debris, digging through great piles of bricks and roof tiles. Underneath, he found all six of them, in one spot. In a final act of love, Maydat had scooped her children up, hoping to shield them from death, offering herself instead.

Imar-Ali buried the bodies of his wife and five of their children before dusk, and the family's relatives reported the deaths to the local authorities. Only five days later, on 13 April, did a helicopter with representatives from the military prosecution office land in the village. They claimed the fighter jets had attacked a group of terrorists hiding in the vicinity. It was a blatant lie. After superficially scanning the ruins of Imar-Ali's house, the officials told him that the explosion had been caused by a gas leak, not a bomb. They also hinted that Imar-Ali himself was handling explosives on his premises. The officials refused to exhume the bodies in order to run forensics tests to establish the cause of death. They warned Imar-Ali and his brother, Minkail, not to take the investigation any further. And perhaps it would have ended there, had Mum not gone to Rigakhoy as soon as she heard the rumour about an entire family being wiped out by a bomb.

Mum didn't have the authority to open a case, but she promised Imar-Ali and his relatives that she would tell the world about what had happened; that even if Russia didn't prosecute the murderers, there was something called the European Court of Human Rights, the last vestige of justice for Chechens. She interviewed the villagers and took photographs of the ruined house and the bomb fragments with a clearly defined serial number: 350Φ 5-90. In any other country, this would be deemed crucial evidence, but not in Chechnya. Then it was time for the hardest part. She asked if she could photograph the bodies and, although exhumation doesn't sit well with Muslim burial traditions, Imar-Ali agreed to it. With help from neighbours and relatives, he dug up the graves of his wife and children whom he had laid to rest only days earlier. I can still see those photographs when I close my eyes, as clearly as the first time I saw them, as a ten-year-old. Five tiny, doll-like bodies, laid carefully next to each other, according to their height. Their colourful, mismatched clothes are covered in dirt from the grave, as are their distorted, red faces. In another photograph their mother lies on her side as if she were slain just moments ago. There is nothing peaceful about these bodies; they don't look as though they have just fallen asleep and could open their eyes at any moment. Although their faces are smoothed by a mask of death, the agony and violence of their final moments rests underneath like a silent scream.

One of these photographs would go on to make international headlines when Tanya Lokshina placed it in front of President George W. Bush in the summer of 2006. Ahead of the G8 summit in Moscow, President Bush met with members of the press and civil rights organisations and, with only five minutes allocated to her, Tanya wanted to make an impact. Instead of giving a speech, she showed the president a blown-up photograph taken by my mother, telling the president, 'When you meet your friend Vladimir later today, ask him about Chechnya.' It's not known if he said anything in response or not. Either way, leaders of the free world were too interested in Russia's money and natural resources to let minor things such as war crimes get in the way of a good working relationship. It would take eight years for Imar-Ali and his only surviving son, Umar, to get any justice for the murder of their family.*

It had come as no surprise when the prosecution refused to open an investigation into the bombing. In 2004, such aerial campaigns still took place in mountain towns and villages – Rigakhoy, Vedeno, Shali, Dai, Zumsoi. They were designed not so much to 'smoke out' the insurgents, who rarely stayed in one place for long, as to discourage locals from sheltering them. Russian forces were using the same tactics as their colonial predecessors, forcing the highlanders to flee their homes and resettle on the plains where it was easier to control them. And in many ways, they succeeded. Today there are some settlements high in the Chechen mountains that exist only on the map: if you go there, you'll be greeted by ruins and abandoned homes, with not a soul in sight.

When Mum saw me on top of the horse, her face lit up. 'Don't get off yet!' she exclaimed, and took a quick snapshot.

The next morning, after we said our goodbyes and thank-yous, Mum, Tanya and I got back in the car. A wave of tiredness slowly washed over me. For a while, I watched as we slowly zigzagged our way down the narrow mountain roads. One wrong turn and we would be flying into the abyss, like with that mad horse. Soon, despite the nauseating turns of the car, I was asleep.

Outside Grozny, we switched to a minibus that would take us into the city. I was just falling back to sleep when I heard a loud chatter start up. It was hard to ignore; all the women were talking at once.

---

*In 2012, the European Court of Human Rights ruled that Russian forces were responsible for the bombing that killed Maydat and her children and that Russian authorities failed to conduct a proper investigation. Imar-Ali was awarded 300,000 euros, a tremendous sum for Chechnya.

Apparently, there had been a terror attack in Grozny. Little by little, we learnt more. A bomb had gone off at the Dinamo stadium where a parade commemorating Russia's victory in the Second World War had been taking place. Terror attacks were nothing new, but this felt different.

'Haven't you heard? Akhmad Kadyrov was at the stadium during the attack. He was blown up by the bomb!'

The president of Chechnya was dead.

7

Putin's Little Dragon
2004–7

I grew more nervous with each passing hour. It was almost nine o'clock in the evening and not a word from Mum and Anya.

Soon, the soft summer sky turned dark, the noises from outside died down and the flat grew quiet. I hated the darkness, hated how large the rooms felt when I was alone. I delayed knocking on the neighbours' door, keen to avoid the embarrassment that came with them knowing Mum had left me on my own so late. I knew that she must have had a good reason, but they wouldn't understand. Adding to my resentment, I recounted all the other times she had had me stay with random people because of a last-minute work trip. It was often obvious they didn't want me there. A few times, when Mum left me alone in the flat, she had forgotten to buy groceries or leave any money to go to the market. And now this . . .

It was much easier to be angry than scared. When the hour hand of the clock pointed to ten, it was time to knock on the neighbours' door. Kameta's parents let me in and sent me straight to bed without much reassurance. I hugged my knees, lying on the floor in Kameta's room, and tried to ignore the cacophony of intrusive thoughts that plagued my mind.

What's taking them so long? She's never left me alone for the night without any arrangements. What if something really bad has happened? What if . . .? No, not going there; no, no, la la la.

Eventually, tiredness overpowered me and I fell asleep.

'Lanuska,' whispered a gentle voice seemingly moments later. 'Let's go back to our flat.' Still heavy with sleep, I quietly followed Mum. Dawn was about to break.

In the morning, I learnt where they'd been all night. Mum told me apologetically that she had had to accompany Anya on an interview. It had been with Ramzan Kadyrov, son of Akhmad Kadyrov, the president of Chechnya, who a month before had been blown up at the stadium. I didn't know how to feel about this. On the one hand, I was proud of my mother's bravery. But through her I had heard stories about Ramzan's viciousness and his violence. He was a dangerous man.

I had long been aware of Ramzan Kadyrov because of his regular appearances on Chechen TV. I thought everything about him was detestable: his cold, small eyes set far too close together; his sparse ginger beard; his bad haircut; his guttural voice that turned the Chechen language into a vulgar medley littered with junk words. But none of that would have mattered if he hadn't been a turncoat who shook hands with the very same politicians who bombed and exterminated his own people. Before the attack that took his father's life he had been the head of his father's security team, and he was already notorious for his cruelty and explosive temper. After his father's assassination, Ramzan was flown to Moscow, where he appeared in a baby-blue tracksuit in front of his new 'adoptive father', Vladimir Putin. He signalled to the president of Russia that, with the Kremlin's backing, he was going to continue his father's political course. In return for his loyalty, he was appointed deputy prime minister of Chechnya aged just twenty-eight – the minimum age for the presidency was thirty – setting him on the path to leadership. Almost every night, this man and a host of sycophantic reporters invaded our living room. That's why Anya had gone to his house in Tsentoroi village. She wanted to take a closer look at the man who would be the future president of Chechnya. Fearing for her friend's life, Mum refused to let her go alone and, after a long back and forth, they resolved to go together.

And this was not the end. Today they were going back to his home for the second part of the interview.

Days after the two trips, I overheard Mum describing to colleagues how Ramzan Kadyrov had turned his ancestral village into a fortress with checkpoints and armed militia. In contrast to the rest of destitute Chechnya, his house dripped with gaudy opulence. Mum kept reiterating with a smile how whoever designed his house had never bothered to remove the price tags from the baroque-style furniture. When, days later, Mum brought home a copy of *Novaya Gazeta*, I instantly snatched it from her bag, eager to read Anya's write-up of the interview. It must have been the first political article that I'd ever read.

I lost track of all the additional characters in the article, and couldn't yet grasp the references to political events. But at the centre of it was a portrait of a brutish, impulsive, ignorant young man who had been handed an extraordinary amount of power. Ramzan was a seething mix of boorishness and insecurity, fuelled by an underlying need for approval. In other words, he was a classic bully. Except this bully had a private army, secret torture rooms and a direct line to the Russian president. Kadyrov might have been uneducated – during the interview, he couldn't remember which branch of law he was supposed to specialise in – but he possessed a calculated, instinctive cunning that would only sharpen over the coming years. He loved dog fights just as much as he loved pitting people against each other. During the interview, he insulted Anya; he taunted her and encouraged his entourage to do the same. He couldn't stand her brave questions that tried to hold him to account. No one dared to speak to him like that. At one point, Kadyrov had raised his hand to hit her and Mum threw herself between them, shielding her friend.

I gathered from the article and from eavesdropping on Mum's conversations that during the interview neither woman was sure they would get out of Tsentoroi alive. As they were walking back towards the car, Anya half expected a bullet in the back. From that first exchange, she had got the measure of Kadyrov and tried to warn the world about 'the little dragon raised by the Kremlin who needs constant feeding so he doesn't breathe fire'. The article sparked a feud between the journalist and would-be dictator; he hadn't liked being challenged and made to feel uncomfortable in his own home. Chechens were aware of his reputation but now Kadyrov's true self had been revealed to the rest of Russia, even if only to the readers of the progressive *Novaya Gazeta*. The 'little dragon' never forgot Anya and the other Russian-speaking woman who came with her that day.

★

In late August 2004, Mum warned me that our new tenth-floor flat wouldn't be ready in time for the start of the school year. I was growing frustrated. Not only would I be missing the first days of school; I still had no idea what our new home looked like. The uncertain, homeless summer was coming to an end and after the usual tour of the three villages and visiting family in the Urals, I found myself staying with a set of relatives whom I'd only met once or twice. It was the family of Mum's aunt Taus, the younger, jollier sister of the imposing Detsi Chovka. They lived in a small village in Dagestan, Chechnya's neighbouring republic, and most of their neighbours were Chechens too. Because of the lack of clearly defined geographical borders, it wasn't uncommon to have settlements with mixed populations at the seams of the Caucasian republics.

I was still in Dagestan, away from Mum, when the unspeakable happened. I couldn't quite make sense of it at first. One day, I found all my relatives glued to their television set, watching as men carried naked, blood-stained children from a burning building. The camera panned to a group of weeping women, their faces contorted with grief. What was happening? And why were the kids just wearing their underwear? I couldn't comprehend how anyone could inflict such horror on innocent children.

On 1 September, parents, teachers and children were gathered to celebrate the Day of Knowledge at school no. 1 in Beslan, a small town in the republic of North Ossetia-Alania located about a hundred miles west of Chechnya. Sometime after 9 a.m., before the festivities were in full swing, a group of armed men poured out of vehicles and started shooting, forcing everyone into the gymnasium, which was rigged with explosives. This was the beginning of one of the darkest chapters of Russia's recent history. For three days the rebels held over a thousand people hostage, most of them children, and subjected them to inhumane treatment, refusing them food and water. The reason many of the children were in their underwear, I found out years later, was because it was so hot inside they had no choice but to remove their clothes. On the third day of the siege there was an explosion at the gymnasium, followed by a second one, after which a fire broke out allowing some hostages to escape. This prompted Russian forces to storm the building and open fire on the rebels, who replied with gunshots. Most of the hostages were killed on that final day, caught in the middle of senseless, chaotic crossfire. The abominable massacre left 330 people dead, including 186 children.

Just a few weeks earlier, Mum had given me her old mobile phone, so that we could keep in touch. Now it started ringing.

'Are you all right, Lanuska?' she cried. 'Don't be scared, nothing will happen to you. I'm coming to get you as soon as possible.'

I was more sad than scared but sensed that Mum needed reassurance. I distracted her with a story about a recent trip to the Caspian Sea, telling her that the water was so shallow I'd had to walk for a long time until it was deep enough to swim, all the while ignoring my relatives' pleas to turn back. The sea had seemed more like a puddle.

'Some people drown in puddles, you know,' Mum interjected.

'No, it wasn't dangerous. Everyone followed me and in the end we dived into the sea from each other's shoulders. And then, we had a picnic on the beach!'

Mum came for me a few days later, and she had more bad news; Anya was in hospital. On her way to Beslan to report on the school siege, she had suddenly become so ill that her plane had to make an emergency landing. Anya had been taken to a hospital in Rostov-on-Don, in southern Russia, with severe toxic symptoms – it was likely that someone had poisoned her tea. As she fell into a coma, doctors fought for her life.

Anya hadn't been going to Beslan solely as a reporter; as one of the few people allowed in when Chechen militants seized the crowded Dubrovka Theatre in Moscow in 2002, she had experience of terrorist negotiations. It was evident someone had wanted to prevent her arrival that day, and although her health gradually recovered, it was never the same. After the attack, her stomach could no longer digest normal food and whenever she came to stay she always brought small packets of oats to eat.

The world soon discovered that Chechen warlord Shamil Basayev and his accomplices were behind the terror attack in Beslan. It was a spectacular failure on the part of Russia's federal security agencies, who ignored every detailed warning about the impending attack. As with the Dubrovka Theatre hostage crisis, most civilian deaths were the result of the disastrous actions of law enforcement agents, who prioritised using force against the terrorists above rescuing the hostages, resulting in a higher death toll. In the aftermath of the Beslan tragedy, the Russian government obfuscated the truth and tried to sabotage attempts at an independent inquiry, going as far as threatening the mothers of the murdered children. Journalist Elena Milashina, who went in place of Anya, spent years investigating the incident. She, too, would become a close family friend.

For us Chechens, the Beslan terrorist attack was a turning point. Now, it was not only Russians but also a large part of the international community who thought of every Chechen as an accomplice to terrorists. Any remaining sympathy towards Chechen independence vanished. I knew what would follow: more anti-Chechen vitriol, more calls for blood, more work for Mum. The school siege had been an utterly despicable and immoral act resulting in the deaths of innocent children, but it was also detrimental to ordinary Chechens. As much as I hated to admit it, I was a little embarrassed about sharing a nationality with those responsible for the attack. Nothing could justify what Basayev and his accomplices had done. And yet, just as in the 2002 Dubrovka attack, when the identities of some of the militants were uncovered, it came to light that some had become radicalised because of the loss of a family member and the destruction of a family home. These militants didn't just want independence for Chechnya, they wanted revenge.

As a child, I counted myself lucky because I hadn't experienced the life-shattering loss of a loved one. Yes, my father had been killed in the war when I was five, but I could hardly remember him; and several of my distant relatives were at some point kidnapped by Kadyrovites, but none were beaten badly and all were released as soon as Mum got involved. But the person who was most important to me, my mother, was alive and well. Sometimes I wondered if, God forbid, anything happened to her, would I want to avenge her by killing another human being? Would I be able to cross that line?

I saw first-hand what being pushed to the edge might look like when I was twelve years old and attending a two-week summer camp on the Black Sea near the town of Gelendzhik. We arrived on two large buses from Grozny – forty boys and two girls – me and Raya, a friend from my class. The gender imbalance was shocking and unexpected; I'd been to a few summer camps and there was always a roughly equal number of girls and boys. 'What a bunch of *kolkhozniki*,' I whispered in a sarcastic tone to Raya, calling them by the derogatory term we city slickers used to describe village simpletons. 'Let's stick with our boys,' Raya whispered back, referring to our classmate Aslan and his brother Amir. At school, Aslan and I were rivals and sworn enemies. Once, after he'd said something mean to me, I wrote a withering poem comparing him to a bison and threatened to make copies unless he apologised. He threatened to kill me. I threatened to come back as a ghost and haunt him. Given the circumstances that summer, Aslan and I tacitly agreed to hold a truce for the duration of the camp.

It was a typical Soviet camp scattered across several concrete buildings with large windows. We stayed in wooden barracks with girls from other Caucasian republics. 'Make sure you shut the windows at night because we get thieves,' the camp supervisor told us. Indeed, several nights later I noticed a white hand reach through a window to grab my phone from my bedside table. Raya reached out and slapped it with all her might. The hand never reappeared.

For the duration of the trip, our group existed in a state of anarchy, our councillor – a man in his early twenties – being more interested in flirting with the Russian girls than looking after us. He came up to me and Raya on the first day and declared, 'You girls, you'll be doing my laundry.'

I laughed in his face.

'You understand that because you're the only females', he carried on unfazed, 'you'll have to help the boys out. That's what their sisters would do.'

'Well, in that case,' I retorted, 'maybe they should all have brought their sisters along.' I added that if he bothered me again, I would complain to my mother.

It was the best summer camp experience of my life. The food was decent (except for the time I found a five-rouble coin in my bowl of buckwheat), the sea was just a fifteen-minute walk away, and unlike the other groups, Raya and I could hang out on the beach for hours, unsupervised. We made friends with three Chechen girls from another camp and spent all our time together. The only thing, or rather person, spoiling our idyll was Turpal, a boy with menacing eyes and a nasty attitude. He was nothing but trouble. On the second day he waved a small knife at two Russian girls because they wouldn't get out of his way. When our supervisor refused to confront him, Raya and I took matters into our own hands. We cornered him by the dining room and berated him for his actions. 'Do you want all the Russians here to think that we are simply stereotypes? That we are all knife-wielding savages?' Raya pressed him.

'I hate Russians,' he replied. 'I will never let them stand in my way.'

We thought Turpal was a lost cause until several days later when Raya and I spotted him slow-dancing with a fair-haired Russian girl at a camp disco. She was clearly besotted with his macho persona, and he was positively beaming. 'What a hypocrite,' I sneered.

Soon afterwards, a bunch of us were hanging out outside when I noticed a ten-year-old Chechen boy hitting a Balkar boy who was much younger than him. I separated them and told off the Chechen for picking on someone smaller than himself, but noticed that Turpal and his gang were watching the whole thing, and had been egging the boy on.

'What are you doing, defending that boy?' Turpal shouted at me.

'I will not let anyone bully small kids, whoever they are,' I replied defiantly.

'You stick up for outsiders. You're not a real Chechen!'

'You can talk! You dance with Russians girls – *you're* not a real Chechen!'

Turpal was mute as his friends laughed and yelled '*Baaahaha*, she got you!'

I walked off hand in hand with Raya with a huge smile on my face. I had really out-sassed myself this time, nothing could top it. But I was anxious too – a humiliated boy is a dangerous thing.

After that episode, it seemed Turpal was steering clear of me. At one of the football matches, he happened to be on a team with Aslan and Amir and he was playing very well. As he weaved his way across the field, never losing control of the ball, we couldn't help but cheer him on at the top of our voices. He scored once, then again and again, and our team won. Afterwards, Turpal, Raya and I ended up sitting on the benches chatting about the game. But I was still wary.

The topic turned to Russians. 'I hate them all,' he said again. 'I hate their language, hate the look of them.'

This time, I tried to reason with him without the sass. I listed the examples of all the good Russians I knew – human rights activists, journalists, my own grandmother. But Turpal was unbending. He told us that his older brother had been kidnapped by the federals and had disappeared; that his father had died during the war (or was it his mother?). He spoke of *zachistkas* in his village, of shellings and the musky smell of their basement. He spoke of hunger, of all the years of school that he'd missed.

'Have you ever heard of the human rights centre Memorial?' I asked when Turpal paused in his soliloquy. 'My mum works there. They might be able to help your family.'

But the boy had different plans.

'After I'm done with school, I'll go to the woods,' he insisted. 'My oldest brother knows some people.'

'What about your family?' we continued. 'Have you thought about them? What if you get killed? What if you're forced to kill innocent people? How would you live with yourself?'

I kept pressing him because there was a chance we could change his mind. There was still hope that he might have been showing off to impress us. Turpal listened patiently to all our arguments but refused to budge.

The last week of camp flew by and we found ourselves back on a bus, heading home to Grozny. My skin was caramel brown and the red holdall with a broken wheel was stuffed with cheap, silly trinkets purchased in seafront shops. Hours later, with my head on Mum's shoulder, I recounted all the adventures of the past weeks, Turpal being just a footnote in the story.

A couple of years later, Turpal came up in conversation. I can't recall who it was that told me that he had gone ahead with his plan; perhaps it was Raya, or her brother Amir. 'Have you heard what happened to that guy with the knife from our summer camp, what's-his-name? Do you know that he followed his brother to the woods? Haven't you heard that he was killed? Only a month later?'

There it was. For generations of young, angry men and women, going to the woods seemed like an alluring route to revenge, in a country where official paths to justice were virtually non-existent. Add helplessness, humiliation and impunity to that volatile mix, and you get people who have nothing to lose. Someone who is hurting and wants others to hurt too. Someone who believes that inflicting pain will restore some sort of cosmic balance.

I would be fifteen, the same age as Turpal, when I learnt the true meaning of rage. How it lives within you like a toxin; how it yearns for release, burning your soul. I also learnt that nothing beautiful can grow from poisoned soil.

By October 2004, after a month of living in our tenth-floor flat, it became clear that Mum had embellished a thing or two about how habitable our new home was. First of all, despite living on the top floor, the view was less than inspiring: a sprawling mud desert with no vegetation stretched all the way to the horizon. Looking left on a clear morning you could see the outlines of tall mountains far, far away. Straight ahead, in the distance, stood a military base, and occasionally we heard faint gunshots. To the right was a building almost identical to ours – a ten-storey tower block with rows of enclosed balconies. In Soviet times, this was supposedly a model neighbourhood in the suburbs of Grozny, with schools and small squares, and because of its distance from the city centre, our building had not been damaged during the wars.

As for the famed lift, it worked about 50 per cent of the time, and when it didn't Mum and I – and whoever was staying with us – had to climb all ten flights of stairs. That would have been fine had our water situation not worsened with the move. There was not a single working water tap in the area. Each day, in the morning and again in the afternoon, a Soviet-era water tanker with a hose at the back arrived at our building and honked loudly three times. All the neighbours hurried down with buckets and basins and the driver filled them up for two roubles per bucket. There was a significant disadvantage to this system – if your flat's window was on the other side of the building, as ours was, there was no way you could hear the horn. And since the driver followed his own unpredictable schedule, the only way for us to know when the water tanker had arrived was our downstairs neighbour tapping on her gas pipe. Whenever the lift was broken, I was forced to carry at least four large buckets of water up to the tenth floor where I poured the water inside a large plastic cistern. Mum usually asked me to leave the heavier buckets downstairs, so she could bring them up when she returned, but I rarely listened – the last thing I wanted was to burden her even more after a long day at work.

I was delighted that we had our own home, but I missed my old neighbourhood and often hung around with old friends and classmates after school. Because of our modest finances, the renovations dragged on – the concrete living-room wall was still covered in bullet dents and there was a watermelon-sized hole right next to my bedroom door. Mum and I spent every Saturday morning watching design shows, debating over which imaginary sofa would look better in the living room and planning questionable DIY projects. We agreed to begin by decorating the kitchen and my room. I envisaged a minimalist blue bedroom with clean lines and white, rectangular furniture, but it seemed as though the whole world (Grozny city market) was against it. In the end, Mum and I decided on bluebell-coloured wallpaper with a tiny pattern – a heavy-hearted compromise for me. When it came to a ceiling light, we settled on a fancy pendant comprising closely packed upside-down triangular leaves.

For months, Mum, our cat Reddy and I were the only inhabitants on the tenth-floor landing. At some point, a young family with the quietest kids in the world moved into the opposite flat, but the apartment next door remained empty, so I could sing as loud as I wanted, gallop around the house and enact scenes from imaginary soap operas. Then, sometime in early 2005, we heard sounds outside our door. The lift was broken as usual, so the young men were hurrying up and down the stairs carrying sacks and boxes into the neighbouring flat. Who were they? Brothers? Students? Seeing no women, Mum grew suspicious. It wasn't long before our new neighbours revealed themselves, exchanging their moving-in-day tracksuits for the black uniform of the Neftepolk – the Oil Protection Regiment. Our closest neighbours were Kadyrovites, members of Ramzan Kadyrov's special forces headed by his right-hand man, Adam Delimkhanov. Their regiment was often involved in the most notorious anti-terrorist operations that in fact were nothing more than *zachistkas*.

At first, everything was peaceful. Although Mum warned me against opening the door to strangers, no one ever knocked. Sometimes, I'd hear noises and look out through the peephole, but all you'd see were the Kadyrovites coming and going, like normal people. Inevitably, we'd bump into each other in the corridor, and they'd smile through their black beards. I met their attempts at friendliness with a stony face. On one occasion, one of them asked where Mum worked, and I replied, 'My mother works at the human rights centre Memorial, got any problems with that?' Smiling awkwardly, he walked away. After that, the Kadyrovites began to melt into the background when Mum passed them. It must seem surprising that I blurted out this information so mindlessly, but Mum never made a secret of who she was and our address was well known to many people. Everyone thought at the time that her visibility and reputation gave her a degree of protection. We despised and distrusted our Kadyrovite neighbours but didn't necessarily fear them – there were such an abundance of armed men on every corner of Grozny that they became part of the landscape.

From time to time I saw mysterious women through the peephole. One of them, a woman in her mid-twenties with dyed strawberry-blonde hair, transparent skin and dark circles under her eyes, appeared more often than the others. Definitely not a sister. Once, Mum had a chance to speak to her about quite an unusual subject. It was the last day of Eid al-Adha, a feast of sacrifice at the end of which meat is traditionally given to disadvantaged members of the community and to orphans. Mum and I were watching TV – we didn't tend to celebrate the day. During the ad break, I went to the kitchen to fetch something. When I switched on the light I discovered a giant chunk of beef lying on the floor. 'Shaitan's work!' I thought instantly, for there was no other explanation for such a bizarre occurrence. 'Maaaamaaa, did you buy any meat today?' I yelled.

'No, Lanusya,' she responded.

'You better come and look at this.'

Mum came through, picked up the meat and thoroughly inspected it. It was a beautiful beef fillet, high quality, fresh, with no fat. Where did it come from? Reddy begun to rub his head on our legs, as though protesting his innocence. 'Reddy, that chunk is twice your size!'

laughed Mum, looking at the suspect. The only place he could have possibly stolen it from was the balcony next to ours, belonging to the you-know-whos. Mum didn't have any choice; meat in hand, she knocked on the Kadyrovites' door. The blonde girl appeared moments later, a vacant expression on her face. She politely refused to accept the return of the stolen chunk, explaining that there was already half a cow stored on the balcony – it was common, when the weather was cold, to refrigerate food outside, saving the fridge space. In truth (quite understandably), she probably didn't want to take back a piece of meat that had been in a cat's mouth.

After we were safely back in our flat, Mum and I dissolved into laughter. The second one of us stopped, the other one would start again.

'See Lanuska,' Mum said, still giggling. 'Reddy made sure that you still got your piece of meat!'

'He's the real man of the house!' I replied.

The cat must have eaten plenty of meat while in the neighbours' flat and then, like a true breadwinner, brought some back home. It would have taken a lot of courage and skill, because to get back to our balcony, he had to balance on a very thin ledge. And what did we do with the meat? Our friend Alik, who came for a visit with other human rights activists the following day, cooked a nice stew with it. The fact that the meat was stolen from Kadyrovites who, for all we knew, could have stolen it from someone else, made it even more exotic.

Our next interaction with the neighbours was in the presence of a police officer. It was one of the few weekends when Mum and I were both at home all day – me at the computer in my room and Mum in the kitchen, doing DIY. The peace was suddenly interrupted by a woman's scream from the other side of the wall. I ran to the living room and saw Mum standing frozen, carefully listening to banging noises and muffled curses followed by even more screams. I heard a man shout, then the sound of broken glass. The woman was begging for him to spare her life. The banging noises grew louder and louder, and the screams were becoming unbearable. Mum quickly dialled a police acquaintance, asking him to come at once. After another blow, the screaming stopped completely.

About fifteen minutes later, the police officer arrived, and following a short conversation with Mum he banged on the neighbours' door. Mum ordered me to go to my room and I gladly obeyed. She later told me that the door was opened by the screaming girl, who had a massive bruise around her eye. She tried to persuade everyone that she was fine, smiling through tears. The officer warned our neighbours that if it happened again, there would be consequences. I overheard Mum whisper, 'They have an arms warehouse in there. The weapons are everywhere, in the corridor, in the rooms.' We never heard screams again, nor do I remember ever seeing the strawberry-blonde girl after that episode. But just in case, Mum sent me away to the village.

There was no escape from the increasing 'Kadyrofication' of our Grozny. Although a man named Alu Alkhanov was appointed president of Chechnya in 2005, Ramzan Kadyrov and his security forces wielded the most influence in the republic. Within a couple of years, Kadyrov had pushed all his opponents out of the way while continuing to attract more men to his battalions. Kadyrovites were gradually replacing Russian federals, whose presence shrank dramatically. By 2006, most law enforcement in Chechnya, including the police force, was under Ramzan Kadyrov's control. None of this would have been possible without the Kremlin's backing, especially the Ministry of Internal Affairs, who lent legitimacy to Kadyrov's private army and integrated it within its own body.

I couldn't even avoid Kadyrovites on the way to school, a lovely half-hour walk through residential streets of one-storey houses shaded by walnut trees. At ten, I was old enough to walk to school alone. I set out early, enjoying the fresh morning air, petting every cat on the way and kneeling to quickly sniff pink and blue hyacinths whenever they were in bloom. During that first year after our move to the tenth-floor apartment, I'd taken the scenic route – it took longer but passed more front gardens – until one morning I was chased by a long-haired old man. He called me by a woman's name and followed me, perhaps thinking I was his missing daughter. I felt for him: war had driven many people insane, and because of the lack of proper mental-health facilities, they were left to wander the streets.

Nonetheless I was spooked and began taking the most direct route to school. Then one day a large military base appeared, seemingly having grown out of nowhere on the side of the road about two-thirds of the way there. Bizarrely, it turned out to be the new headquarters of the infamous Neftepolk – the same Oil Protection Regiment to which our neighbours belonged – where Kadyrov's elite forces were stationed. Bored Kadyrovites guarding the building often catcalled passing girls, and although I'd been propositioned since the age of eleven – thankfully nothing too sexual, but enough to make me want to disappear – this felt different. After that, I walked right the way around the military base, extending the journey by ten minutes.

Mum's work at Memorial was not getting any easier. The flow of kidnappings, illegal imprisonment, disappearances and extrajudicial executions continued, except now it was carried out by the Chechens themselves. The number of law enforcement agents operating in Chechnya was completely disproportionate to the several hundred militants hiding out in the forested mountains. In order to justify the existence of salaried men with a monopoly on violence, they had to show that their efforts in counterterrorism were effective, even if it meant torturing and disappearing innocent young men.

Most of the rebel commanders had been eliminated one by one: Saudi warlord Khattab had died in 2002, after opening a letter poisoned by the FSB; Aslan Maskhadov, the former president of Chechnya turned rebel leader, was killed in Tolstoy-Yurt in 2005; and Shamil Basayev, the monster behind the Beslan terrorist attack, was killed by Russian special forces in Ingushetia. Anyone suspected of affiliation with the militants, including their distant relatives and neighbours, became a target. Another practice that Ramzan inherited from his father Akhmad was hostage-taking, which was supposed to force the militants to surrender. One of the most notable examples of this was when eight members of Aslan Maskhadov's family, including his sixty-seven-year-old sister, were detained on the same day. Seven of them subsequently disappeared. Somehow, those who had fought for Chechen independence and sought shelter from Russian bombs less than a decade ago were now killing and torturing their own people.

Memorial collected thousands of testimonies from innocent people who were kidnapped from their homes and subjected to brutal torture so they would sign confessions admitting to being members of unlawful armed groups. The more fake confessions that were produced, the better Kadyrov looked before his Kremlin superiors. In return, he was given carte-blanche power and generous funds from the federal budget. Women were not spared – mothers, grandmothers, sisters. In 2006, a video of a twenty-three-year-old pregnant woman, Malika Soltayeva, made the rounds, shared by text. It showed her being tortured by Argun city police, who accused her of taking a Russian lover. Severely beaten with wooden sticks and lashes, Malika suffered a miscarriage. Mum tried to raise the case with the local authorities, but they threatened to prosecute Malika for false reporting of the abduction. This was not uncommon – increasingly, victims and family members were too scared to talk to human rights organisations and journalists, fearful of what the Kadyrovites might do to remaining family members.

As Chechnya fell more and more into the grip of Kadyrov, Mum's dedication to her work deepened. In autumn 2005, Mum's colleagues practically forced her to take a break. She'd put her neck on the line too many times, especially after Anya's interview with Ramzan Kadyrov, and was not slowing down. Reluctantly, Mum took a few days off. We hadn't had a holiday together in ages, but our scramble to catch some sun by the Caspian Sea turned into a spectacular failure. Not only was the weather disappointingly cloudy; on our first day Mum nearly drowned in the stormy sea (she was a terrible swimmer) and I suffered food poisoning from an Olivier salad. On the second day Mum's phone exploded with calls. Back in Grozny, families were being evicted from the temporary housing where they were staying because their homes were about to be bulldozed. In an attempt to 'beautify' Grozny, the local authorities were throwing people out on the streets and destroying their makeshift homes, but they weren't so keen on paying compensation. Naturally, Mum took it upon herself to campaign for the poor families and embroil herself in fights with the mayor's office, and so we boarded a bus back to Grozny. Sitting by the window – green-faced, nauseous and cross with Mum – I wondered why she had bothered to make this trip anyway. Our lives were built around other people's needs. Mum never knew how to say no. She never switched off and rarely found time for herself – or for me, for that matter.

Since joining Memorial, Mum had received several prestigious human rights awards, including the Right Livelihood Award from the Swedish parliament in 2004 and the Robert Schuman Medal in 2005. She was proud that her work was recognised, and displayed her medal and the diploma on a bookshelf. However, her instinct was to give away the monetary rewards that came with them. Even when Memorial colleagues begged her to keep at least a little so we could finish the flat renovation, she refused. 'It's not my money,' she would argue. Instead the funds were distributed among a long list of those who needed it more than us, while Mum and I lived in a flat with bullet holes in the walls and a living room that had no flooring. I would have remained oblivious to this had she not developed a habit of giving away her salary too. Mere days after payday, Mum would strut in and announce that we must tighten our belts until the end of the month. 'But you just got paid!' I would cry in disbelief. 'I need new trainers, mine have holes in them.' She would assure me that I'd get a new pair next month, and would seal the holes in the old ones with super-glue. Sometimes she'd get defensive and angry, calling me a clothes-obsessed materialist – which, in all honesty, wasn't far from the truth. But occasionally, she did go too far. When I was eleven, she gave away my favourite stuffed dolphin to an orphanage ('You're too old for it anyway!'). And there was the time she let a runaway stay with us for a week.

It was quite common to see large groups of Roma beggars, often children, on the streets of Grozny. Sometimes they even made their way into more residential neighbourhoods like ours and knocked on every door asking for small change. Mum had first spoken to Alyona when she'd knocked on our door one Sunday morning. I peered out of my room to check who was there and saw an olive-skinned young woman in a long, patterned skirt surrounded by several children. Mum rarely gave money to beggars – only clothes and food – but she told Alyona that she could come to her for help, should she find herself in trouble. And, not long after, she did – with another knock at the door, this time at about 6 a.m. Alyona told us that she was an orphan and that her abusive aunt beat her and forced her to beg. Her fiancé, Vitya, was doing mandatory military service and her aunt was planning to marry her off to an old man. Mum let her stay with us for a few days and asked me to teach Alyona to read – an unusual request. Having never attended school, Alyona barely knew the alphabet at the age of eighteen. I happily complied and patiently sat with her for hours at a time, showing her building blocks with letters Mum had brought home. Not paying any mind to the fact that her teacher was only eleven, she proved to be a keen student and soon we moved on to simple children's books. About a week later, Mum came home from work and told us that she had found Alyona's distant relatives, who lived in Russia. They agreed to host her until her fiancé came back from the army, which made her very happy. The next morning Mum handed her a train ticket and her phone number – just in case. It was a tearful goodbye, with Alyona crying and promising that she'd keep in touch. About a year later Alyona wrote to Mum saying that Vitya had come back from the army and that they had married; our Cinderella got her happy ending.

Mum brought me up to be generous and kind to others but my sense of self-preservation was stronger than hers – which is a nice way of saying that I was more selfish. I saw Mum give herself away to others and felt very protective of her. 'She takes care of everyone, but who is taking care of her?' I reasoned. Mum didn't just deserve a break, she desperately needed one. And, most importantly, no matter how much she tried to laugh it off, she was really shaken by her meeting with Ramzan Kadyrov. And then, just at the right moment, Mum and I were given the opportunity to escape it all – for a little while at least. We were going to travel abroad – to Ireland.

In October 2005, I ate buttered toast for the first time, and it was a heavenly, life-changing experience. Bread had always been a staple, but toasters were not often seen in Chechnya and Irish butter tasted so different. It was salty! The moment that combination of flavours hit my tongue – the warm, crispy white toast dripping in melted butter – I fell in love with Ireland. We were staying at a bed and breakfast, which meant I could have as many helpings as I liked. And there were all kinds of cereals on offer that I'd never seen before, like Rice Krispies. Several days later, Mum and I moved into our own little flat in a picturesque Dublin suburb. Thanks to Memorial and a fantastic Irish organisation, Frontline Defenders, we were going to have several months of peace and quiet, all expenses paid. It was part of a shelter programme for human rights activists from dangerous regions, that allowed them to rest and recuperate in a safe environment, along with close family.

Mum had already been abroad, but for me going to Europe was like flying to another planet. I wasn't even entirely sure that 'abroad' was real until our plane hit the tarmac. Everything looked and tasted different. Every day, Mum and I walked the seafront and inhaled the fresh, invigorating air, as if it had been prescribed by a doctor. The sea was different here, compared to the overcrowded beaches near Sochi or the muddy, shallow waters of the Caspian coast. It was pensive and powerful, waves angrily crashing into the barnacled pier and exploding in thousands of droplets. When the tide was out, I explored the narrow sandy beach in search of seashells and put any whole ones I found in a special plastic bag that I kept in the corridor because of the increasingly pungent smell.

Everything in and around Dublin was so different, but I was quickly getting used to living in a place where nothing reminded me of my homeland. One of the best things about being there – apart from a wider range of chocolate and a massive, cheap Penneys store – was having Mum close to me. We spent days in museums, strolled through parks, visited medieval castles and gazed at the gorgeous Christmas decorations adorning every building. We found it amusing that Christmas trees appeared everywhere towards the end of November, but the jolly, festive atmosphere was very contagious. Mum was relaxed and chirpy, and most importantly, because she wasn't torn by millions of obligations, she was present – not only for me but for herself.

But she wouldn't be Natalia Estemirova if she didn't find ways of being busy and productive. Mum insisted on participating in various talks, seminars and human rights conferences that gave her a chance to talk about what was happening in Chechnya. On top of that, she sent me to a local Catholic school, so I didn't hang around at home. I found out many years later from someone who worked at Frontline Defenders that normally they didn't arrange schooling for the children of human rights activists because they were only in Ireland for about three months at a time. 'But Lanka must practise her English,' Mum had insisted, and so I joined a class full of children my age who spoke English with a strange, incomprehensible accent. I didn't make many friends but everyone was nice enough and once I was even invited for a sleepover. The girls made a point of speaking veeeeryyyy sloooowlyyyy so I could understand them and showed me how to play Twister. As we contorted our bodies into funny shapes, trying to place our limbs on colourful circles, we had no need for a complicated vocabulary – laughter was a universal language.

Mum also attended language classes each day, but became very self-conscious when using the new words. She panicked and forgot the most basic phrases, such as 'thank you' and 'hello'. It was endearing seeing my fearless mother, who knew how to answer every question, turn to me when it came to speaking English. Whenever she forgot a word, I would tap her hand and whisper it in her ear. Because I was more confident, I ended up ordering food, chatting to cashiers and asking people for directions. As a rule, Mum made a point of not praising me too much, fearing it would spoil me, but she couldn't help herself. 'Lanuska, you are so brave,' she told me, almost inadvertently. 'I don't think that at your age I would have the courage to put myself out there, unless I spoke the language perfectly. But it never stops you!'

I knew this about Mum. She was too self-conscious to speak the impossibly difficult Chechen that she never learnt as a child, and now she was struggling with English because of that old mental block rather than her lack of ability. I was happy to watch her confidence grow week by week, though, and by the end of our stay she was ordering food at McDonald's without my assistance.

Those months stretched into eternity, but Chechnya was calling us back. It was only meant to be a short stay. We both missed Grozny and left beautiful, unbroken Ireland with light hearts.

There was a lot of catching up to do at school. I had missed an entire term of physics, a subject new to me. By then, it was clear that I was no scientist and maths problems filled me with dread. Most nights I prayed for the lessons to be cancelled because the teacher hated my guts – she even told me as much.

Ireland may have given us a chance to get away from Ramzan Kadyrov, but the Kadyrovites were still living next door. While Mum and her activist colleagues typed up reports on human rights abuses in our kitchen, our neighbours were very likely committing them elsewhere. We completely lost track of how many people lived in the flat – sometimes there were as many as twenty squeezed into the two-bedroom apartment; at other times the place was quiet for weeks. But soon enough, Mum and I became the victims of their dirty business.

Above our flat was a dark attic that spanned the whole floor. I knew that the vents in our bathrooms led directly to it, because one day two unfamiliar cats had fallen through them, one after the other. They had clearly been in the middle of a fight because the second they both landed, they ripped into each other there on the bathroom floor. I grabbed a mop, opened the front door and escorted them out as they temporarily stopped to hiss at me. (This is necessary background information.)

It was a warm spring evening, and I was studying for a test. The window was open as usual, allowing a light breeze into the stuffy room. While I was tackling a tricky maths exercise, I heard a strange gurgling sound; it was accompanied by a foul stench. I slowly turned around, trying to locate the source. Looking up at the ceiling, to my horror I could see the glass leaves of the pendant light filling with brown liquid, which soon spilled over and started to drip on the carpet. Fighting nausea, I yelled 'MAMAAA!' and ran for a bucket.

I'd never seen Mum so angry. Her face bright red, she began spitting insults. 'You sons of bitches!' she yelled. 'Bastards! I'll show you!' (Mum cursed as infrequently as she cried.) She sprinted into the corridor in her dressing gown, hurriedly shoving her feet into slippers. 'Lana, you're coming with me!'

I trailed behind, anticipating catastrophe. Mum's wrath moved tectonic plates, eliminating anyone unfortunate enough to stand in her way. I worried about her target. We flew up to the attic of our block, the so-called 'technical' floor located right above our flat. In order to get in, you had to duck through a hatch half a metre high. When we stooped to do so, we immediately spotted a pair of men's legs in Adidas tracksuit bottoms and a hand beside them holding a *gumakh* – a jug that's used in Chechnya instead of a bidet. Then the rest of the body emerged. It was one of our next-door neighbours with his black bushy beard.

Mum yelled for an eternity. Standing on the lower step, she told off this giant of a man who now stood like a boy by the wall, gripping his *gumakh*.

'Are you all careless children down there?' Mum shouted. 'Couldn't you just call a plumber when your toilet broke instead off shitting on your neighbours? That gunk could have ended up spilling all over my DAUGHTER!'

I looked up, gave the neighbour a stare, and then studied my feet. It was such a bizarre situation that I felt embarrassed for that idiot in his stupid slippers.

'I went through that door,' she told me later. 'Turns out they've turned half of the floor into a TOILET! And because they are running out of space, they've found a new spot above your room!'

She ordered me to air every room in the house and wait in the kitchen while she handled the mess. Not only did my poor mum have to deal with the Kadyrovites' crimes at work, she literally had to scrub their shit and piss off her rug.

On 28 April 2006, at a meeting of NGOs and the authorities held at the Chechen parliamentary assembly, my mother directly addressed one of the representatives of the ORB-2 detention facility: 'Your establishment has such a bad reputation', she stated, 'that the mere threat of being taken there can absolutely break a human's will.' The room erupted in applause.

ORB-2, an abbreviation for Second Operational Investigative Bureau, was originally established during the second Chechen war to investigate the activities of organised criminal groups. In reality, it had become an illegal prison in which detainees were beaten and brutally tortured in order to extract false confessions. Chechen men were plucked from their homes, streets and places of work by ORB-2 operatives who never showed their identity papers. They threw detainees into vehicles without number plates and took them straight to the detention facilities, where they interrogated them without lawyers present. The families of those men were left completely in the dark about where they had been taken. Survivors spoke of chilling abuse: electric shocks, severe beatings, suffocation with plastic bags, even rape. After days of violence, victims were handed a piece of paper to sign – their 'charge' would be filled out later, most often 'participation in illegal armed groups'.

Mum was the first to raise concerns about this illegal prison at national level. That's why her statement caused such a big reaction. The then president of Chechnya, Alu Alkhanov, and prime minister Ramzan Kadyrov, whose own troops were in competition with ORB-2, condemned the facility. As a joint project, the Chechen authorities and NGOs set up a special commission to inspect the detention centres and prisons, with Mum as one of its members. I found out about the latter when leafing through a local newspaper where Mum had occasionally published her articles. There was a picture of her wearing a green long-sleeve top, standing next to a group of people I didn't know – except for one to the left, Alu Alkhanov.

'Oh, Mum, you have a picture with our president, it's a historical record,' I proclaimed. She was typing away on her laptop and ignored my comment entirely. It didn't matter to her who was sitting opposite, as long as they had the power to make a difference and she had all the necessary facts at hand.

Mum continued to investigate the secret prisons and Anya Politkovskaya carried on writing about them – the meetings with Chechen officials hadn't amounted to much. On 10 June, Mum gave an extended joint interview with Anya for the liberal radio station Echo of Moscow. They talked about ORB-2 and another secret prison in the Oktyabrski district that had been left behind by the infamous Khanty-Mansiysk unit – the unit responsible for torturing and disappearing our friend's son, Zelimkhan Murdalov. At the start of the second war, Khanty-Mansiysk had appropriated a building from an orphanage for deaf children to turn into their prison, and now, as it was about to be demolished, Mum rushed to document the crime scene. She recorded torture instruments and blood-stained walls with horrifying recent messages – one read, *Who am I? What happened to me? Am I alive or dead? 27 March 2006*. Another interviewee on the radio show was Alaudi Sadykov – a former schoolteacher and a quiet man whom I had met several times as a child. He too had been tortured at the Oktyabrski prison. As he spoke I could see that the hair on the right side of his head covered a hole – his ear had been taken by his torturer as a trophy.

During the interview, Mum and Anya disagreed on how to best deal with secret prisons. Anya didn't think that cooperating with the authorities, who were often implicated in human rights violations, was the best move. But Mum made a strong case:

'Of course, we are not only talking about torture at ORB-2. Torture is taking place throughout Chechnya. People are tortured in various prisons – legal, illegal, semi-legal. But the ones who created the system, who played a huge role in it, are those responsible for ORB-2. This prison is completely legal, but for some reason it is unsupervised and not controlled by anyone. We managed to rescue people from there and they are no longer tortured. I don't want to say that all is good now. But on 6 June there was a committee meeting during which it was decided to create a commission that would monitor the state of the Executive System. And we thought it was right that we should do this. If we can help someone, that's great.'

The host asked Anya if she believed that the commission could change the situation in Chechnya for the better.

'No, I do not believe it,' she responded, 'because one of the most terrible torture centres in Chechnya is Tsenteroi – Natalia Estemirova knows this, we all know this. Tsenteroi is, as it were, Ramzan Kadyrov's kingdom.'

She had understood Kadyrov from that very first meeting with him and was working to expose the nature of his regime at every opportunity. For her, official meetings with the authorities were little more than window dressing; they wouldn't change the fundamental situation in Chechnya, not while Kadyrov was in charge – a fact proven by the absolute impunity with which torture and murder took place in his hometown and personal fiefdom of Tsenteroi.

'What is the Chechen parliament? This is the place where people are gathered at the request of Ramzan Kadyrov. It's full of Kadyrov's relatives, Kadyrov's acquaintances; this is Kadyrov's parliament. How will this parliament fight Tsenteroi? Well, that's just ridiculous. The truth is that we cannot do anything with Tsenteroi; they laugh at us.

What power do we human rights activists and journalists have? There's nothing we can do. To say anything else is to sugarcoat the truth.'

Her conclusion was sobering: 'Until people in Chechnya stand up against this lawlessness, nothing will change.'

On 7 October, Mum and I were boarding a minibus near the Grozny Drama Theatre to go home. It was one of those rare autumn days when the air seemed to be illuminated by the buttery sun. The bus was about to leave when Mum received a phone call. I watched in horror as her face turned white, just as I had read in books. 'Anya has been murdered,' she whispered in a strange, hushed voice.

She shouted at the driver to stop the bus and let us off. It was a very long walk home; as the world around me blurred, I was too shocked to say anything. Mum didn't cry. She made phone call after phone call, never giving herself a second to stop and process the fact that Anya – her comrade, her friend, her ally – had been killed, shot in the head in the lift of her Moscow apartment building.

I didn't know how to approach my grieving mother, how to comfort her. Her phone would only stop ringing for about ten minutes at a time, and then it would start again. She left for the funeral the next day, leaving me with the downstairs neighbours. There was a pile of dishes in the sink that neither of us could face tackling. I kept telling myself that I must do them, but something prevented me. I went to school as always, came home and then went to the neighbours for the night. I leafed through the last book that Anya had given me – an enormous art album for children with famous paintings from London's National Gallery annotated with little arrows explaining the symbolism. I was mesmerised by *Bacchus and Ariadne* by Titian, always heartbroken by the fact that Theseus is forced to abandon Ariadne because of a prophecy. But seeing the youthful eagerness with which Bacchus jumps out of the carriage towards his new love always gave me hope that maybe they were a good match after all.

The dirty dishes were still untouched in the plastic basin three days later. I decided to stop going into the kitchen altogether. That evening, when I went to the neighbours, there was a commotion in the neighbourhood – sirens and gunshots. A counterterrorism raid was taking place in the tower block beside ours. I watched footage of our building on the TV with amusement. We weren't allowed outside for several hours. 'Are you okay? Are you safe?' Mum screamed down the phone from Moscow. I was okay. But everything that was happening in those days was happening to a different Lana. I did everything I was supposed to do, but it all felt like a dream. The next day, I went home after school and finally washed those neglected, crusty dishes.

I didn't realise back then that Anya's murder would change the course of our lives. Anya was a champion of the Chechen people and Mum vowed to carry on her friend's work, to build on her legacy. Her Memorial colleagues in Moscow were worried about the safety of their Grozny colleagues. Anya had been murdered on Putin's birthday – too much of a symbolic act to be considered a coincidence. And only one man could be responsible for giving his 'father' such a brazen, barbaric gift. When Mum started writing for *Novaya Gazeta* about human rights abuses in Chechnya following Anya's murder, at first under a pseudonym and then under her own name, she was taking on a serious enemy. But her desire for justice always trumped her instinct for self-preservation. She didn't have time for fear – having wiped away her tears for her fallen friend, she simply put it aside.

After being appointed president of Chechnya in February 2007, Ramzan Kadyrov found myriad ways in which to impose himself on my life. He had a habit of turning up in the most unexpected places, with a fleet of journalists. Traffic would stop as his black motorcade flew through the city at speed. Three times I had the opportunity to see him in the flesh, and all three times my body refused me, my stomach starting to tighten in a knot, my vision blurring and my legs taking me in the opposite direction. 'Let him live in the television,' whispered the voice in my head. 'That way we can pretend he isn't real.' When it was rumoured that Kadyrov would come to our neighbourhood to see the renovated tower blocks, I stayed in my room. When my classmates and I attended a festival in the city square and someone yelled 'Ramzan is nearly here!' I boarded a minibus and took off. When, in a last-minute schedule change, he decided to pay a visit to my school and I heard the sirens of his convoy, I slipped through the school gates and ran as fast as I could, so fast I forgot I was wearing a classmate's jacket that she had lent me because it was cold. It was enough being hounded by Kadyrov on television and posters and hearing about him every day. I wanted to reserve the right to never see him in person.

The only place where I could escape the incessant propaganda, other than home and Memorial, was the Youth Library. My closest school-friends had discovered it, and eventually I decided to tag along. The library occupied a few rooms on the third floor of a rather grim-looking Brutalist building, but once inside you were transported to a cosy sanctuary with rows of colourful books, comfy chairs and three welcoming custodians. The librarians were chatty, jolly, middle-aged women who treated us like family, rushing to put the kettle on and fetching a plate of biscuits whenever we appeared. Once gathered around the table with cups of tea, it was time to discuss the agenda – what event should we put on next? We organised presentations, poetry competitions and even a stand-up comedy show, which made me particularly excited. On 23 February, the anniversary of the deportation, we read poems and excerpts by authors who had lived through it and were encouraged to talk about how our own family members had been affected. I told the story of my grandpa Hussein, recounting his grisly journey to Kyrgyzstan, the death of his parents of which he was unaware, and how he lost touch with his sisters for decades. Every single person in the room had a family story like this, and in a strange way it was comforting that there was something that united us all, old and young.

The library was a welcome outlet after a string of cancelled after-school activities. No matter what was happening in our lives, Mum had never given up on her quest to turn me into a 'real lady'. I was her project, and she wanted to make sure that I grew into the best version of myself. But just as with the house renovation, she had neither the time nor the money to see her project through as she wanted. Singing lessons ended abruptly when she had to send me to the village for a long period of time. Art school was too far away for me to travel alone. And while she never abandoned her dreams of turning me into a pianist, when she bought me second-hand keyboards that I had no interest in learning how to play (because she never found me a teacher) her enthusiasm fizzled out, the keyboards collecting dust in the corner of the room until she gave them away. I enjoyed French classes and made a lot of progress, but they, too, ended when one day our sharp and sarcastic young teacher, who usually wore a dark-coloured hijab and always made jokes about me being the youngest in class, didn't turn up. At home, Mum sprang the news on me: 'We had to evacuate your teacher and her daughter to France. Her husband used to be a militant during the war – he was disappeared. But now those bastard Kadyrovites are bothering her, accusing her of having connections with terrorists.'

'Is it too much to ask for normal French classes without all this craziness?' I whined in response.

But perhaps the most soul-destroying after-school activity that Mum inflicted on me was Caucasian dance classes at the folk school. The sessions took place in a gym close to my house where, thankfully, there was no chance of bumping into any classmates. Caucasian dancing is a powerful and singular style of dancing that varies from region to region. Some Chechen youth dance groups even toured abroad during the war, showcasing their talent to the rest of the world. But as much as I liked watching others perform, and occasionally danced at parties and weddings, I detested dance school with a passion, not least because of my innate inability to copy other people's moves. Compared to the elegant, swan-like girls in my class, I moved like an awkward duckling, constantly bumping into everyone, all the while suffering the withering smirks of teenage bunheads who had been performing professionally since they were little. Mum, however, was convinced that dance classes would turn me into a lady and told me off whenever I skipped class – which I did often. My humiliation was compounded during a short end-of-class showcase that I normally avoided by leaving early. The dance teacher became wise to my trick and put me in the middle of the line. Each of us only had to perform one movement – a graceful tiptoe to the end of the room in tiny-tiny steps, as if floating, while gently moving our outstretched arms. It seemed basic enough, but my stomach was in knots. I watched the first girl float so seamlessly she appeared to have small wheels under her skirt. The second one was even better. I grew more and more nervous as my turn approached. When the girl before me glided across the floor, I was seriously considering faking a faint. But while

I was assessing the safest trajectory for my fall, I heard the deafening shout of my moustachioed teacher: 'ESTEMIROVA! NOW!' I felt instantly dizzy, but there was no choice. I lifted my soft leather-slippered heels, stretched my arms out as if I was about to lift off, and waddled along, cursing the day I was born. Thankfully, the accordion was so loud it drowned out some of the laughter I heard behind me. Those were the longest twenty seconds of my life. When I got to the other side of the room, I caught my teacher giving me a look – he was not disappointed but almost pitiful, as if I were a kitten freshly rescued from a sewer. 'Estemirova,' he sighed. 'You sing, right?'

'Yes, I do.'

'You should stick to singing then.'

So thanks to a decent (or loud, at least) singing voice, I joined the choir at the folk school. It meant less dancing, but singing didn't turn out to be very exciting because all the solos were given to the older girls. And with my alto I was consigned to belting out simple harmonies consisting of two or three notes. My inner diva was distraught. Gradually, I abandoned the folk school altogether, and Mum accepted it.

Meanwhile, I was doing quite well academically. At home, I would sit at my computer and draw very detailed pictures in Microsoft Paint – landscapes, portraits, interiors, even political posters. I still made up stories in my head, although I was too lazy to write them down, and I wrote poems and essays that Mum took to local newspapers to be published. She always encouraged my writing. My French may have faltered, but I was learning English independently, dreaming about being fluent one day – with the help of an electronic dictionary, I translated the lyrics to my favourite songs, trying to make sense of them. A few years later, I would even read my first novel in English, *Bridget Jones's Diary*.

At school, I attended the English club, where we put on small plays. Why go to snooty dance classes when I could play a bunny, a princess or a witch? I even went so far as to write a play for the school's New Year party (in Russian, of course), subverting a typical plot that involved Ded Moroz looking for his kidnapped granddaughter, Snegurochka. In my version, Snegurochka was abducted by a group of pirates, who carried her away on their ship demanding a ransom. They 'tortured' her by showing her horrible colour combinations – pink with orange, for example – and rubbing pieces of Styrofoam together. But by the end, Snegurochka realised that she didn't want to play second fiddle to her grandfather, and instead went off to explore the seas with the gang of pirates that she had befriended. Naturally, I played the pirate captain and also acted as director, playwright and set manager. My classmates were happy to participate, and the cast was assembled in a single day. Our gym teacher lent us her office for rehearsals, and we even built a passable pirate ship out of wooden chairs. The play was becoming more political as I included provocative jokes about Putin and the then prime minister Dmitri Medvedev, and my classmates and I had heaps of fun during the read-through. But then came the shattering news that the head teacher, Fatima Magomedovna, had dropped our play in favour of her own form's stage production. As seniors, they held a higher position in the pecking order than a bunch of ninth-graders. But I believed something else was at stake: my play was too political, too avant-garde. This was a blatant example of censorship, or at least that's what I grudgingly relayed to my classmates, who seemed rather relieved that they didn't have to participate in my over-the-top experiment. The head teacher's production was a classic, toothless retelling of the story in which Snegurochka is kidnapped by Baba-Yaga (the witch) and is 'rescued' after Ded Moroz encourages the audience to call her name. I was even offered the role of Baba-Yaga as a consolation prize, as I had played it on two previous occasions, but this time I refused, choosing instead to sulk in my room with a giant bar of chocolate. 'They weren't ready for your play,' Mum reassured me, having read my scribbles. 'Don't let this stop you from writing.'

By the winter of 2007, Grozny was bedecked in banners sporting the faces of Ramzan, Putin and Akhmad, Ramzan's late father. 'Look at them,' Mum whispered as we passed. 'The father, the son and the holy ghost.' Chechen TV broadcast never-ending tributes: Ramzan had single-handedly taken down a nest of terrorists; Ramzan had adopted the son of his fallen friend; Ramzan had awarded his mother a medal. Thanks to Mum and her colleagues, I knew what was going on behind this facade; how he personally beat and tortured people at his home. How he took concubines on a whim and fathered children with different women. How he robbed his own people of their pathetic salaries to enrich himself and those close to him. A gulf was opening between my carefree school life, with its English classes and new-found interest in celebrity magazines, and the way my homeland was descending into authoritarianism. Having eliminated most of his rivals, Kadyrov now ruled Chechnya as if it were his own private kingdom, with the complete blessing of the Kremlin. In exchange for Russian money and political power, he ensured that no one caused any trouble.

The personality cult seeped into everything. One day, a portrait of Akhmad Kadyrov appeared in my classroom. On another, I was asked to participate in a TV quiz show for schoolchildren, and we were asked to wear red T-shirts which bore images of Ramzan's face. I called Mum and cried: 'What should I do? If I put on this T-shirt, I betray our principles and if I quit, I betray my team.' Luckily, my teacher found an alternative and we graciously lost to a team while wearing plain aquamarine T-shirts. They ended up wearing T-shirts with Kadyrov's face.

The final blow came from where I least expected it. We were at the Youth Library, debating what event we should put on next. As usual, the lovely librarians had greeted us with a pot of tea and a plate full of biscuits. We spent some time catching up and chatting and then one of the women stood at the head of the table and put an index finger on her lips, asking for quiet.

'Dear girls,' she started with a big smile. 'You are all so proactive and talented that we don't always know how to keep you entertained. And how great you are at coming up with all the events! But I have some special news for you. Our Ministry of Culture has announced a competition between all the education establishments. It can be an essay or poem, whatever form you prefer. The topic is "Why Akhmad-Khadji Kadyrov is my hero".'

I felt nauseous. This couldn't be happening. I looked around; my friends seemed to be puzzled too. I was too grown up and polite to make a scene. Instead, I mumbled, 'Excuse me, I have to go', grabbed my satchel and walked out of the room, turning away from the stunned faces. This was supposed to be our safe space. But nowhere in Chechnya was safe from Kadyrov anymore. Apart from one place.

Instead of going to the flat, I caught a bus to the Memorial office. Mum wasn't in but everyone else was there.

There was Shamil, thirty-something years old in his impeccably neat outfit. Whereas Mum was the heart of Grozny Memorial, he was its soul – courteous, modest and endlessly brave. He often accompanied Mum on her risky trips but also made sure she made it home safe whenever she worked late. Despite their decade-wide age gap, Shamil at times took on the role of a protective older brother when Mum encountered a particularly rude and dismissive official or a pesky 'suitor' who assumed that her being a single mother was an open invitation for improper advances. After all, Chechnya was and remains a very patriarchal place where even the strongest and most independent women require an occasional brother figure who speaks a man's language. Shakhman was the other man of the office, softly spoken and more serious than his colleagues, perhaps because he was in his fifties. He always asked me about school and promised to teach me how to pray when I was older. Whenever it was time, he would stop what he was doing, discreetly slip into an empty room and perform *lamaz* on his roll-out prayer mat.

Of course, I got along best with the girls – a rather frivolous description for these experienced and courageous young women, mostly in their mid to late twenties, without whom Memorial would not have functioned. There were not one but two Zaremas – one tall and the other short. The latter was a talented filmmaker and always lugged a melon-sized Sony camera around with her. There were Taisa and Zareta, who documented the testimonies of dozens of daily visitors and gave them legal advice. When I walked into the office that day, it was strangely empty but then I heard a burst of laughter and the murmur of voices coming from the kitchen. I walked in and was greeted with jokes and comments – and an obligatory cup of tea. Even when Mum wasn't there, this place was my home away from home.

A few days later, at school we were given the chance to participate in a less contentious essay competition titled 'My Future Job'. On my walk home that day, I found myself lost in thought, reflecting on my life and imagining all the different paths it could take. Now that I was thirteen, my old fantasies about being an interior designer seemed childish and superficial. I couldn't dedicate myself to something so un-serious after Anya's murder. Up until then, I had seen Mum's activism as a background to our lives, but now I felt drawn into it, as if following in her footsteps was somehow a duty. Once I got home, I went directly to my desk and started to write.

On October 7, 2006, journalist Anna Politkovskaya was killed. Since then, I have started to think about what is happening in the world, in the country and in our republic.

A lot is happening. People start wars because of disputes between politicians, they kidnap people in order to extort confessions from them about something they did not do. People are being kicked out of their homes, pensioners are dying of hunger. And all this is covered with the magic word 'democracy', which does not exist anywhere in Russia. It took me many months to understand all this . . .

Inspired, I filled an entire page. In the months after Anya's death, I hadn't quite been able to process the murder; I wasn't sure how you're supposed to feel when someone who is a part of your life dies. I berated myself for feeling numb. But suddenly, all these hidden feelings translated into a new plan. I wanted to become a journalist, just like Anya.

I will tell the whole truth to people. My articles will bring about a revolution. I know that there will still be enough injustice in our lifetime for me to fight against.

In order to become a journalist, I read a lot, study English and French, and try to write articles. I think that a journalist should be smart, well-read, courageous, prone to rebellion, have a good imagination and a sense of humour. One must also possess a little bit of cynicism and cunning.

I don't think my desire to be a journalist will change; my commitment is more serious than ever. My mother supports me in this. I am very grateful to her for it. And if something doesn't work out and I decide to deviate from my path, I will remember Anya Politkovskaya, a journalist who died for a just cause.

After asking Mum to proofread my essay, I handed it in to my teacher and tried to put it out of my mind – the winners would be announced after the summer holidays.

Meanwhile, there was another surprise coming my way – and this one wasn't very pleasant. Mum came home one day and handed me a sleek brochure. 'Lanka, look at it carefully,' she instructed. 'It's a very special school in the woods outside Moscow. You would stay there; it would be just like Hogwarts. And there is a swimming pool too, can you imagine?'

'But what about you, Mum?'

'I'll be fine. But you have to go away for a bit. I can come and visit you.'

Months later, when I was far away from Mum, I got a phone call.

'Lanka! You'll never believe this! Remember that essay that you submitted before the summer break? You won first place! They were supposed to send you to a literary camp but since you're in Moscow they'll be sending Raya instead. It's such a big achievement, Lanuska! It's the best essay in the whole of Chechnya!'

8

The Headscarf
February–May 2008

'Mum, I'm only going to say this once,' I said quietly, so that no one could hear me. 'You must come and take me away from this school right now. If you don't, I'm going to run away.'

The hellish boarding school outside Moscow, hidden by a thick pine forest, was a far cry from the 'Hogwarts with a swimming pool' Mum had promised back in August. After five months of loneliness, isolation and relentless xenophobia from my Russian classmates – to which I'd been forced to respond with fists and fingernails – I started planning my escape. I'd listened carefully to the stories of other students who had ventured out to neighbouring villages to stock up on alcohol, noting how they got past the house warden and the locked doors. All I needed to do was pick a good time – five or six in the morning – and make my way out of the school gates and through a small wood to the motorway beyond, where I'd catch a bus to Moscow, or just hitchhike. But I was hoping that it wouldn't come to that.

There was silence at the end of the phone.

'Mum?'

'Yes, I hear you. Are you really sure about this?'

'Absolutely, 100 per cent.'

'Okay then,' she said quietly. 'I'll hop on a plane and come and get you.'

And she did. Several days later Mum stood at the door of my isolation ward with a flustered, confused look on her face. That's where I had spent the previous week, stricken by a horrible cold and high fever. Despite my weakened state, I leaped towards Mum. Her eyes widened in horror. 'Lanka . . . You've lost so much weight, oh my God . . . Turn around!' Her thirteen-year-old daughter was so skinny her ribs were poking through her tight top, sunken grey cheeks covered in small angry spots. There were dark circles around my black eyes, which were dull and lifeless like burnt candles. I avoided showing her the leopard-like marks of faded bruises on my stomach and back — some fights are best left in the past. I wanted to go home.

'Just grab all the essential stuff and I'll come and collect the rest. It's school time, everyone's in classes — do you want to wait, so you can say goodbye?'

'No.'

'All right then.'

She took me by the hand, and we trudged towards the main gates through the dark, snowy forest. I turned around for the last time to look at the neat brick cottages. My lips stretched in a glorious smile: I would never see that place again.

A few days later, in early February, we flew back to Grozny. The flat seemed different — as everything does when you've been away for a long time. New books and souvenirs inhabited many of the surfaces, and the centrepiece of my room was now a monstrous, plush orange sofa bed. Mum nervously introduced it: 'It's much bigger than the previous one and you now have a proper double bed!' My wardrobe shelves had been invaded by Mum's clothes — which I immediately took out, throwing her a look — but my posters were still there, the actors from *Lost* and the Pussycat Dolls still pouting down from the walls.

The lift kept breaking down, as usual, and the smelly tap water still left brown stains in the bathtub. If you left the tap running for about ten minutes, Mum explained, there was a chance the water would clear, but when this experiment failed, we headed to the tap outside and lugged full buckets of water back up to the tenth floor, just as we'd always done. The building had undergone renovation the year before, but it seemed papering over the bullet holes had been enough for the city authorities.

On the first evening after my return, I cuddled up next to Mum in her sparsely furnished room with bare walls and read her some of my recent poetry. I wrote of my first snow, of unfulfilled hopes, of loneliness. Each poem became increasingly dark — one even contained a swear word that rhymed with 'bad', but Mum gave me permission to say it out loud. She was shifting uncomfortably next to me as I read. 'Lanuska,' she said in her little girl voice. 'I had no idea it was so bad there. Some of these poems . . . They're really good, shall we enter them in a competition? You should carry on writing poetry.'

Mum clearly didn't feel comfortable probing me further; the angst and longing that emanated from my poems said enough. I would rather have her believe that I was weak and homesick than tell her what had really happened in that school. Sending a Chechen girl to a school full of Russian kids was always going to be a recipe for disaster, but we didn't have to go into details. She didn't have to know about all the insults – 'Hey terrorist! Terrorist, are you going to blow me up? TERRORIST!' – about the teachers who used to smirk and say, 'Oh, so you're a Chechen? That explains it!', or how my 'breaking point' had been breaking a boy's nose after he'd insulted my mother (and threw me against a wall). It was time to put away those unpleasant, dark memories and go back to being a cheerful teenager. I knew deep down that those months had changed me forever. For the first time in my life I experienced true suffering and felt alone and unwanted. But I also learnt something crucial that made me feel very proud. Even in the toughest circumstances, I stayed true to myself and picked solitude over conforming to the will of others. Inside me there was a deep well of resilience that I could always draw upon. I would never let anyone bully me.

Grozny had changed, too. For having efficiently handled terrorism (torturing people in secret prisons), Moscow had rewarded Kadyrov with a tidal wave of money. The city was full of quickly erected, clone-like buildings covered in yellow and grey plastic cladding. The rebuilding made me sad. What I was seeing was nothing like the new, magical city of my imagination. All that time growing up among the ruins, the slums and piles of rubbish hadn't bothered me, partly because I knew little else, but also because I believed the city would someday be rebuilt into something better than before. I had imagined exquisite houses with large windows and plaster cornices. Whenever I travelled, I memorised beautiful buildings, trying to picture how they would look in Grozny, conjuring vistas of green parks with giant trees, promenades, museums and playgrounds. Before the wars, Grozny had been known as the Pearl of the Caucasus, all grace and greenery. How disappointing it was now to see the spread of mediocrity – painfully symmetrical squares of dying grass, tacky boutiques, badly designed rectangular buildings that looked as if they'd been cut out from paper. But what upset me most was the thought that these ugly buildings would stand forever – or until the next war, at least.

On my return to Grozny, I was once again struck by the sheer number of propaganda posters depicting the Kadyrovs and Putin in various settings, spouting words of wisdom in quotation marks. However, there was a new addition to the usual messaging – a woman in a headscarf. She never looked at the camera but down at the pavement. Modest, pious and quiet, she was everything the authorities thought a woman should be.

It was now common to see women and girls wearing headscarves, and to hear a woman's place in society discussed on Chechen state TV, usually by middle-aged men in grey robes. Young women were getting out of hand, the grey robes claimed; they were no longer listening to their parents and were wearing inappropriate clothing that barely covered their knees.

Historically, Chechen women had been depicted in long dresses, with headscarves covering their two plaits, but things had changed in the twentieth century and unmarried women were forgiven for wearing their hair uncovered and their skirts (slightly) above the knee. After marriage, long hair was often concealed by a scarf (which in many ways is the Muslim equivalent of a wedding ring), and in religious families male relatives still had the power to force girls to wear a headscarf, but that situation tended to be the exception. However, when Ramzan Kadyrov became president, in February 2007, Chechnya rapidly changed. To consolidate his authority, Kadyrov began a so-called Islamisation campaign, pushing through a revival of traditional values. In interviews, he would assert that women bore a double duty when it came to virtue since they represented their entire family – they were responsible not just for their own conduct but for that of their husband and their children. By the autumn Kadyrov had announced that he expected all women working for official institutions to wear headscarves. Soon enough, television station directors, university deans and school headmasters began forcing women and girls to accept the new dress code.

'They're concerned about women's virtue, as though it's up to them to decide!' Mum would comment angrily, and she took her opposition to the headscarf regime to the newspapers, writing: 'During times of war, while men killed and destroyed, women gave birth, searched for water and baked bread. Despite the obstacles, they delivered food to blockaded villages, rushed to help when men were being kidnapped.'

She believed that the war had significantly changed the role that women played in society, and that it was only now that the fighting was over that men had realised this: 'And now they decide on revenge, demanding a return to century-old traditions? But is it really just that? Because, according to Caucasian customs, only a close relative – a father, a husband or a brother – can tell a woman what to do. So, have all Chechen men given this right away to one person?'

This wasn't the first time that Mum had had to resist the pressure to wear a headscarf. During the nineties, when she was working as a history teacher, the then president, Aslan Maskhadov, had also wanted all women to cover their hair. She recalled shrugging off armed men at the school entrance who demanded that she wore a headscarf. She refused to wear it and she refused to force it upon her female students. In the face of war and political turmoil, Maskhadov's initiative had been forgotten, and I don't think Mum thought she would ever face such demands again. Yet in 2007 she found herself fighting another guard, one who refused her entry to the prosecutor's office because her hair was uncovered. 'Some pimply twenty-year-old with a Kalashnikov and too much power,' my mother told me when she got home. Mum had caused a scene until the embarrassed guard stepped out of her way. She had survived the horrors of war, visited the most harrowing crime scenes, worked in dangerous conditions and raised a child on her own – no man could tell her what to do.

That didn't mean that she never wore headscarves. When visiting rural villages on work assignments, especially in the highlands where attitudes were much more conservative than in the cities, a headscarf demonstrated respect and won trust. Besides, Mum always tried to make herself invisible on these investigative trips, especially if accompanied by a foreign journalist, and a headscarf was camouflage. Most days, however, she showed off her chestnut-coloured shoulder-length hair, leaving her scarves hidden away in a special wardrobe drawer.

As soon as I stopped looking like a starved ghost – which took about two weeks on a steady carb diet of *chepalgash* – I was ready to go back to my old school. I carefully folded and tucked away all my jeans at the back of the wardrobe, knowing I was now too old to wear them in Chechnya.

'But you're only thirteen, that's nonsense!' Mum protested, rolling her eyes. 'I know it is but I keep getting stares on the streets and one man even told me off!' I replied. Mum wanted me to stay a child for as long as possible, and I wasn't in a hurry to grow up, but the world saw me differently. Sometimes the worst thing you could do in Chechnya was draw too much attention to yourself. In the end, Mum gave in and let me wear a plain black skirt.

The familiar light-pink building of N7 was exactly the same as always. I admired it from the other side of the road, watching sleepy students trot towards the gate. Inside, a strong smell of fresh paint lingered in the air, a promise of something new and exciting. On the way to my classroom, I was bombarded with questions from friends, teachers and even pupils I'd never spoken to: 'Where on earth have you been this time?' 'Are you here for long?' 'Are you at least staying until the end of the year?' After being in the enemy camp for so long, it was great to bask in the warm spotlight of attention and not be treated like a pariah. I felt overjoyed to be catching up with schoolfriends. There was beautiful and giggly Zareta, who looked a bit like Audrey Hepburn. And two bubbly sisters, Madina and Seda. And sardonic Raya, who always had a great quip handy. It was as if a special place of warmth was waiting for me, just where I had left it.

This new-found popularity lasted for two days, and then the spotlight shifted to a recently married ex-classmate, Fatima, who strutted into school for a visit wearing high heels, her fingers covered in rings and with a distinctly *womanly* aura about her. Just a couple of years earlier we had chased each other in the schoolyard during breaks and moaned about homework, but now she was an entirely different person with adult responsibilities. I had noticed that more and more girls were marrying young – Fatima was the second girl from my class who had chosen to opt out of school aged sixteen. I melted into the background and observed her graceful, almost regal mannerisms and restrained laughter. She seemed very mysterious, but I didn't want to know her secrets.

One of the first things I noticed when I returned to N7 was that the girls now covered their hair. 'You know that they won't let you into the school without doing it, right?' they told me. They all wore headscarves, of different shapes and colours, constantly readjusting their fine hair, which kept escaping from under the silky fabric. Reactions to the decree were mixed. 'It's annoying when it's hot but other than that we've kind of got used to them,' my friend Zareta said, smiling. 'I look awful in it, it makes my face look strange,' complained Raya. 'No, it doesn't!' somebody reassured her. 'We do need to cover our hair, it's written in the Quran.' 'Many things are written in the Quran, Zareta! Do you see men following all the rules?'

'Have you seen Makka?' someone else asked, pointing to a tall girl in dark clothes. 'She looks completely different.'

I couldn't believe my eyes. Ever since I'd known Makka, she'd worn baggy jeans, hoodies and beanies. People took her for a boy. And here she was, dressed in a tight black skirt and shirt, hair covered with a dark headscarf. Something about her hunched back and stiff movements told me that she was uncomfortable. Raya looked on with humour, 'At least now she's dressing like a girl! And she can still be a Goth even in a headscarf.' And it was true, for she somehow looked menacing in the grey, drape-like scarf that covered her black dyed hair.

Most girls had accepted their fate. I couldn't really blame them. In Chechen culture, young people are brought up to obey their elders, especially girls. If my girlfriends voiced their discontent – or, worse, organised some form of protest – they could get into serious trouble at home. Another complication was that all my friends were religious despite a limited understanding of Islam, and they did not want to appear to be bad Muslims. Kadyrov's headscarf decree skilfully manipulated that instinct, not only by forcing submission but also by making girls feel guilty and unfaithful if they voiced any opposition to it. Even so, the scarves always vanished after the day's last lesson, forgotten at the bottom of bags until needed the next morning. There's always a way.

At the end of February, Mum brought some unexpected news: 'Looks like you'll be seeing me on Chechen TV more often than usual.'

'What do you mean?' I replied

'I've been made the Chair of the Grozny City Council for Assistance in Ensuring Human Rights and Freedoms.' She laughed. 'It's quite a mouthful.'

The council had been set up just a few weeks prior to Mum's appointment by the young-faced mayor of Grozny, Muslim Khuchiev, who seemed to only care about three things – money, his hair, and Ramzan Kadyrov's goodwill. Countless committees and new government departments with clunky abbreviated names burgeoned under Khuchiev's rule. It was one way of demonstrating that the money flowing from the federal budget wasn't wasted, despite the fact that a lot of it ended up in the 'charitable' foundation of Kadyrov's mother, Aymani.

'But doesn't that mean you'll be working with those crooks and sycophants? Are you going to stay at Memorial?'

'Of course I will, Lanka. And I will be independent. The city administration needs a shake-up. Maybe they will finally do something about ramps for the disabled, or Khadizhat's orphanage . . .'

Mum always had a special relationship with the orphanage that was set up by Khadizhat Gaytayeva and her husband, Malik. Throughout the two wars, the couple searched for orphaned children and gave them a caring home. They survived through grants and donations and often struggled to get by. The very fact that the orphanage existed contradicted Kadyrov's proclamations that there were no orphans in Chechnya because they had all been adopted by their relatives. Time and again Mum would visit Khadizhat with bags of donations and small sums of money.

Mum's work didn't stop at documenting human rights abuses; she wanted to fix everything and help everyone – whether it was street access for disabled people, an underfunded orphanage or the closure of Shanghai, temporary accommodation for the homeless. She really thought that joining the council would give her more official power to tackle these social issues – and to talk about the kidnappings. It was an unpaid position – Mum would never take money from the corrupt mayor's office.

On the surface, it looked as if Mum was mostly tasked with resolving social issues, as if she was a local councillor rather than a human rights activist. The long queues outside Memorial's office now consisted of people who wanted a consultation about compensation for unlawful evictions. Mum took on each case with the same level of commitment, regardless of whether it was ramps for the disabled or textbooks for disadvantaged students. Cases concerning abductions and torture carried out by law enforcement never went away, but now the victims were even more hesitant to speak to human rights organisations or to journalists – they knew that, unlike the federals, the Kadyrovites were not planning on leaving the republic at the end of their rotation; they were ruling it now. Memorial continued to document human rights abuses, but it had to do so even more carefully.

It was decided by Memorial's board that, for their personal safety, Chechen employees should not work on cases relating directly to Ramzan Kadyrov. In reality, however, the staff were too entangled by now. One case was particularly sensitive. Mum had come across a rather eccentric but brave preacher, Mohamad-Salah Masayev, who believed that speaking truth to power was his God-given mission. He came forward with testimony about his abduction and torture at Ramzan Kadyrov's secret prison at his home village of Tsentoroi, claiming that, on 27 January 2006, he and two acquaintances had attended a mosque in Gudermes, a town located about thirty kilometres east of Grozny, where he prayed and preached. The three of them were abducted directly afterwards by local policemen, and taken to the station where Mohamad-Salah was severely beaten and accused of being a radical Islamist. Two days later he and his cellmates were taken to Tsentoroi and then transferred to a large bus. This vehicle became their prison for a month. Mohamad-Salah was subjected to continuous beatings, torture and even a mock-execution. On one occasion, he was placed in front of Kadyrov and the future president of Chechnya lifted his boot, as if ordering Mohamad-Salah to lick it and beg for mercy. Mohamad-Salah spent four months as a prisoner in Tsentoroi. By the end, he could barely stand. He was released as abruptly as he had been abducted.

After Mohamad-Salah returned home, he vowed to take Ramzan Kadyrov to court for his crimes, whatever it took. When he came to Mum with his story in 2008, she involved her other colleagues, including her boss, Oleg Orlov, Katya Sokirianskaia and Svetlana Gannushkina. Mohamad-Salah proved to be an exceptionally courageous man who wasn't afraid to confront the Chechen authorities over what had been done to him. With the help of his lawyer, Stanislav Markelov (the same man who had led Zelimkhan Murdalov's case), he filed an abduction report and was deemed the victim of a crime. The activists became friendly with Mohamad-Salah, and he would spend hours on the phone with Mum, giving her details about his imprisonment and delving into his interpretations of the Quran. As with many of her clients, she readily took on the role of therapist.

Every winter our finances were dire, and especially so before our two birthdays. But this year we had so little money that Mum warned me she might not be able to get me the guitar she had promised. 'But I will still get you something small,' she reassured me.

For her fiftieth birthday, which came first, I made a colourful sign on pink paper emblazoned with the English words *Happy Birtday!* (unfortunately, misspelt). Mum's friends Alik, Varya and Ieva happened to be in Grozny, making the celebration all the more special. In a snapshot taken on the day by Varya, Mum is wearing a white satin blouse, her green eyes highlighted by grey eyeshadow. I am leaning into her – thirteen for three more days – with a slightly grumpy facial expression half hidden by a shaggy haircut.

Mum said that for my fourteenth birthday she would let me treat my girlfriends to a lunch at the best (and only) pizzeria in Grozny, Rafaello Esposito, which was located in a beautiful nineteenth-century red-brick building. Nicknamed the Landlord's House, it had been built for English oil refinery workers in 1923. I loved its classic architecture; it seemed like a little glimpse of what Grozny could have been – quaint, ornate, interesting. But most of all I loved pizza. Real Italians would probably consider it an insult – the thickness of the crust, the roughly chopped sausage from a packet, cheese that was as far from mozzarella as Grozny was from Napoli. But this combination of piping-hot cheesy bread with meat (there was also mince) was still one of the most satisfying delights for a group of teenage girls.

I took snapshots of us on Mum's digital camera, which she'd let me borrow for the day. I felt very cool and grown-up in my white long-sleeved T-shirt and knee-length denim skirt with a frayed hem – the closest thing I had to jeans – fiddling with a small pendant that hung around my neck. Mum had surprised me with it for my birthday. The day before, we'd strolled through the market, heading in the direction of the jewellery – I'd never been there before – manoeuvring through the narrow rows of laden stalls. Mum stopped and pointed to a small table with all kinds of charms in silver and gold – animals, shoes, tiny flip-phones and flowers. Among all the gaudiness, I found what she was pointing at – a tiny silver guitar encrusted with tiny crystals. 'I want you to have that as a promise that as soon as I can afford it, I will buy you a real guitar,' she said. 'For now, you can hang this one on your necklace.' I loved it – it would be my lucky charm.

Later that day, as the capricious March weather turned grey and rainy, I sat at my computer looking through the photos from my birthday. I noticed that the new pimple near my nose was very visible, despite my best efforts to cover it with Mum's foundation. Loading the photos into Microsoft Paint, I was attempting to conceal the pimple with skin-coloured digital paint, hoping no one would notice the difference unless they zoomed in, when I heard the key turning in the lock. Mum was home. I jumped up to greet her. Her hair, wet from the rain, stuck to her face and her mascara was running. She handed me a large cardboard box. 'What is it?'

Mum smiled. Impatiently, I ripped through the soaking cardboard and gasped – it was a guitar! A beautiful, glossy, birch-coloured thing of beauty with a chestnut neck.

'It's yours!'

'But – but you said we didn't have any money!'

'I scraped some and borrowed the rest from Shamil!'

I couldn't believe it. I put the guitar on my bed and carefully stroked her, like a precious animal. Mum was standing in the doorway, still wearing her rain-soaked coat, beaming like the sun.

★

The first time my form teacher, Tamara Arbievna, mentioned my lack of headscarf, I ignored her. The next day I went to school with uncovered hair, and the day after too. Every now and then, Tamara Arbievna would ask, 'Estemirova, where's your headscarf?' but I just smiled and changed the subject. For a while it seemed like a farce. Deep down, I hoped the decree would be temporary and soon things would go back to normal. I hadn't planned to make a fuss.

My tiny rebellion received mixed reactions. People loved or hated me, and sometimes both. Some of my male classmates had started to go through a religious phase when they hit their mid-teens, and clearly didn't approve. During breaks, some boys listened to Arabic *nasheed* music on their phones and one of my classmates even wore a *pes* – a traditional Chechen skullcap. As their voices broke so did their sense of humour, and every joke I made in class was met with cold stares and whispers. I was a very inconvenient kind of girl – a loud, know-it-all tomboy, happy to poke at an opponent's vulnerability. I acquired several frenemies among the boys in class; we'd be gossiping about teachers and drawing caricatures one minute, fighting and insulting each other the next.

'Hey monkey, do you want a banana?'

'What's that ginger dog? All I hear is barking . . .'

'Hey egghead!'

'Hey shorty, drink some milk, it might help you grow up!'

Unsophisticated insults, yes, but since none of us cursed in front of the opposite sex, we had to be inventive. Gradually, my not wearing a headscarf turned into an ongoing joke.

But if there was one person at school who detested me, it was the ethics teacher, Kesirat Khasanovna. A sixty-something Aunt Lydia type, she had a cutting, high-pitched voice that echoed through the entire school. She would walk around like a hawk, waiting and hoping for obscenities to happen. Kesirat Khasanovna's favourite pastime was catching and reprimanding girls engaged in behaviours deemed 'un-girlish', such as running, shouting, fence-climbing and fighting. 'STOP RUNNING!' she would scream at the top of her voice. 'YOU'RE A GIRL. GIRLS WALK!'

Ethics was a mysterious subject that kept appearing and disappearing from the curriculum. From what I remember, the first lessons were dedicated to table manners and the importance of hygiene. On my return from boarding school, however, I discovered that we were a few weeks into studying the particularities of Islam. I couldn't help but find it entertaining when, in a monotonous voice, Kesirat Khasanovna would interrupt reading from her photocopies to embellish them with improvised monologues. She was obsessed with the topic of women's virtue and the proper way to behave: 'Girls, you are valued for your modesty, obedience and piousness . . . Any rudeness or insubordination is whispered to you by Shaitan. Are you really going to fall for Shaitan's scheming?' she would ask, trying to find my face in a crowd. 'Estemirova, do you understand me?' Kesirat Khasanovna enjoyed letting me know who she was *really* talking about.

She didn't tolerate bad discipline. If I objected to anything, she would start shouting or simply expel me from class. I usually resolved school problems independently, but Kesirat Khasanovna's crusade got to me. So, I explained the situation to Mum, choosing my words very carefully.

'We're going to school tomorrow,' she said with the fierceness of a lioness protecting her cub. 'It's one thing that they berate you about a stupid headscarf, but this is bullying! It's absolutely unacceptable!'

'It's not bullying, I always fight back!'

'You shouldn't be fighting all the time, you should be studying! I should never have brought you back from that boarding school.'

'Believe me, I did more fighting there,' I said gloomily.

In the end, we compromised; Mum gave me permission to stop attending ethics classes (the subject didn't count towards our final grades anyway).

Although my form teacher turned a blind eye to my uncovered hair, it was harder to escape the dean, Fatima Magomedovna. Before the headscarf decree she had worn a short blonde bob, but this was now hidden under a tiny multi-coloured acid-shade fabric triangle. I'd clashed with the dean before and was aware that the topic of headscarves would come up, so I tried my best to avoid her. The problem was that her office was only one door away from our classroom. She cornered me several times and threatened to send me home the next time I 'forgot' my headscarf. I told myself that I should get better at being invisible. Finally, however, she caught me off guard with a gentle tap on the shoulder, 'Estemirova, come to my office for a chat after school.'

After my last lesson, I knocked on her door. 'Come in!'

Fatima Magomedovna looked up with a sweet smile and offered me a seat. 'Lana,' she purred. 'I get it. You don't like headscarves; you don't agree with the politics. It's your right, you're a smart girl. But do you think I like it? I mean, it doesn't even suit me! I never wore a headscarf, not in the Soviet Union, nor after marriage. Things were different then, we were freer. I didn't wear it during the war either, and I know your mother doesn't. But Lana, with this law, a lot of things are at stake. It came from above and they actually send people to ensure that rules are being followed. They don't give us any warning, they just turn up! Recently one of them came to the school and said, "I saw a girl without a headscarf in the corridor, how's that? Didn't you tell her?" What was I supposed to say? You know that we may all lose our jobs because of you? Please, think about it. Please . . .'

I was silent. As with the television quiz the year before, I felt torn. Did I stand by my school or by my principles? I wanted to cry.

'Just think it over, okay? You can go now.'

Walking home, my empathy for the dean turned to anger: *How could she be so manipulative and pretend to be my friend? But she wasn't a bad person . . . How was it fair that I needed to make this choice? How was it fair that I was being forced into submission by someone I'd never met?*

When I got home, I rushed to my diary. 'Everything sucks!' I wrote. 'Today I had another interrogation regarding headscarves. I DON'T KNOW WHAT TO DO!!! To wear, or not to wear – that is the question. If I don't wear it the school authorities might get into trouble, and if I do – it means I'm submitting to that bastard. Living here sucks. Why must I suffer?'

I wrote a lot more, over several pages, but sometime later I ripped it out. That evening I came into the kitchen, where Mum was as usual working on her laptop. I climbed on the sofa, put my head on her knees and told her what had happened. 'Lanusya,' she said softly, stroking my hair. 'I think it's brave of you to fight for what you stand for, but you shouldn't feel obliged to do so. I'm a grown woman and my reputation allows me to be stubborn when I have to be. You're only fourteen, you don't owe anything to anyone.'

I listened silently, but inside me there was a struggle. Part of me wanted Mum to tell me to carry on, to make the decision for me. But she was giving me a choice. It was too overwhelming, and one teardrop followed another.

'Why are you crying, silly?' she asked with a look full of love.

'I can't . . . I just can't . . . I can't give up,' I muttered through tears. I cried because I felt sorry for myself; sorry for my mother, for the dean, for my friends. I cried because life couldn't be simple, and it would get worse. I was crying about everything.

'*Shhhh* . . . Calm down, Lanuska. Everything will be fine, you'll see. We should go to bed, the morning's wiser than the night.'

The next morning, I walked into school without a headscarf, my right eye hidden behind a spiky fringe. My girlfriends were surprised. Hadn't I talked with the dean? I said something sarcastic, something along the lines of her not being able to tame me. I had to pretend. During break time I was standing in a corridor chatting and laughing with friends when suddenly I noticed the dean staring at me. Her look froze my insides.

Several days later, in the middle of a lesson, a knock on our classroom door announced an unplanned assembly.

'Lessons are cancelled! Everyone to the assembly hall.'

Some moaned; others were pleased. My girlfriends and I climbed the stairs and stood chatting outside the hall until they ushered us in. The stream of students slowly took up every corner of the room, the noise and laughter becoming ever louder. These assemblies had become part of the school routine and were mostly used for event announcements and discussing mundane topics such as bad discipline. Finally, the dean came on stage, accompanied by the headmaster. Fatima Magomedovna's round, red face radiated annoyance.

'Silence, everyone!' she shouted. 'Okay, I will start calling out surnames and those I name must come up on to the stage straight away.' She began, her voice echoing around the hall. 'Aliev! Gaitukaev! Dadaev!' Boys gloomily dragged themselves towards the stage, heads down. *So, it's to be an execution*, I concluded. The dean called out a few more surnames, then suddenly somebody pushed my shoulder.

'I repeat once more, ESTEMIROVA!'

Confused, I headed towards the stage, wearing a mocking smile. I climbed the steps, my classmates chanting approvingly behind me, and stood in the second row.

'Don't be shy, Lana, stand at the front!' said the dean. 'Gaitukaev, swap places with Estemirova!'

Still smirking, I obeyed.

'Please, have a look at these students everyone,' Fatima Magomedovna began. 'They are the disgrace of our school: slackers, under-achievers and those who think that rules do not apply to them.'

The dean continued in the same tone, but after a few minutes I stopped listening. There were about fifteen of us on stage, and only two of us were girls: Madina and me. *What's she up here for?* I wondered. *Ah, trainers! I'm wearing Converse too. And black nail polish. But she's wearing a headscarf . . .* Standing on the metre-high stage, I surveyed the room, carefully examining every girl, not missing a face. Was I really the only girl in this school who didn't wear a headscarf?

Soon the headmaster joined in, emphasising how we were ruining the school's image. With an external inspection due, we had to re-evaluate our choices. *So that's why we're here*, I thought. *The notorious school inspection!* It's a peculiar talent of mine to switch off completely in boring situations. Walls disappear, noise becomes quieter and quieter, and suddenly I'm somewhere far, far away. As the lecture droned on, I zoned out, but was brought back to reality when the dean began calling the boys out one by one, reciting their sins.

'Eskerkhanov,' said the dean. 'You've missed school twelve times this term. You never do your homework, and all the teachers complain about you. Have you anything to say in your defence?'

Eskerkhanov couldn't put two words together.

'Are you ashamed of your behaviour?'

'Yes, I am,' Eskerkhanov replied. I think he wanted to disappear.

'You must apologise before the entire school and promise to change, you may only leave after that!'

'Sorr . . .' Eskerkhanov mumbled, his voice trailing off.

'What is it? Louder, I can't hear you!'

THE HEADSCARF

'SORRY!'

'All right, you may go.'

The execution continued. Awaiting my turn, I tried to prepare witty responses. The crowd on stage began to thin.

'All right, I haven't time for everyone, therefore you must quickly apologise and I'll let you go. Dakaev, are you sorry?'

'Yes!'

'Shakhgiriev?'

'I'm sorry!'

'Great, go now.'

'Ilyasov, are you sorry?'

'No.'

'No, what?'

'I'm not going to apologise.'

'Wonderful, you will stand here till the evening! Estemirova, apologise and leave!'

'I don't know what exactly I'm accused of,' I responded, mischievously.

'You know perfectly well,' Fatima Magomedovna replied wearily.

'I demand a lawyer!'

The room exploded in laughter.

'Stop being a clown, Estemirova! Look at you! Black nails, no headscarf, trainers . . . You think this is how a girl should look?'

'These are Converse. Trainers are not in fashion,' I answered.

'So smart, huh? How many times have I told you to wear a headscarf? I said it nicely once, twice, your head teacher has spoken with you too . . . And still you don't care, it's all a joke for you!'

'You don't have the right to force me to wear a headscarf,' I said coldly, fists clenched. It no longer felt funny. 'There's no official edict about headscarves, it contradicts the constitution of the Russian Federation!' (I wasn't entirely sure about that, but when in doubt I always mentioned the constitution.)

'We have our own laws in Chechnya,' she snapped.

Our squabble went on for several minutes, until finally Fatima Magomedovna ran out of patience.

'All right, Estemirova, that's enough! You'll stand here until you apologise. I can wait. You don't want to do things the easy way, so you can have it the hard way! And you, Ilyasov, will stand here as well! Everyone can enjoy that!'

But nobody wanted to. All anyone wanted was to leave. So we stood there, just the two of us, for ten minutes, then twenty, then forty. Slowly, students began to abandon the room. The dean said nothing. From time to time someone would shout, 'Estemirova! We're with you,' or, 'Just apologise,' and I smiled. An hour passed. Soon there were only a few students in the room and a couple of teachers, the former out of curiosity, the latter for supervision. Every ten to fifteen minutes we were asked if we would like to apologise but each time we silently turned our heads away. My fellow dissident was looking exhausted. Students kept entering and leaving the hall to make sure we were still there. Eighth-graders started placing bets on who would give up first.

Then, Ilyasov cracked. When one of the teachers again asked whether he wanted to apologise, he suddenly said yes and quickly left the stage to join his friends. That left just me now.

It seemed to last an eternity. The dean visited a couple of times, but I was adamant. The longer I stood there, the less likely it was I would apologise. I had refused to wear a headscarf from the moment I returned to my school and this was the climax of my dissent. Stubbornness and pride would not let me apologise – but there was more. *If I apologise now*, I thought, *I'll betray Mum and our common struggle. If she complicates her life every day by arguing over headscarves with security guards and officials, can't I stand on a stage for a few hours?* We were both convinced that girls and women must have freedom of choice and I was ready to stand up for that freedom. My mother never actively encouraged me to go against the school rules, but she respected my decision to challenge them. And besides, I had a reputation to maintain – always a good motivation for a fourteen-year-old. My girlfriends visited during class breaks. 'Lana, please, say sorry,' they urged. 'They're just words!'

'I can't.'

My history teacher brought me water when no one was watching, never pressurising me to apologise. Gradually, as everyone grew bored, I was left on my own in the empty white hall. Soon it seemed that time had stopped, and I would stand there forever. I went into my usual trance and began to make up stories.

THE HEADSCARF

I didn't even notice when somebody called. 'Estemirova!'
The dean was standing in front of the stage, looking up.
'Go home!'
'I'm not going to apologise!'
'The show is over. You don't have to apologise. You've proven yourself enough.'

Fatima Magomedovna looked at me with the dislike reserved for an old but, now, respected rival. We understood each other. She turned on her heels and left the hall. It took a few seconds for me to realise I was free. As I made my way down the steps of the stage, my knees began to shake, simultaneously stiff and weak.

Before leaving, I looked at the clock and could hardly believe what I saw. I had been standing on that stage for almost four and a half hours.

Following the 'execution', there seemed to be a quiet acceptance about me not wearing a headscarf. In the meantime, my maths grades improved, my reputation as the school rebel was rock solid and I finally discovered the name of my favourite music genre – indie rock. But things were far from calm: I even got hit by a car and received a marriage proposal in the same week.

It all started with a whisper of a school fight. As I was waiting in anticipation, looking at the clock, the story finally emerged. We (the boys, not the girls) were to fight the rival school in the closed-off basketball court behind the school building. It was part of an ongoing feud the origins of which were obscure. I thought that it was a perfect opportunity to try my hand at conflict journalism since, by pure coincidence, I had Mum's old Sony flip camera at the bottom of my bag. The camera captured very bad-quality videos that were impossible to edit, but that didn't stop me from using it from time to time. I'd recorded about a dozen videos of myself – nothing groundbreaking, just monologues about anything that came to mind, soulful song recitals and a couple of interviews with my very reluctant and very shy relatives, plus occasional cameos of Mum and the cat. But recording a real school fight would take me to a whole new level.

After the last lesson of the day was over, things started moving quickly. The fight would begin sooner than planned, so I found myself in a crowd of excited girls, walking, or rather half jogging, towards the spectacle at a very unwomanly pace, all the while recording everything that was going on.

'Excuse me, sir,' I said to a very serious-looking tall boy, 'what are your expectations regarding the fight?'

'We're gonna mess them up,' he replied while covering his face with his hand.

'No comment,' others said, among less polite responses.

Then, as I was climbing the fence to get closer to the action, I heard a scream: 'Kesirat Khasanovna is coming!'

The orderly ten-year-olds in front of me unlocked their hands and scattered like sparrows. I looked back to see the ethics teacher galloping towards us, hand on headscarf to keep it in place. 'Stop iiiiiit!' she yelled. She grabbed a few girls by the elbows and ordered them to go home because 'fighting is not for girls'. She didn't appear to have minded the fight itself; her biggest concern was that we girls were so eager to watch – unfeminine and immoral, this had to be stopped immediately.

So as to avoid the teacher's wrath – I knew I was walking on thin ice after the headscarf rebellion – my friends and I hid in our favourite snack shop. I chatted to the shop owner, munching away on chocolate and poking my head out from time to time to check if Kesirat Khasanovna's hunt was over. Someone said that the fight had been called off, but we refused to believe it.

Moving on to our favourite bench under a chestnut tree – a perfect observation spot – everyone seemed to have forgotten about the fight, but then, suddenly, we saw a boy running towards us with panic on his face. Stopping in front of us, hands on his bent knees, he tried to catch his breath, then managed to exclaim, 'The fight is still going ahead!'

Quick! We must move quickly! A crowd of students once again ran towards the basketball court, all the while trying to act casual. I switched on my camera and started recording, walking backwards so as to capture the size of the crowd. At that moment I heard an engine roar and caught something grey moving right at me. But before I could think about it:

BAM!

The back of the car slammed into me and up in the air I flew. My first reaction, as I lay on the dirty pavement, was to cover up my exposed thighs. Then, as horrified friends ran towards me, I started to assess the damage. Surprisingly, I was feeling fine. Moreover, this had to be the least dramatic car accident ever – the driver had only just started up his engine and begun backing out of a parking space. When my friends got me up, I managed to take a few steps.

'THE PRESS HAS BEEN HIT BY THE CAR!' I heard one of my classmates, a boy called Tomayev, yell. 'THIS IS THE END OF INDEPENDENT JOURNALISM!' The crowd that had been heading towards the fight now doubled back to watch a more exciting spectacle – a girl had just been run over, live news.

'Are you okay?'

'Are you hurt? Should we call a doctor?'

The driver was standing at the back of the crowd by now, not daring to come closer. 'Is she okay?' he asked one of my friends in a shaky voice.

'Of course she's not okay, you dumb idiot, you just hit her with a car!' Raya yelled back bravely.

A doctor wasn't required since I was perfectly fine, apart from several scratches and a barely noticeable limp. I was escorted back to the bench and one of my classmates, who lived nearby, ran home to fetch clean water and plasters.

'So, what's your first comment after this horrendous incident?' asked Tomayev, a cheeky smile on his face.

'An official statement will follow later,' I replied. 'All I can say at this time is that it feels awful that my life is under threat, just because I was trying to tell the truth.'

We all laughed and continued to banter like this. The fight was called off.

When I got home I decided not to tell Mum anything – why worry her if I wasn't really hurt? However, my limp didn't go unnoticed, and she immediately asked about it. I ended up telling her the truth, trying to make it appear as light-hearted as possible. 'Can you imagine, I was hit by a REVERSING car; isn't that ridiculous!'

Mum didn't find it amusing, and was going to go to my school the next day. I can't remember whether I persuaded her to let the matter lie (the incident was partly my fault) or whether she had too much work to do; either way it ended up being forgotten about. But, later that evening she said 'Lana, after school, I want you to come straight home, no hanging out in the schoolyard.' As she said this, I knew that I was going to completely ignore it: *I mean, it's not like she's ever going to be there to check my whereabouts!* Yet, at the back of my mind I knew this was about more than just the accident, aware of the true horrors of Kadyrov's regime that lurked like a spectre in the background – the young men who disappeared in torture chambers, the houses burnt down in acts of collective punishment – and the fact that Mum was a constant nuisance to the regime because she kept investigating it all.

I really didn't want to leave my bubble – my friendships; the laughter; the evil teachers, old benches, cheap chocolates, music magazines and gossip. Nothing could keep me at home; nothing, apart from a marriage proposal that came out of nowhere, just a few days later.

I was heading towards our favourite after-school bench as usual, when I heard someone call my name. There was the tall, smiley boy of about seventeen who I'd spoken to the day before when he and his friends had been very keen to make themselves known to my pretty girlfriends. I had relentlessly mocked the whole group (as I always did), so I was surprised to see one of them here again.

'Hey,' he said. 'I have something serious to discuss with you.' I wanted to reply with a joke, as usual, but, seeing a solemn expression on his face, I changed my mind. He continued, 'Remember my friend Apti? The one who was quiet yesterday?'

I did. He was the one I had called a *guron*, a country bumpkin, behind his back but hadn't dared say so to his face because he had looked at me with such intense hatred that it seemed he wanted to burn a hole through my face.

'I think I do. He's not much of a talker, is he?'

'No, he's very shy. But he really, really liked you. And he asked me to ask you if you would consider marrying him?'

'What? Is this a joke?'

'No, he is serious. You need to give me the answer now and I'll pass it on to him.'

'But . . .' I still wasn't quite sure if this was a prank. 'Does he know that I'm younger than my classmates? I'm only fourteen and they are sixteen.'

THE HEADSCARF

'That's perfect, he is seventeen. Look, he is a good guy. He doesn't smoke or drink, studies the Quran, and his parents are building him a house in the village.'

It wasn't unheard of to receive such proposals, and by then I knew of a few sixteen-year-old girls who were married, but their bridegrooms tended to be older and they were exceptions. Mostly, young women were married off at eighteen or nineteen, and engagements were often relatively short. But that was for others; I didn't see myself as a good candidate for a wife, and I'd have to be at least twenty-three at any rate. I was wearing a skull ring and an anime T-shirt for God's sake! But I had to choose my words carefully because the honour of a Chechen man, even a seventeen-year-old, is a very precious thing.

'Listen,' I said as gracefully as I could. 'Sorry, I can't remember your name. I'm sure that Apti is a good man and I wish him all the best, but I'm not looking to marry at the moment. I need to finish my studies and I'm only fourteen.'

'Suit yourself,' replied No-name with a big smile. 'But just to warn you, Apti is very serious about marrying you. And while it's your choice to say no, he might still take you in another way.' He turned away and started walking quickly towards the school gate.

I froze on the spot, replaying these last words in my head. 'Another way' could only mean bride-knapping, something that had happened to a couple of my cousins. Were they just toying with me because I had made fun of them the day before? Or was this boy serious? I started to panic and decided to take the bus home instead of walking. On the bus, I looked out of the window nervously to see if I was being followed. My stomach hurt and my heart pounded in my throat. After my last teenage heartbreak at the age of twelve at a summer camp, I'd closed my heart to everyone (apart from unattainable celebrities, specifically, Sawyer from *Lost*). I loved the idea of love, but whenever a boy showed any interest the fantasy evaporated, and it seemed way too real to be appealing.

I found it ridiculous that one of Mum's biggest fears was that I would get bride-knapped, since I considered myself to have neither the looks nor the reputation for it. But this fear was the reason she tried to delay my adolescence by insisting that I keep wearing jeans, even when I was getting aggressive comments from strangers on the street. I couldn't possibly tell her about what had happened. Mum did everything she thought was right to protect me from danger, and in return I protected her from the knowledge that I was already in danger.

'It's probably a prank anyway,' I reassured myself. 'What village boy would want to marry a city girl who doesn't know how to make *zhizhig-galnash*?' I got off the bus and practically ran home, looking across my shoulder every other step.

'Lanuska, what's wrong?' Mum asked when she came back from work. 'You are so pale. Come, let me check your temperature.' She placed a cold palm on my sweaty forehead. 'You are so hot! Does your throat hurt?'

The *Schrödinger* marriage proposal had sent me into a psychosomatic frenzy, and in the few hours before Mum arrived at the flat I had made myself ill. I stayed indoors for a few days praying that Apti would find another bride and forget about me altogether; that it had been just a prank after all.

I didn't waste any time while in self-imposed confinement – my resistance against headscarves had to continue. The fight had to be taken to the next level, and I had an idea: I picked through my mother's drawers until I found an old black silk headscarf with a pattern of gold coins. I burnt holes in it, nailed it to my bedroom wall and added a small paper handwritten sign. Although Mum gave me a symbolic telling off – claiming it was her favourite – my art installation moved her. She took all our guests into my room, so they could appreciate my work. 'I came into her room and look what she's done to my headscarf!'

However, my revolutionary actions, I decided, needed to reach beyond the walls of the flat. After the latest 'execution', I was fired up. But when I shared my ideas with friends, they laughed – it was often hard for them to tell when I was being serious. Undeterred, I locked myself in my room and started to plan. Running a solitary underground campaign wasn't easy, however, and the floor was soon covered in crumpled sheets of paper. Sometime later, I came up with a call to arms:

THE HEADSCARF

Headscarves suck, headscarves are lame,
Girls, let's go, let's join the game!
Let's not listen to those cowards,
We look best with hair uncovered!

Let's untie our hair
And shout like no one's there:
'Kadyrov, if you are the boss,
You should wear the headscarf first!'

I devised a distribution plan. Mum would print dozens of copies on her work printer, and take them to school. There, I'd distribute them among allies – though admittedly, I still needed to recruit allies. Then, on a prearranged signal, we'd throw the leaflets around like confetti during break time, preferably from the top of the stairs, as they did in the movies. Everyone would read the poem and embrace the revolution. My imagination went into overdrive: national television reporters would arrive and run an urgent story about a spontaneous student protest breaking out in one of Grozny's top schools. The teachers would panic; the dishonoured head teacher would resign. But then a traitor betrays my confidence and I'm taken away in a black van. There's an interrogation with a strict but stupid prosecutor. Human rights organisations appeal on my behalf and Mum punches somebody's nose, shouting, 'Don't you dare touch my daughter!'

At some point in my reverie Mum entered the room and I excitedly began telling her my plans. She grew serious. 'Lana, no one can see this, neither friends, nor relatives. It's a wonderful poem but now's not the time to publish it. Let's wait a little and then we'll see.'

My enthusiasm evaporated instantly. I was developing an intuitive sense of the line between risk and danger, and my protest plans had clearly crossed it. As much as I tried to pretend that we lived an ordinary life (which worked most of the time), as I grew older I became more aware of the dangers. There was no further discussion. I hid the poem in a computer folder.

'Lanka, RenTV asked me to do an interview about headscarves,' Mum told me.

'On TV? Really?'

'Yes, on one of the evening programmes!'

Mum rarely appeared on TV because of her council work, and when she did, it was just a general shot with some middle-aged man talking over her. Now she was going to be on Russian TV, which would be broadcast to many more people.

Mum was pictured walking with a reporter through the Grozny market. With cheesy music playing in the background, I heard her say, 'I don't want to wear a headscarf. I don't like it, it constrains me. That's why I don't wear it, especially when I'm being forced into it.' The music continued, so did Mum's commentary: 'We can't follow the same traditions that we were born into, otherwise we would still live in caves. That used to be a tradition, too.'

Watching, my stomach grew ice cold and my fingers began to clench in a fist; I struggled to breathe, and when I tried to speak only strange, guttural noises came out. I was scared. Something about seeing my mother's face on screen had made me realise the scale of her battle. For most of my life, I'd thought of Mum's work stories as tales from a book in which she was cast as a fearless hero fighting the forces of evil. The rules of the genre meant that she could always escape, untouched, and return home. But now I suddenly saw a petite woman in a white windbreaker, a woman who had just declared insurgency on national television. *How many potential enemies have seen this piece?* I wondered. *Have my classmates? Now everyone knows what she looks like!* Yes, she'd appeared on screen before, but this wasn't the same. Mum was just like everyone else, I realised. There was no magic protecting her from threats, beatings or murder. She was mortal.

'Mum, why did you have to do it so openly?' I mumbled.

Her look told me that she hadn't expected that reaction. We went silent. I went to bed early and straight to sleep. The next morning began with my usual ritual: I opened my window wide and took a deep breath, drinking in the fresh morning air. It was an ordinary day because I had decided it was. We both forgot about the interview.

Then, several weeks later, it forced itself back into our lives, and it changed the course of them forever. Mum was summoned by Kadyrov himself.

★

Memory is a treacherous thing. Our brain might remember an old plot line from a Brazilian soap opera we watched ten years before, the name of a neighbour's second cousin whom we've only met twice, but the most important moments and conversations, the life-defining incidents, often disappear. Trying to remember, you walk through a forest in fog, barely seeing the contours of the trees.

I can't remember the details of the day on which Mum was summoned to meet Kadyrov. I can't remember whether she seemed frightened on her return. All I have are fragments lodged in my brain from snippets of overheard conversation or what was shared later with me by her friends and colleagues.

'He summoned her . . . Started to yell!'

'I told him to stop speaking to me in that tone of voice, I could be his mother.'

'He went quiet . . .'

'. . . like a bad student scolded by a teacher.'

'He fired me from my position on the Human Rights Council.'

'. . . said his hands are elbow-deep in blood and he's killed people, but he's not ashamed of it because they were enemies of Chechnya.'

'He asked me if I am not worried about my daughter. Said that he knows which school Lanka goes to.'

'. . . called me a liar.'

'Ordered me to wear a headscarf in front of him. I refused.'

She told the same stories of her misadventures over and over again to different sets of people until her delivery was perfectly polished, like pebbles on a beach. A little joke, a dramatic pause, a clever retort. When the stories were dark, she shone a bright, surgical light on them, even made them sound funny to show that she wasn't scared. And Kadyrov she turned into a spoilt school bully who had to be put in his place.

Mum rarely told me her anecdotes face to face. I usually heard her telling them to someone else as I stood by her, like an assistant. I almost believed that she wasn't shaken by her encounter. But she told me again and again: 'Come straight back home after school.' She didn't have to tell me not to talk to strangers – I'd known that since I was little – but she began checking in on me several times a day, not just with a text but a proper phone call.

'She was absolutely petrified,' recalled her friend and colleague Katya Sokirianskaia. 'She would always act according to her conscience and not think about the consequences. But that time she was really scared because he threatened to do something to you. I don't remember why she didn't leave straight away – it was something to do with your passport.'

'No, my passport was the reason why we couldn't leave the following year. That year it was exams,' I replied.

While I had been having the time of my life that spring – hanging out with friends and maintaining my rebel status – Mum had been going through something very different. Later, Katya told me more about that uneasy period. In February 2008, Kadyrov had arranged a series of meetings with the team at Memorial. The first encounter was unsettling. Inviting the group to his palace in Tsentoroi, the president had accused them of blackening his new image of Chechnya and undermining him personally. He had suggested they face each other in a televised political debate, the winner determined by an audience vote. There was only ever going to be one winner, of course, and having lost, Memorial's employees would have to work for Kadyrov. Thanks, however, to the diplomatic efforts of my mother's boss, Oleg, the TV debate was replaced by a round-table conference. Then, at the next meeting, Kadyrov appointed Mum chair of the Human Rights Council. She lasted several weeks. The day after the headscarf interview was broadcast, sometime in April, Mum was tricked into believing that she was having a meeting with Muslim Khuchiev, the mayor; instead, she was taken to Kadyrov's home, where she found the president boiling with rage.

Life went on as usual. I went to school, hung out with friends, revised for exams, played the guitar and continued my headscarf resistance. Mum would periodically ask me to come straight home from school, but as usual I ignored her. Bad things happened to other people, never to us. I rarely felt anxious. Something told me that, after my exams, things would change again, but I brushed such thoughts aside.

One warm evening in May, Mum sat me down for a talk.

'Listen, Lanka,' she said, 'I have wonderful news. This summer we're going to England. But don't tell anyone at school. Can you imagine? You'll finally see London!'

'And what happens after that?'

'Remember every now and then we've discussed that it would be great if you moved to live with your Auntie Sveta in Yekaterinburg, in Russia? Just for a year or two?'

'I suppose so.'

'Schools are much better over there and I would feel happier if you were somewhere safer.'

Yekaterinburg, it was, then. I accepted my fate. Those periods in Grozny would end up being some of the best times of my life. But I knew they couldn't last.

On 3 August, Mum and I were still in England when she heard the news. Mohamad-Salah, the preacher she had helped just a few months earlier, had disappeared. While in hiding in July, he had spoken to a journalist from *Novaya Gazeta* about his abduction and detention at Kadyrov's secret prison, and on 2 August he had returned to Chechnya to attend his older sister's funeral. The following day, several unidentified men wearing camouflage had abducted him for the second time in his life, this time from his family home. No one had heard anything since, but it was not hard to imagine what might have happened to him.

In the end, I did have to put on a headscarf. I had no choice. Heading into school one morning for my history exam, quietly revising as I went, I discovered the classroom door blocked by an unfamiliar woman.

'Where's your headscarf?' she threatened. 'You were told that you can't enter the exam room unless you're wearing a headscarf.'

True, but I'd ignored it. I looked around in panic and noticed Tamara Khasanovna coming out of the teachers' room. I was hoping that she would let me through but instead she whispered, 'Estemirova, run and look for a headscarf, hurry!'

With only minutes before the start of the exam, I panicked. I rushed to the schoolyard, heart thumping in my ears. This was no time for principles. It was the end of May, school was over and no one was outside. 'What should I do? How much time did I have?'

And suddenly, a miracle – I saw a group of primary-school girls in tiny headscarves. I ran up, struggling to catch my breath, and began begging to borrow one: 'Please, please, I'll return it right after the exam, I'll buy you chocolate, too!' Finally, one girl timidly handed over her colourful headscarf. Grabbing it, I ran back to the exam room.

The scary woman was still on guard but this time, noticing the cloth in my hand, she let me through. My classmates were already at their desks. I carefully looked at the headscarf. 'Is this it? Am I really going to just put it on, after months of fighting?' I racked my brain, considering my options, until I came up with a compromise. After some fumbling, I folded the headscarf into a ribbon, put it around my head and tied it into a big knot on my forehead – I may have looked silly, but hopefully also victorious.

After the exam, I took it off and went to look for the kind little girl, but she was nowhere to be seen. She's probably still out there, waiting for her headscarf and chocolate!

9

Yekaterinburg
2008–9

'Just for a year or two,' echoed Mum's words as we boarded the Moscow–Yekaterinburg flight.

For years, there had been a vague plan to send me to live with Mum's younger sister Sveta in Yekaterinburg, 'for better schools and maybe university'. But the sobering thing is, abstract plans sometimes come true. Mum and I landed in Koltsovo airport in late August 2008, about two weeks after the Georgia–Russia war began. The news channels played footage of Russian tanks driving through the streets and old Georgian women weeping before the fresh ruins of their homes. Somehow, though, it didn't feel like a real war, perhaps because it was so short compared to ours. I was also confused about what was going on and my attempts to find the truth on the Internet ended where they always did, at the indie rock page of a pirate music website. Listening to Mum's conversations, it was obvious that Russia was in the wrong, but the whole situation seemed very complicated.

Only a couple of weeks previously we had been in Oxford, enjoying the mild English summer. We had spent two and a half months in England, staying in London for the first week and then moving to Oxford for the remainder of the trip. I flicked through my favourite memories, starting at the beginning. 'Sloaaaan Squeaaa . . .' I would repeat the name of the bus stop after the announcer, trying to copy the funny-sounding accent. The upstairs seats on the red double-decker – which, I had discovered, was very much a real form of transportation – were full, so I glued myself to the window downstairs, greedily observing the fast-changing kaleidoscope of city vignettes. There was a red telephone box and a red postbox; over there was a black cab driving passed a pub with ivy-covered walls. Everything was so perfect and pretty and so much better than I'd imagined. And then I saw *it* and lost my power of speech entirely, disintegrating into dozens of indistinguishable squeals. Standing there majestically – sitting at the most strategic spot on the right-hand side of Westminster Bridge – was Big Ben, the symbol of Britain. In theory, I knew it existed – it adorned the cover of my English-language textbook, stared out from our box of black Akhmad tea, and featured in countless news reports. Yet because of its grandiose symbolism, it had seemed to me as mythical as Camelot, the Shire or Hogwarts. I tried to take it all in but couldn't – my gaze kept jumping from the intricate, lacy facade of the Houses of Parliament to the clock tower with the gilded roof. In the end, my eyes began to hurt.

'Lanka, you've been standing there for half an hour,' I heard Mum say behind me. 'Come, Joy wants to take us for a walk along the Embankment.'

Joy became our guide and friend throughout our stay in England. Mum had met her the previous year through a mutual friend, Mariana Katzarova, the founder of the Anna Politkovskaya Award of which Mum was the first recipient. A few years older than Mum, she had an unruly mane of salt-and-pepper hair and astonishingly blue, almost turquoise eyes. She was cool – faded leather jacket and vintage jeans kind of cool, casually dropping in the word 'shit' in the middle of a conversation. It was not surprising that Joy and I bonded so quickly; despite being in her early fifties, she was a teenager at heart. To me, she was as big a part of the London magic as Camden Town, Hyde Park, Tate Modern and those delicious scones.

Quaint and idyllic, Oxford was Mum's domain, her ideal of a city. We stayed in an old Victorian mansion with a massive garden that had been turned into a boarding house by a group of nuns. We had the basement room, and, although it didn't have much of a view beyond people's feet walking back and forth, it was charming and cosy. In the evenings, Mum and I cooked meals in the communal kitchen while chatting to the other residents – mostly PhD students. Mum's English had got much better since our stay in Ireland, but she would still throw me a questioning look whenever she couldn't remember something.

A tiny family unit, Mum and I always did plenty of things together, but we grew even closer in Oxford. We raided the local Primark, tried new cuisines, attempted yoga, spent hours chatting about everything under the sun or simply read together in comfortable silence. Being a nature lover, Mum was thrilled by our proximity to the University Parks, excitedly studying every tree and flower, dragging me through garden centres to stock up on seeds to take home. We took full advantage of every free museum and sightseeing attraction, splitting our time between Oxford and London and even making the journey to Shakespeare's birthplace in Stratford-upon-Avon. Overcome with passion for history and literature, Mum existed in a state of fangirl euphoria, excited to see all the places that she'd only ever read about. As for my own fangirling, I nearly fainted when Joy surprised me with two tickets for Panic! At The Disco, my favourite band on earth. Days later, I found myself in an orderly queue in front of Coco, Camden, accompanied by the fifteen-year-old daughter of one of our Oxford acquaintances. Once we were inside and I caught a glimpse of heart-throb Brendon Urie, my high-pitched squeal instantly blended with a choir of screams from the other over-excited teenagers.

Back in Yekaterinburg, I carefully unpacked my luggage, pausing to look at all my treasures: the coveted ticket from the Panic! At The Disco concert, postcards from Tate Modern and National Gallery, a pair of authentic black Converse All Stars, a navy hoodie with *Oxford* on the front and an outrageous T-shirt with fluorescent skulls and bones that glowed in the dark – a parting gift from Joy.

'Don't forget to email Joy,' Mum reminded me. 'You two really got on, you must keep in touch. And it will be good for practising your English, too.'

'Of course I won't!'

Mum didn't stay for the start of school. On a cold August morning, we embraced one last time and she was gone. I was to start another chapter of my life with Auntie Sveta, her husband Andrey and my cousin, Sasha. They were still living in the tiny two-room apartment that had sheltered us during the second war, but a decade later every inch of the space had been masterfully utilised. Sasha and I were to share a room, which of course wasn't ideal for a pair of teenagers of opposite gender, but it showed the length to which my aunt was willing to go to keep me safe. She put up a few shelves on the left-hand side from my bed (for *Lana's* things only!) and cleared half of the wardrobe for my clothes. There was no space for two desks but I could use the other room for all my needs, including the computer, when Auntie Sveta and Uncle Andrey were at work. There was no special fuss made about what was, objectively, a very big change; everyone just fell into their roles. Mum's immediate family were never ones for loud pronouncements or protracted emotional conversations. At the age of fourteen, my ever-changing living situation – Grozny to Oxford to Yekaterinburg – seemed normal precisely because I didn't know what normal was. It was always clear to me that Mum and I had a peculiar, extraordinary existence that was different from everyone else's, and that the only way of thriving was to adapt and focus on the positives.

Sasha looked very Russian, in my opinion, with shaggy, straw-coloured hair, blue eyes and soft features. I could always read his mood by the expression of his mouth – whether he was sceptical, overjoyed, interested or irritated. He was two years older than me and already accomplished – he had written short stories that had won competitions, played the piano, drew beautifully and had read serious books on philosophy. Although I tried not to make it too obvious, I was very eager to keep up with him intellectually. He felt like the big brother I never had. There were other cousins, too, of course – Yura and Ruslan, the sons of Mum's second sister, Lena, but they were three and four years older than me respectively, an age gap that proved too big for proper friendship. With their brown hair, dark eyes and skinny frames, they certainly looked more Chechen than Sasha, but neither had ever visited their grandfather's homeland. By bloodline, Lena's sons were a quarter Chechen yet they were all Russian. I was a quarter Russian and the rest of me was as Chechen as could be. But we were a family all the same. In Soviet times, some intermarriage took place between Chechen men and Russian women (almost never the other way around), but after the wars unions between the two nations almost ceased.

When it came to being taken seriously by my cousins, I had the unfortunate disadvantage of being fourteen and a girl, whereas they were sixteen, seventeen and eighteen and on the verge of becoming men. They accepted me into their group, and I tried to play it cool when they made fun of me or dismissed what I had to say. But when the ridicule went too far, I hit back. One time Sasha and I started bickering while unpacking groceries and, before we knew it, we were furiously battering each other with baguettes. Auntie Sveta had to jump in to separate us. I ran from the room crying, leaving a trail of breadcrumbs behind me.

The fourth largest city in Russia, Yekaterinburg's main claim to fame continued to be rooted in being the place of execution of the Romanov family, Russia's last royals. In the Soviet era it had become one of the most important industrial centres in the country, especially known for its metallurgy. The city centre, a forty-minute to an hour bus ride from our home, depending on the traffic, boasted a few handsome streets with neoclassical architecture and a beautiful promenade along the river Iset. In winter, the wide river was covered in a thick sheet of ice, and we could cross it on foot to get to our favourite cinema. But beyond the city centre it was one featureless, concrete sprawl, each district blending into the other. The neighbourhood where my aunt lived was a far cry from the leafy, picturesque streets of Oxford. On the outskirts of the city, it was the final stop on several bus routes. In the evenings, my cousins and I would go for long strolls in this foggy industrial cityscape, trailing through a labyrinth of identical tower blocks, sparse woods littered with syringes and empty beer cans, and busy motorways covered by flattened brown snow. In the distance, the shadows of old Soviet factories growled like dragons, releasing charcoal smoke. I clung to the faint smell of pine trees – the pitiful, shrinking woods were being replaced with a vast expanse of multi-storey beehives. My cousins drank cheap tinned alcohol (in secret). I stuck to soft drinks.

I didn't mention these walks to Mum when I spoke to her on the phone; there was no need to worry her.

On 1 September, I started tenth grade at the same school as Sasha. New beginnings always filled me with excitement, but this time I was anxious too. After having had my fingers burnt at the boarding school, I didn't feel as confident as before. And besides, I'd come to realise that my age difference from the rest of the class could be a problem since I'd started school early and skipped a grade. Would sixteen-year-olds want to be friends with a fourteen-year-old? Would anyone like me at all? Each time I changed schools (this was my seventh transfer), I resolved to become a better version of myself, which I had decided meant cooler and wiser, with a devil-may-care attitude. But I could never figure out how to be anything but awkward, strange and a little wild – less party animal than feral kitten hiding under a truck. For better or worse, I only knew how to be myself.

After a month at the new school, I still didn't have any friends. I did make attempts. I told funny stories about my past. I carefully challenged the teachers' authority, making sure everyone could see how fearless I was. I even created my first profile on Vkontakte, Russian Facebook, and posted an album of London photos, *because it's the coolest city in the world, right?* Everyone loves London. Nothing worked. The class I'd joined already had close-knit friendship groups. It seemed as if whatever door I tried to knock on was sealed shut. And besides, after several weeks of quietly observing my classmates, I concluded that they weren't that great anyway.

'You're so quiet,' a teacher told me once. I'd been many things, but 'quiet' was new. Such a contrast to the class clown and rebel of a few months ago.

It took me a few weeks to discover that the school I was attending focused on maths and sciences rather than my beloved humanities. This was not good. In classes, I was frequently completely lost, as if the teachers were speaking a different language.

estemirova lana <angrygroznygirl@googlemail.com>   03.10.08
To: estemirova

Mum, hi! How r u? I'm not great. We got our reports back and I got five As, five Cs and 5 Ds. Don't be upset, I fixed it. Mum, I exposed this school. It's a **POLYTECHNIC SCHOOL!** It means that their focus is on stuff like maths, chemistry etc. And I, the most humanities-oriented, anti-science person, have ended up in hell! Sorry but I'm probably gonna get lots of Cs this term. I really try. Auntie Sveta helps me but she wants me to focus ALL my time to maths! And it's more important that I read and learn languages!! I haven't made any friends. I have acquaintances but that's it. You know, it's not fun out here. I'm at such a fun age but I'm not having any fun. I'm again becoming mean and irritable (but the worst thing is that I don't know how to release my aggression). It's, like, SO lame, but I understand that Grozny would have been bad for me and no fun too. AAAAAAAAAAAA!! SEE YA!! Please reply when you see this, or I'll feel blue.

Natalia Estemirova <estemirova@gmail.com>   03.10.08
To: me

Hi, Lanuska. Love the photos you sent me!

Regarding the school – it's a pity but you still have your after-school activities. You can read, and we'll sort out French. And when it comes to anger, you have to literally run from it. Find out if there are any sport clubs, maybe even martial arts. You and Sasha would benefit from it.

I'm currently in London at Masha Karp's flat, the one who works for the BBC. You remember her, of course. Masha is not here, she's in St Petersburg and her flat is in the process of renovation. Everything is covered in books! I met up with Joy yesterday – she was sorry you weren't there.

I preferred to spend my school time alone. During breaks, I would walk the hallways, headphones in my ears, quietly humming along to the Libertines or Strokes. Cringing, I remembered my failed attempts to make friends at the boarding school the previous year: how I'd offered my classmates chocolate, made thoughtful comments about their style, and listened to their vapid boy dramas. And how did they treat me in return? People always take kindness for weakness, I told myself, as if being nice means you're a push-over. Not this time. Better to be a proud loner than demean yourself for a pack of girls with half a brain. And besides, I had my cousins.

I missed Mum, though, and resented the fact that she never had time to call me during the day, when I was alone and could speak privately. I could dial her number with my eyes closed – 89287864751, 89287864751, 892 . . .

'Hello, Lanuska!'

'Hi, Mama!'

She told me how cold it was in Grozny and that she had had to turn on the gas stove to warm herself up. About a brave Afghan activist, Malalai Joya, whom she'd met in London in October when she became the second recipient of the Anna Politkovskaya Award. Mum had presented her with a small white statuette shaped like a dove. And how she'd gone back to the National Gallery to revisit her favourite paintings – no, she hadn't had time to go back to Tate Modern.

I told her about the books I'd been reading – John Steinbeck's short stories, Erich Maria Remarque's *All Quiet on the Western Front* – and that I had bought the most outrageous lime-green tracksuit bottoms, which I wore with purple trainers. Bitterly, Mum would note another bizarre change made by Kadyrov in the city. In my first months of Yekaterinburg, I tried not to dwell on the fact that, just months ago, the president of Chechnya had threatened my mother to her face. Instead, I would reminisce about our embarrassing morning jogs at the University Parks, and how Mum insisted that we exercise together, just like all those years ago when she dug up the old Jane Fonda aerobics tape.

But Kadyrov, and the threat he posed to our family, never truly left my mind. While Mum tried not to burden me with stories from her work, I knew that people were still being kidnapped in Chechnya. She continued to write for *Novaya Gazeta* under her own name.

People Are Still Being Kidnapped in Chechnya
Natalia Estemirova for *Novaya Gazeta*
20 October 2008

On Thursday, 16 October at 18.30, the special Kadyrov police regiment detained Muslim Musaevich Utsaev, born in 1984. Muslim Utsaev is a former foster-child from Khadizhat Gaytayeva's celebrated orphanage. Grozny native Khadizhat created the orphanage at the beginning of the first Chechen war for children who were left parentless due to the hostilities in Chechnya.

Many of her pupils remained living in the orphanage even as they grew up, since they had no other housing.

Muslim Utsaev, whose parents and close relatives were killed during the war, grew up in this orphanage. He worked on construction sites in Grozny and handed most of his earnings to the orphanage. The employees and children of the orphanage have long since become a real family for Muslim.

On Thursday, three cars drove up to the orphanage, from which twelve armed Kadyrovites emerged. They were accompanied by a man whose face was covered by a hood. They demanded that Muslim identify this person. Muslim replied that perhaps he had seen him somewhere, but he did not know who he was. After that, Muslim was ordered to get into one of the cars and was taken away to an unknown destination. The orphanage staff could not remember the licence plates of the Kadyrovites' cars because the orphanage was cordoned off and no one was allowed to leave.

This wasn't just any story – Mum had known Khadizhat for years and had helped her in every way she could to keep the orphanage afloat. I too contributed by putting together donations of old clothes and toys. They'd witnessed so many horrors during both wars, and still it wasn't over. In the days after the kidnapping the orphanage staff – Muslim's only family – filed a missing person's report at the police station with help from my mum, but they never saw the young man again.

A typical day in Yekaterinburg would begin at 6.30, when I'd wake barely believing that I'd slept, and wondering whether to invent another headache excuse for my aunt. No one at school cared if I showed up. Once I'd resigned myself to going to school, I'd start the slow process of getting ready for the day. I'd dress and make myself a cup of the instant coffee I had begun to drink because constant tiredness was making me fall asleep during lessons. I'd watch MTV while munching on toast. It would still be dark outside when I left to catch the bus, so I'd wrap myself in endless layers, feet crunching pleasantly on the snow. I'd wait amongst strangers in the dark, all of them in matching black puffer jackets. When I got to school it was still dark, and it wasn't until the end of the first lesson, at around 9.30, that the darkness would finally fade to grey, then to a paler grey, and it would remain that way until about four in the afternoon. On some days, I had music school in the evenings. Afterwards, wrapped in my twenty layers, I would walk back to the bus stop, squinting to see the correct number – I should have worn glasses, but I already had pimples and the combination would have turned me into a complete nerd – I still had my pride.

In the evenings, Sasha and I followed a regular routine of plonking ourselves in front of his computer screen, armed with fizzy drinks and chocolate, and slowly making our way through every film in the IMDB 250 list. We watched and rewatched *Forrest Gump* six times, froze to our seats as Brad Pitt yelled 'WHAT'S IN THE BOX?', failed to figure out the meaning of 'rosebud' and couldn't for the life of us understand what Ilsa saw in washed-out alcoholic Rick. I was mesmerised by *The Godfather* – a film that seemed made for people who hated gangster films. I rewatched the Sicily section on its own because it reminded me of Chechnya – it even had a hasty marriage proposal and a car explosion, just like back home.

Most school breaks were spent plugged into headphones and wrapped in melancholy, slowly making my way through the entire Radiohead discography on my MP3 player, imagining all the things I would say to Thom Yorke if I ever met him: that he had changed my life; that he understood the loneliness I felt better than anyone else; that maybe I would play him my version of 'Karma Police' (one of the first songs I learnt to play on the guitar) and we would make a record together.

'Hey you!' I looked to the far corner of the corridor and saw a tall chubby boy from my year gesturing at me to take out my earbuds.

'Yeah, I'm talking to you,' the boy said again. He was surrounded by friends who sniggered when he spoke.

'What?' I replied indifferently. I'd never spoken to him before but from snippets of overheard conversations I'd gathered that he was a nasty piece of work.

'Come here,' he commanded.

'What for?'

'I said, come here.'

'If you want something from me, YOU come here,' I responded. 'I'm not a dog.'

The school bell interrupted this strange interaction and soon enough I'd forgotten about it. Until a couple of weeks later, when I was waiting for class to start and he walked by with a group of acolytes. I glanced up and was met with smirking eyes. He whispered loudly to his friend, 'Here's that terrorist. She's going to blow us up.'

Did he really just say that about me? A familiar adrenaline rush and a surge of fury I hadn't experienced since boarding school coursed through me. I knew what happened when you let this kind of thing slide.

'Hey!' I yelled at his broad back. 'Turn around.'

The boy stopped and turned in disbelief. I walked up to him.

'Did you just say something about me?'

'No, you must be crazy.'

'So who did you call a terrorist, then?'

'What, are you deaf? I didn't say anything about you.'

I see how it is. He's not committed enough to this tiff and didn't expect me to respond.

'I'll tell you what,' I said through gritted teeth, although my voice was shaky. 'It's not the first time I've had to fight assholes like you. So, you better just leave me alone and let me be. But if you want to start something, I'm ready. Bring it on!'

'You've lost your marbles,' he replied, screwing a finger against his temple. The boy was clearly embarrassed more than anything. I may have been awkward and anti-social but inside me burned an angry fire just waiting for a match. 'Escalate, always escalate,' was the main lesson I took away from boarding school. 'Show your bullies that you're even crazier than them.' After that episode, I saw him occasionally gawking at me, but he never said a word. So I went back to Radiohead.

It didn't occur to me to tell my aunt about this exchange. I often found myself telling her details of my life that I didn't have a chance to tell Mum, because she was there and would listen. But as for painful experiences, they were my burden to bear, no need to ask anyone to carry them for me. At least, that's what I thought at the time. My relationship with Auntie Sveta was uneven. There were fun moments, as when she dyed a strand of my hair red or took me to my first bowling alley for my birthday. We did girly things together – a novelty for her and me both, because Mum never had time. As Auntie let me buy the clothes I wanted, I ended up with T-shirts with silly prints and an outrageous turquoise puffer jacket to complement my neon-green tracksuit (I had a rule to wear at least three colours at once).

'I should have been more patient with you,' Auntie Sveta said years later, reminiscing on a peaceful summer night in Andalucía. I have heard that phrase often, but the truth was, my pouting expressions, extreme defensiveness and sarcasm would have driven anyone up the wall. Inevitably, she and I clashed. We clashed over my unwillingness to study maths, my strong opinions, my 'sneaky' ways of avoiding school. She never screamed; even when she was angry, she remained softly spoken. But although we didn't always know how to communicate, her unconditional love shone through in the little things she did: when she patiently followed me around shopping centres as I window-shopped; when she spent hours trying to break algebra formulae down for my stubborn brain; when she made me pizza, or when she trusted me with her own problems. She made me feel part of the family, never differentiating between me and Sasha. But however hard she tried, I longed to be with my mother.

estemirova lana <angrygroznygirl@googlemail.com>   09.11.08
to: estemirova

Hi, Mum. Oh god, I feel awful! I cut a straight fringe but it turned out so lame (I mean, Auntie Sveta cut it, not me). I still look like an emo and don't look like a beauty (although I've long accepted the fact that I won't be beautiful). See the photos below. All is good, I'm working on my maths homework. Gosh, I'm so sick of everything, I don't want to go back to school, I don't want to see those faces again. I don't know what I want. I want to travel; I hate living in Russia, I just hate it. I tore some pages from my diary, the ones where I documented everything happening to me, my grudges and other silly stuff. From now on I will only write my thoughts about the world that I have no one to express to. How's Georgia? Tell me. All my classmates hate the Georgians now. A bunch of nobodies. They watch propaganda on the news and think of themselves as clever politicians. Also, I think I have a split personality. Inside me there is this fun, bright, crazy person who's ready to change the world. And also an insolent, mean cynic ready to destroy it. But I try not to get upset and to improve myself instead.

And the fringe ... SUCKS!!!! It's been snowing here. I stole Uncle Andrey's hat that's twice my size. And I keep wearing it. And it makes me happy.

Please, can you send me a long letter, in which you describe in detail everything that's happening in your life. Well, bye! I think my long, silly email will make you as happy as yours make me (but yours are not silly). And now, bye once again!

Natalia Estemirova <estemirova@gmail.com>   13.11.08
To: me

Hello, Lanuska! I had such a busy day yesterday, not a second to write to you, I had to come home early. I'm torn between things and my hands can't move anymore. Did you hear about the shooting at the Youth Palace? A security guard was murdered. He worked in the building. I pity the guy, but they behave really awfully over there.

The fringe doesn't suit you; you don't suit any haircuts that you pick, they ruin you. But, perhaps it's for the best – who do you have to impress over there?

I made your balcony photo my background picture on my computer.

My communication with Mum was becoming more and more erratic. I couldn't talk to her as much as I wanted to because mobile phone operators charged extortionate sums for phone calls across Russian regions, and since there was no Internet in the Grozny flat, Mum had to use the office wi-fi to email me. When I missed her more than I could bear, I called Mum from my mobile, stealing her away from work. The phone bills rose exponentially. I would wrap myself in a coat and sneak out to the communal balcony outside Auntie's flat, feeling her stare burning into the back of my head. As I stood out in the cold, looking at the bleak urban landscape and blowing out my breath like smoke, a factory in the far distance mimicked me, releasing brown clouds into the twilit sky.

'Hello, Lanuska.'

I suddenly felt warm. I told her about my day, complained... As always, we spoke about trivial things. I told her about school, music lessons, exaggerating my achievements in French. The most important stuff – the loneliness we shared, the isolation, uncertainty and heartache – slipped into the long pauses.

'Vanessa the cat is looking poorly. Her fur is not shiny and she has lost weight, maybe I should take her to a vet.'

I knew she never would.

'I got an A for literature.'

Sometimes she didn't pick up and I retreated, defeated, into the flat.

After a while, when costs spiralled, we switched to landlines. The Internet in her office was too weak to use Skype.

13.12.08   Lana's diary

I don't know what's up with me. I think that nobody cares about me. I try not to say anything unnecessary, so no one gets tired of me. I don't trust anyone. I know that Mum cares about me but the job is more important to her and I've long accepted that. Gosh, here I am, sitting and feeling sorry for myself. Why am I always blaming and justifying myself?

All her life Mum worked, worked, worked, helped people and completely forgot about me. And then, after she sent me to the boarding school, I at first resented it and then resigned myself to it. Her job is very important, she's helping people and I'm just standing in the way. Let's stop pretending: I get in her way. Sometimes I regret ever being born. She'll probably only need me when she's old.

Oh my God, what is this nonsense that I am saying? My Mum loves me and wants to protect me from her work. I can't live in Chechnya and I don't want to wear a headscarf. But we can't be together now. I'm just lonely.

Four months after she left, Mum arrived for the Christmas holidays. We met her at Koltsovo airport and when I finally saw her, black puffer coat in hand, I ran forward with the same eagerness as all those years ago in Kamyshlov. Our reunion felt cinematic.

Later, when we sat drinking tea, I glued myself to her, head on her shoulder, her hand in mine. She was delighted. But in the evening I made a point of going through and watching a movie with Sasha – after all, I was a grown-up now. Those two Christmas weeks flew by. She promised to return in the summer. 'Keep studying French and English,' she urged. 'They're very important for your future.'

Four months to go until we see each other again.

It was not long after the Christmas break, and Mum had already disappeared into her work. My safety had always been her main source of anxiety; having sent me away was giving her a false sense of security and dulling her instinct for self-preservation. She continued to investigate and document human rights abuses, writing fearless articles that drew more and more attention to her.

In January 2009, my mother reported in *Novaya Gazeta* that many young people were joining illegal armed groups. These young people, aged eighteen to thirty, had 'gone to the woods' to join the rebels in huge numbers – the estimate in her article was as many as 1,000 in the previous two years. The fight against these young rebels was now being carried out by militants – former Chechen independence fighters who had been amnestied and now held power in Chechnya. My mother wrote that the federal government had 'managed to pit one generation of Chechens against another'.

As always, she didn't shy away from risk, writing directly about the head of Chechnya: 'Ramzan Kadyrov is responding with force to those joining the rebels. Fewer men are now arrested on suspicion of connection to the rebels, but the number of extrajudicial executions has increased. The familiar fear that Kadyrovites might break into your house and kill anyone there has returned to Chechnya.'

This is what happened to the family of Datkhu Ilayev. After Datkhu had left for the hajj, Kadyrov's men came to his house and killed his three sons. Neither Datkhu nor his sons had any connection to the rebels. Most likely, someone had sent in a false denunciation about their family. Snitching, which flourished in the ancestral village of the Kadyrovs, Khosi-Yurt, was another feature of Ramzan's Chechnya.

The principle of collective responsibility, in which the families of those who joined armed groups were punished, was first implemented in May 2007. The president of Chechnya, Kadyrov, and the mayor of Grozny, Khuchiev, appeared on TV and declared war:

> We will no longer conduct a dialogue based on state laws. We will act according to Chechen customs . . . The evil that your relatives are doing will return to you in your homes. Soon you will feel it in your own skin. Everyone who has relatives in the woods will feel the responsibility. Everyone! Everyone!

Around a hundred relatives of the rebels were called to the Chechen Ministry of Internal Affairs. There, the deputy prime minister, Adam Delimkhanov, announced that none of those who went to the woods would be forgiven. 'Their heads will be chopped off,' he insisted, adding that the responsibility for these children's actions lay with their families. They and their neighbours would bear the punishment. At the end, the families were forced to publicly denounce their loved ones. At first, there was a heavy silence in the room, but then an old man stood up and said: 'If my son gets caught, I give you my permission to kill him.' Hearing that, a woman whose four sons had gone to the woods started to cry. She begged for forgiveness for her children, but Delimkhanov replied, 'All will be responsible for one.'

That summer, President Kadyrov appeared on local television. 'It is no secret that many people are relatives of young men who have gone into the forest,' he said.

> I know that they keep in touch with them, even send them food. I warn that if these young people are not returned home within ten days, all their relatives will be put on trial. I forbid the burial of those who fight against us. If I find out that someone who was in the forest is buried in some village, no one will remain in their positions: neither the head of the police, nor the head of the administration, nor the imam of the mosque.

Words were followed by actions. The head of administration in the city of Argun, Ibragim Temirbaev, the elders and police chiefs compiled a list of seventeen families whose sons had gone to the forest. These people were ordered to leave the city. As Mum noted at the time: 'The fight against the militants has grown into a war against our own people.'

The principle of collective responsibility took an even more sinister turn when the houses of relatives of the alleged rebels started to go up in flames. This barbaric punishment was of course supposed to send a message without attracting media attention, but Mum followed the trail of arson with a voice recorder in one hand and a phone in the other. She encouraged petrified victims to talk about what had happened to them. One was Yakhita, whose house was gutted by fire in July 2008, along with her brothers'. Mum noted how, although it was now December, the house still emitted a smoky, corrosive smell.

Both Yakhita's brothers' sons had gone to the woods and she was being punished along with them. This was becoming a common practice in Chechnya, and Mum had explicitly covered it in a piece for *Novaya Gazeta* titled 'Cleansing with Fire'.

> Arsonists in camouflage uniforms and masks have been breaking into the homes of Chechens at night. They drive people out into the street, douse the houses with gasoline and wait until the burning roof collapses. Firefighters and police do not come to the scene on call. Criminal cases (few victims of the fire dare to file complaints) are not investigated. The prosecutor's office does not interfere.
>
> From July 2008 to December 2008, twenty-four houses have been burned down in Chechnya.

Thanks to Mum, media outlets and human rights organisations also turned to the topics of collective punishment and house burnings, undermining Kadyrov's plan to keep things quiet. But unlike many of her colleagues, Mum lived and worked in Chechnya. And to some, her courage was coming across as a provocation to the regime.

On 19 January, I received an unexpected call from Mum. 'Lana,' she half whispered, 'I don't know if you saw the news ... Stas was murdered. He was shot.'

I was quiet, completely startled. Stanislav Markelov, whom everyone called 'Stas', was our wise-cracking friend and a brilliant human rights lawyer. He'd been shot coming out of a news conference in Moscow, half a mile from the Kremlin. He was only thirty-four. Two children and a wife. Anastasia Baburova, a journalist for *Novaya Gazeta*, had tried to come to his aid, but she was shot and killed too. Mum was saying something else, but her words didn't make sense. 'I'm going to the funeral soon . . . I don't think you should come.'

'Mum, I beg you, please, please be careful!'

'Of course, Lanuska, I'm always careful.'

After we said goodbye, I sat motionless, phone in hand.

I hadn't seen Stas for a few years but my memories of him still carried a warm glow. He had a serious side, but the Stas I knew made me cry with laughter. He was the funniest person I'd ever met. A chill crept over me, as if someone had left a window open in winter. It was the same feeling I'd had when I heard the news of Anna Politkovskaya's murder.

At first, I was convinced that Stas had been killed by the Russian secret service, people who hated the fact that he was helping Chechens, but it turned out to be more complicated than that. I only knew him as a lawyer who helped the victims of human rights abuses, but he had also been a staunch anti-fascist, and anti-fascist activists were often targeted by neo-Nazi groups that had links to the authorities – so in a sense, they were part of the regime. These thugs often attacked non-Slavic-looking immigrants, many of whom were beaten to death. But these murders didn't gain much sympathy among ordinary Russians.

I tried to read up on Stas and the murder investigation, but it was too painful, too close to home. I sobbed over Mum's article dedicated to him:

> He lived his life without looking back. He enthusiastically took on any difficult case, especially when it was necessary to protect the innocent. He hated the violence that fascism represented for him. I only once saw Stanislav angry, when people spoke lightly about this in front of him. And then I understood why he so desperately

rushed into battle against those who do evil. To him they were all fascists.

The fight against the fascists, in whatever guise, whether it was a skinhead youth or a warmonger, was the meaning of Stanislav's life.

He was the second person I personally knew who had been murdered. Sometimes, in bed in the weeks that followed, I'd be overcome by a huge wave of anxiety. I'd gasp for air and place my hands on my stomach, which always mirrored how my mind was feeling. And the inevitable thought would cross my mind: *what if something happens to Mum?*

When I forced myself to imagine what it would be like if Mum was killed, it felt like torture. What would happen to me, to Memorial? To her computer, where she kept all her work? Sometimes I would have out-of-body experiences where I imagined being told that Mum was gone. The emptiness of everything. And there was always the laptop – her open laptop on the corner of a table. I watched these scenes as if I was a tiny fly in the corner of the room, part of a terrible timeline in another universe.

No, that's impossible. That won't happen, because I'm the narrator of my life, the pilot of my spaceship, and tragedies like that are not going to happen. Bad, inconvenient, character-building things will happen, but they will only strengthen me, not destroy my life. Mum will be fine; she is always fine in the end.

Besides, they wouldn't dare do anything to Mum. She's too high profile.

But Anya had been famous too.

To cope with the anxiety, I retreated into my bubble of books, films, music and Internet surfing. Reading up on Russian neo-Nazi groups, mindful of my altercation with the boy who had called me a terrorist, reminded me once again that I was living in the enemy camp with very few allies.

During this time, I watched *A Streetcar Named Desire* with Marlon Brando and Mum's favourite actress, Vivien Leigh. While I could hardly relate to the journey of an ageing Southern belle who goes through a series of traumatic events, the final line really stayed with me. At the very end, as Blanche DuBois is being led away by a doctor, she says: 'I have always depended on the kindness of strangers.' To me, it encapsulated how it felt being a Chechen in Russia. I was at the mercy of strangers who got to decide whether they saw me as a human being or a stereotype. I never knew which would win, ignorance or compassion. I could have toned down my 'Chechenness' – after all, I wore jeans and had a red streak in my hair – but I didn't want to hide my identity. I was proud of where I came from. However, when I started coming across certain online chat rooms, I was shocked by the virulent animosity between Chechens and Russians.

Access to the Internet was the saving grace of being in Yekaterinburg, because it had barely reached Chechnya. I spent hours surfing the Web, greedily devouring it like fast food. I registered on multiple social-media sites only to forget half my passwords. I discovered the nichest indie bands and downloaded their music from dodgy websites, flooding my aunt's computer with viruses. I obsessed over early YouTube classics, laughing at 'Charlie bit my finger' and the absurdity of 'Llamas with hats', and fawning over close-ups of Panic! At The Disco's frontman, Brendon Urie. I expanded my knowledge via Wikipedia, trapped in an article loop before I realised what it was. I even left comments! But I also discovered a darker side to the Internet: controversial discussions, uninformed opinions, conspiracy theories, creepy videos, pop-up ads – and, of course, racism. As I surfed through Chechen news and message boards, I came to know a different side to my homeland.

estemirova lana <angrygroznygirl@googlemail.com>   06.02.09
To: estemirova

Hi, Mum! I've been reading various chat rooms, where Russians are squabbling with Chechens. It's a nightmare. These bastards are slinging mud at us and invent stupid facts like how we sent Hitler a white stallion as a gift or about the genocide of Russians. And in response, Chechens write naive threats and mention every swear word they know. Because of the war, many of our people couldn't get a proper education, so they write nonsense. But the Russians are dumber. To be so zombified by the state media!! I hate this country that thinks it's the best! A country of evil, stupid, jealous cowards! This year that I'm spending here will be the longest time I've spent in Russia. Among thousands of Russians only a few are normal!!! At least no one is bothering me; I've only had a couple of run-ins. I'm reading books about Chechnya at the moment because I want to know the history of my people. It pains me to see what's happening in Chechnya, but I hope that our spirit hasn't been crushed completely. I know that it can't be independent yet, but it revolts me to think that we are attached to this disgusting stain on the world map.

As much as I criticise Chechnya, it's still the best place on earth for me and I really regret being born in Russia. Sorry that this email turned out so Russophobic :), but still.

Your loving Russophobe (who's v angry)

Natalia Estemirova <estemirova@gmail.com>   07.02.09
To: me

Poor Lanuska! It's so easy to find reasons for hatred. But you can't put everything in one pile. You're surrounded by Russian people now. And you must understand the most important thing: my sisters, their husbands, my brother, they could have easily told me I must sort my problems myself. But not only have they supported me, they are constantly helping out. And this is a form of protest against what the government is doing. In Russia, there was a wonderful period of perestroika, after a decades-long period of despotism and stagnation. During those times, anyone willing to protest was eradicated and exiled. In Moscow and St Petersburg, there's a youth movement that Stas was a part of. He and his friends really loved Russia. He had many reasons to hate it, but he chose laughter instead. Look up his website and see for yourself. Scrolling through these idiotic websites is unproductive. It's beneath our dignity. It's for soap opera lovers. You shouldn't waste your time and emotions on them. You've introduced yourself to this phenomenon and now it's time to quit. You have so many more interesting and important tasks to attend to. Please, be responsible with studying French. And don't foster negativity within yourself. It's time to get smarter. You'll damage yourself if you revel in it.

Something had started to shift when I thought of Chechnya. I was trying to understand if my nostalgia and homesickness was due to being away from my mother, or if it was me missing home. Deep down, I knew that romanticising Chechnya was a way of coping with having been torn from familiar surroundings. Some days, I resorted to old fantasies about the future of Grozny and my place in it: I pictured green parks, quirky architecture, cultural centres, museums and animal shelters. I wanted to make some of those dreams a reality, to be part of the much-needed change. But a little voice inside my head reminded me of the alienation that I'd often experienced in Grozny, with its soulless buildings and shiny new squares. The Chechnya I'd left was already changing, and not for the better. Spending two months in England had opened up new possibilities. What struck me most was how normal it all felt, living in that foreign country. As I stared out of the schoolroom window in Yekaterinburg, I tried on dreams as though they were dresses that I could put on and take off. One began to assert itself: returning to Grozny, living with Mum and our cat again, reuniting with my friends, becoming a journalist, riding around on a red Vespa, and writing exposés about the establishment; meeting The Boy, who would not only understand me and share my interests but also look like Brendon Urie. There were other dreams too, though: packing up suitcases and buying a carrier for Vanessa. Saying our goodbyes and moving to . . . England? France? Germany? In the end, it didn't really matter, we would learn to adapt. Home was where Mum was.

I missed her with every cell of my body but I also knew that I was growing up. Traces of an observant, independent thinker had started to appear, and for the first time Mum was not responsible for the person I was becoming.

I didn't need her as much as I had done; I had learnt to figure things out for myself. One of the threads that held us together had frayed. Mum noticed nothing, and how could I have explained in our few minutes on the phone? How could I put it in a clumsy email? I was changing, I was growing, and my mother, the closest person in the world to me, was thousands of miles away. With this feeling of loss came another realisation: if I can grow so much so fast with Mum not around, then perhaps I can grow up entirely away from her. I was scared that we'd lose our bond if we spent much more time apart. I decided to write Mum an email. I must have deleted it afterwards, because I have only this confused remnant:

> Mum, if you don't have time for skype or something else, whenever I call you, you're busy and you call me very late, when everyone's home and it's too cold to go out on the balcony. Call me once a week. Or don't call me at all, until I go back. Then all problems will resolve themselves and you won't have to talk to me because the rest of the stuff that I . . .

After I pressed send, I began pacing the room, unable to focus. For the first time I had said what was truly on my mind. There was no reply, and after several hours I stopped frantically checking my inbox. Then Mum called. Her voice sounded muffled.
'I don't know where to start,' she said. 'You broke my heart.'
I could barely breathe.
'Did your Auntie Sveta tell you to write that email?'
'No.'
'So, it was your own initiative to write those hurtful words and to shame me like that?'
I didn't reply.
'Do you think it's easy for me?' Mum asked quietly. With that my anger and hurt evaporated. Mum sounded subdued as never before. I had defeated her. But there was no pleasure in it. All I wanted was to cry on her shoulder.
'I'm so sorry,' I whispered through tears.
In the end, we agreed never to talk about it again. I realised that Mum wasn't ready to have a frank conversation about how complicated, hurtful and plainly absurd our lives were. There was only ever one winner in arguments with my mother. The best policy in this case was to continue ignoring the subject altogether. She never admitted fault and she always demanded an apology. Yet, I learnt to see past her stubbornness. Certain signs – the tone of her voice, the sequence of accusations and criticism, her behaviour after fights – demonstrated how she really felt. Behind her defensiveness, I saw someone overwhelmed with guilt, someone who struggled to express emotion.

Admitting guilt, apologising, would have placed us on the same level – as friends, perhaps. But in my mother's mind, she couldn't be my friend – she was my protector.

In the end, the focus of my anger returned to the circumstances that forced Mum, time and again, to send me away. When the hurt faded, I saw the real perpetrators – Yeltsin, Putin, Kadyrov, the war, law enforcement, the kidnappers, the murderers and all the bastards who tried to silence those telling the truth. Angry at the circumstances that drove us apart, I was sometimes also resentful that Mum's colleagues didn't make the same sacrifices (or so I then believed). These thoughts manifested as querulous questions.

'How come Mum is the one taking the hit all the time?'

'How come so-and-so's family is unseparated, unbroken?'

'How come we don't get to have a normal life, while a lot of Mum's friends and colleagues do?'

I was ashamed of that voice in my head. I had always been my mother's greatest champion. I looked out for her when she, as people on missions often do, forgot to look out for herself. Whenever she won an award or received recognition, I was happy. But it was always obvious that she should receive all the honours and medals because She's-Doing-a-Dangerous-and-Thankless-Job-and-She's-the-Best-at-It.

'There are no winners in this, Lanuska,' Mum would laugh. 'We all work as a team; everyone has a part to play. It's very destructive when in our line of work people become self-obsessed performers. That defeats the purpose!'

'Yeah, but you ARE the best.'

Mum came for me on 15 June and we went back to Chechnya. For how long remained to be seen.

Walking into our flat, I was struck by the familiar feeling of unfamiliarity: after nearly a year, I was a guest in my own home. The first thing I noticed was the new doors to the living room; they were a beautiful rosewood colour, with frosted glass panes.

'Ready?' Mum asked, placing her hands on the handles. 'Surprise!'

The doors opened in a swift motion. I gasped. For years, this room had been a renovation project that we could never finish. The sage-coloured gold pattern wallpaper was still there, but somehow it looked new. The corner by the window was now occupied by a large L-shaped couch – an unbelievable couch, the queen of all couches: deep, comfy, the perfect balance between softness and firmness, with plenty of storage room beneath. There was even a matching coffee table that opened like a chest.

'We'll change the curtains and put in a TV soon,' Mum said, almost apologetically. Beyond the doorway, a tall, dark-brown bookcase now stretched from one corner of the room to the other. It was spotless and smooth to the touch. Some of the shelves had doors, others were exposed. The book collection seemed entirely new – I recognised none of the titles, and some were in English. On a lower shelf, I noticed a bowl of pinecones. Where had she got them? I picked one up, almost in disbelief. I turned around with a cone in my hand and Mum was smiling at me. We had dreamt about this for so long, discussing the imaginary curtains, taking notes from design programmes, making endless sketches. Now, here it was: our beautiful living room.

On one of the top shelves, I noticed the familiar flutes with their pattern of forget-me-nots. Beside them were two unframed pictures propped on the shelves, one with flowers and the other a small painting in earth colours, depicting a traditional Chechen tower against a backdrop of light-grey mountains. Staring in disbelief, my mind scrambled through memories to locate it. I hadn't seen that painting for ten years. I'd been five years old when it hung above my bed in our tiny studio flat.

'I thought we'd lost it during the war,' I whispered. How had I not seen it since? I used to know the location of every object in our home better than my mother. From time to time, I would meticulously reorganise all our files and photographs and check the contents of the boxes and suitcases hidden out of sight. I would arrange photos in albums or try on Mum's old clothes, and pore over documents and telegrams. Never had I come across this painting.

'I'd been keeping it somewhere safe,' Mum smiled. 'I wanted to take it out when this place was ready.'

I smiled. The picture made me feel as if everything was going to be all right.

And so we settled back into our old lives, with one or two differences. One evening, for instance, Mum summoned me to the kitchen and pointed to a catalogue on the table. 'Can you help me out?' she asked, looking at an open page. 'I can't decide which dress to order.' Mum rarely asked my advice on clothes. There was something official about her request, as if she was appointing me to a new role. I looked at the rather boring dresses and pointed to a cream-coloured one. 'This one. I think it will go with a lot of stuff and you look good in that colour.'

We had the whole summer ahead of us to decide what to do with our lives.

10

15 July 2009

'Lana, where's my perfume?' I hear Mum's voice. Squinting against the bright morning sun streaming in through the window, I am too sleepy to see her properly. The blinding light contours her silhouette.

'It's there, in the bottom drawer,' I mumble before going back to sleep. Mum rustles around in the cupboard for a few more moments, and then I hear the sound of a closing door.

Or did she ask me to lock it instead? Did she say something about my French class? Did she ask me to buy bread?

I guess it doesn't matter anymore. Ten years ago, I could recall that day minute by minute, but now the details are fading.

'Where's my perfume?' Quick words with a hint of reproach. I had my own way of putting things in order, unlike Mum. I had a system. Maybe if I'd left that goddamn perfume where it was, she would have said something else, in a different tone of voice.

'Where's my perfume?' were the last words I ever heard from my mother. She left, trailing the scent of Nina Ricci's Premier Jour behind her, and I never saw her alive again.

Why did she seem to glow so much in the final days of her life? Was there a hidden meaning, or am I grasping for signs?

Every evening, when I heard her key turn in the lock, I left whatever I was doing and greeted her in the corridor. I would notice it as she stepped towards the kitchen – her skin shimmering in the rays of the setting sun, as if lit up from inside. Tiny golden sparkles in her chestnut hair, while around her, specks of dust danced in the air, adding more magic to the moment.

'Mum,' I gasped. 'You're all . . . *glowing*!'

'Oh, stop it, Lanuska,' she replied, embarrassed. I remember her hesitant smile, a touch of melancholy on her face caused by constant tiredness. How beautiful she was!

I wake with my eight o'clock alarm and run through the day's schedule in my head. Breakfast. Clean the flat a bit. French class. Later, I would need to pack a bag and head for the Memorial offices – the plan was for Mum to meet me there and together we'd go to the village where I would spend a week with relatives. *Okay, time to get moving!*

I loved my French classes. My teacher, beautiful, slender, and in her mid-thirties, had been recommended by a friend. She seemed like a real French woman, although she was as Chechen as can be. I liked her so much that I gave her a copy of my favourite book, a collection of fairy tales by Eleanor Farjeon. She always reminded me of one of those characters – mysterious, dreamy and unique. After the hour and a half class I would stay behind to chat about life – I always got on best with grown-ups. *I should really be leaving soon!*

I text Mum to ask if she is at Memorial. No reply. I text her second phone, a cheap Nokia. *Why is she always so hard to reach?*

Back home, I ransack my wardrobe, choosing clothes to pack for the week. After a lot of thought, I settle on an outfit I hate – a white dress with a blue and pink check pattern and green and pink flats – which makes me look like a little girl. In Yekaterinburg, I can wear jeans every day, but fifteen is too old to wear them at home. My Chechnya-appropriate wardrobe is sparse, filled with skirts and dresses that are getting too short and betray me by exposing the two centimetres of flesh above my knees, skin I shouldn't be showing at my age.

Still no reply. I call Mum again, but she's not picking up. I try her second phone again, with the same result. *Why does she always do this? She was the one who asked me to call . . .* I try again and again. *Fine. I guess I'll just head over to the office and wait there.* It was always nice to catch up with her colleagues anyway.

I take a bus to the city centre, trying to get through to Mum every fifteen minutes. *Strange. Neither phone is working now.* My frustration

15 JULY 2009

grows – she had better come to Memorial soon, or she might delay our trip for another day. I get off the bus. A two-minute walk under a merciless midday sun and I'm at Memorial.

Most of her colleagues are there, but Mum is nowhere to be seen. 'Do you know when she is coming back?' 'Have you seen her today?' Everyone seems a little worried although they're trying their best to conceal it. No one can reach Mum, and both her phones are unavailable. Something must have happened. She's probably in some official's office, unable to charge them. Maybe she's been detained. These things happen to Mum, and she'll return with a good story.

The clock is ticking: 3 p.m., 4 p.m., 5 . . .

More and more people arrive at Memorial, many of whom I don't know. Everyone reassures me: nothing bad has happened; your mother will be fine. *Why tell me this? Of course, she'll be fine, she's Mum! Whatever life throws at her, Mum bounces back.* I just hope she's back today.

Someone suggests I stay with one of Mum's colleagues, Taisa, for the night. But what about our cat? Mum was meant to drop me off and come back to the flat. Who will feed her? Great: someone tells me that the cat has been sorted. I'll go to Taisa's, and Mum will undoubtedly come back during the night. *She better come and get me straight away – I want to hear what happened.*

Taisa's family is lovely. They make me food and we start watching *Lord of the Rings*. 'Any news, Taisa?' I ask every fifteen minutes. There isn't. She'll tell me if there is.

I try Mum's phones again, and again no answer. *What the hell is going on?* If she's been detained then surely they would let her call, to let her family know that she's safe. *It's okay. It's okay. It's okay.* I close my eyes and trace her number with a finger on my right arm – I know it by heart. *Eight nine two eight seven eight six four seven five one. Eight nine two eight seven eight six four seven five one. Eight nine two eight sev . . .*

I open the message folder, scrolling through endless texts. 'WHERE ARE YOU???' 'WHY ARENT YOU ANSWERING??' 'CALL ME BACK!!!'

With shaking fingers, I type: 'PLEASE, LIVE!'

'Taisa, is there any news?'

There is still no news.

I try to eat the dinner that Taisa's mum has prepared for me. It's delicious, but I struggle to swallow. Anxiety is taking up all the space in my stomach. Bite after bite, I try to calm myself. *It's okay. She'll come back. No news is good news. Just watch 'Lord of the Rings', relax.* I remember when I watched the film with Mum a few years back, she'd had a terrible migraine and was unable to move. At one point, when Frodo was screaming with pain, weighed down by the ring, Mum moaned: 'Frodo, I understand how you feel.' I would have done anything to take that pain away from her, feeling silly and helpless before her suffering.

'Can we please turn the movie off? I'm sorry, it's stressing me out.' Taisa switches it off instantly. They're so nice, and I'm grateful for their hospitality. They're feeling sorry for me, but there's no need; Mum will come for me soon. *It's okay.*

And then I receive a call.

I hear that wretched woman crying on the other end of the line. Mum used to work with her, but we were never close. How did she even get my number?

'Lana . . .' she sobs. 'How . . . how *are* you?'

'Why are you crying?'

'Didn't they tell you? Don't you know?'

'Know what?'

'Your mother is gone. She's been killed.'

'SHUT UP! SHUT UP! IT'S NOT TRUE!'

'Oh, Lana.'

'SHUT UP! AND NEVER EVER CALL ME AGAIN!'

Hurling my phone at the wall, I run to the bathroom and vomit in the sink. *NO NO NO! This cannot be! This cannot be! No!*

'What did she say?' Taisa looks so scared. 'No, don't listen to that stupid woman. She doesn't know what she's talking about.'

Suddenly the room starts to fade. All turns to black. As if through fog, I hear the screams of Taisa's mother.

I wake up on the couch. It turns out I fainted. I've never fainted in my life. I sit up and remember – Mum has been killed. But it's not true. *What if it is? No no no no no!* This is my nightmare come true.

15 JULY 2009

So many times I've woken in a cold sweat; so many times I've imagined someone saying those words to me. *So many times, I feared for your life, Mum; so many times I prayed to God, asking him to protect you. This cannot be.* The most bizarre thoughts come into my head, terribly practical ones.

'What's going to happen to me now?' I ask Taisa numbly, looking through her. 'Where am I going to live? What's going to happen to my cat? What about Mum's laptop?' For some reason, whenever I'd imagined this scenario, I had always thought about Mum's stuff – her electronics, her clothes, her documents. Their fate worried me almost as much as my own, as if they would be orphaned, just like me.

'Natasha is going to come back,' Taisa tries to reassure me, but I don't hear any confidence in her voice. I feel sorry for her – she barely knows me. But it's okay. 'Maybe she heard it wrong. Mum will come back tomorrow.'

'I beg you, Taisa, for the love of God, don't talk to anyone. Don't pick up the phone, don't call anyone. Because you won't be able to hide it and I'll KNOW.'

'Lana, of course! Whatever you want!'

'Don't switch on the news. Don't talk to your neighbours.'

'I won't, I promise.'

We sit together in silence, for how long I don't know. Later, someone looks in. I hear voices in the corridor.

'Who is it? What do they want? Please, tell them to go!' I yell.

'It's nothing, Lanochka, it's nothing. Let's put you to bed, okay? Tomorrow we'll go to Memorial and your mother will be waiting there. And we'll laugh about it!'

Oh, but she won't . . . I lie in bed next to Taisa. *Music, I need to listen to some music. What's the most uplifting track that I have?*

Hey now now, they'll find you when you're sleeping, now now
Mum is dead.
They'll reach in and grab what you're dreamin', now now
Mum is dead.
Hey now now, the smallest things are crushing me now
MUM IS DEAD.
The crush, crush, crush is so comforting now

No. I can't listen to this.
I fall asleep.

Why is there a crowd outside Memorial? Hundreds of people are blocking the pavement, some crying. *Who are they?* We go up the stairs. 'That's her daughter,' I hear someone say behind me. A hand touches my shoulder. *Leave me alone . . .* The office is packed with people, but as soon as I enter there's silence. Everyone looks at me. They must think that Mum is dead too. *But no, this cannot be. I need to call my aunts and reassure them.* Pushing everyone away, I run towards the landline in the kitchen. I dial my aunt Lena's number and wait for her to pick up. 'Hello, Auntie?' I hear a cry. 'Don't believe what they're saying, Mum is not dead. Don't believe them.' Then suddenly, as I scream down the phone, as I look at the pale, petrified faces around me, faces that I've known since I was little, faces that I love, I understand. Mum is dead. In the middle of the crowd, I see Shakhman, and he calls to me.

He takes me to an empty room and shuts the door behind us.

'Lana,' he says gently.

Oh, God, she's really dead, isn't she . . .

'Lana, I'm so sorry. Your mother has been killed.'

He goes on about Allah, saying something about heaven and martyrdom. I raise my hand and stop him.

'Tell me one thing, Shakhman. And I need you to be honest with me. Did they rape her?'

'No, no, no. They didn't.'

'Did she suffer? Was it quick? Did she suffer?'

'We've been told that she was shot several times, in her head. She died instantly.'

'That's all I need to know, thank you.'

My soul has left my body, leaving an empty shell to deal with what comes next. Or so it seems. I don't cry. I go to the room full of people and call over a few of Mum's colleagues.

'Please go to the market,' I ask. 'Buy me a long skirt and a dark headscarf. I can't be wearing this dress.' They leave promptly.

Talking, talking, everyone around me is talking. I sit there and wait for the funeral attire, trying to cover up my wobbly, vulnerable knees. Mum was killed yesterday, and she will be buried today. Her cousins are on their way to pick me up and take me to Alkhazur village. I'm acutely aware of the fact that, right before my eyes, my life has been reduced to a map of destinations and actions, point A to point B. Thinking about anything is not just painful, it's impossible.

The women are back with a bag of clothes. An ankle-length navy skirt, a stripy T-shirt and a plain black scarf – a total mismatch, but that will do. Mum's cousins have arrived and are escorting me through the crowd towards the door. Everyone steps aside to let us pass. When we come out onto the porch, I see hundreds of people gathered outside and that overwhelms me. I feel weak and start to faint again. Kind, strong hands catch and support me as I go down the steps. We get in the car and head towards Alkhazur in silence. Somewhere behind me, my mother's body is being carried to a van and taken through the streets of Grozny. Slowly the van moves along Putin's Avenue, the one that used to be called Victory Avenue, the one that Mum refused to walk along. Hundreds of people follow it, sobbing, weeping.

He killed her! I scream inside. *He killed her, he killed her, he killed her, he killed her.*

He killed her.

We are waiting for her body to arrive. According to Chechen tradition, a person must be buried on the day of their death, but we have to wait until the next day. The men separate themselves from the women, performing the mystic *zikr* dance ritual.

I sit in a large semicircle of women and try to utter a cry. Each woman entering the yard comes up to me and joins the crying circle, adding their lamentations to the chorus of wails.

In a moment of surreal detachment, the thought occurs to me: *a princess of sorrow, that's what I am.* With a black headscarf for a crown. Everyone treating me like royalty. 'That's the daughter, that's the daughter, that's the daughter.' I feel numb.

They come up to me, these unfamiliar women, and look me in the eye as if they've known me forever. Men cry. I've never seen so many men cry.

Her body arrives in a white minibus. According to custom, she is to be washed by the women. 'You can go and look at your mum,' someone whispers.

No.

I will not look at my mother's dead body. I don't want my last memory of her to be that. I won't let them do that to me.

This is the longest day of my life.

Her friends and colleagues keep arriving, and I feel crazed. Every person we have known, from every walk of life, appears in that courtyard in a grim procession. At the table, I am served by my family. They have killed several rams, spilling blood on the tiles. The amount of attention I am getting makes me uncomfortable; I feel unworthy. But I greet everyone, thank them for coming.

'Say goodbye to your mother,' I hear a voice say from somewhere behind me. And then Mum emerges from the shade into the sunlight, carried by six men. I can see the outline of her body, wrapped in a thick green blanket with beige and pink flowers. *Is this really happening now, or did it happen a hundred years ago?* I am trying and failing to grasp that this is the last time I will see my mother. I just need some time to let it sink in. But in an instant, the six men are taking her away. A flash – that's all it was. As she flew past me – for the last time – I thought I saw something. It will stay with me forever. Through the fabric, I saw her clenched fists. *Could they not have unclenched her fists? Was she struggling so hard when they were about to shoot her, that she put all her strength and will into her fists?* My own fingers begin to clench, overgrown nails digging into my palms.

There is a huge crowd of women behind me, some holding my arms, supporting and patting me from all sides. Slowly, the men take my mother through the gate. The women are wailing, like an orchestra without a conductor. I follow them as if in a dream. The sun is shining, stupidly, and birds keep chirping away, as if they don't know that Mum is being taken away.

As I walk out of the gate, I see a yellow mini-van. Somebody holds me tight. 'You cannot go with them.' *I know that. You don't have to tell me that I am not allowed to watch my mother's burial because I'm a woman.* I can't walk any further. Silently, the men approach it with their precious cargo. In a few seconds, the green blanket disappears in the belly of the vehicle. My mother is gone forever.

The engine starts.

'Mama!'

15 JULY 2009

The car slowly begins moving down the street.

'MAMA!'

The car disappears behind the corner and the women, kind, sympathetic and cruel, cling to me. God forbid I were to run after the van or collapse on the ground.

'MAMA . . . MAMAAAAAAA . . .'

I scream and cry, my whole being dissolving in a primal, desperate wail. *I will never ever in this life see Mum again.* I collapse sideways, a sea of women's hands gently preventing me from falling.

What's the point of living now?

After locking the door behind her, Mum took the stairs. The lift was broken as usual. What was going through her mind? Perhaps she was listing all the things on her busy schedule. She could never have imagined this would be the last time she would go down those steps.

As Mum stepped into the sunlit street and headed towards the bus stop, four men appeared, grabbed her and started dragging her towards a white car.

'I AM BEING KIDNAPPED!' she screamed at the surrounding tower blocks, hoping someone would hear. There was no way on earth I could have heard her, even if I were awake – our windows faced the other way. Someone did, though, but they did nothing: they were too scared to knock on my door and tell me. Everybody knew where we lived.

Mum fought. She clawed at the men, wriggled and writhed, broke their skin. Their DNA was later found under her nails.

They shoved her in the car and drove towards Ingushetia. I wonder what went through her mind in those moments. Did she beg them for her life? Perhaps she was just relieved that it was her and not me.

Two hours later, once the white VAZ-2107 crossed the border into Ingushetia, the car stopped. They dragged my mother out on the dusty side road and shot her five times – in the chest and in the head.

11

The Balcony
July 2009–February 2010

In late February 2010, just before Mum's birthday, I stood on the eighth-floor balcony outside my Auntie's flat contemplating the efficacy of hitting the ground from that height.

Seven months had passed since her murder. The temptation came whenever I was anywhere high, alone. My diary entries were becoming desperate: 'I think that what I'm living right now is not a life. It's an excuse, a facade. A real life is happening somewhere deep inside me, among ruins and terrible grief that is trying to rise to the surface . . .'

On that cold winter night, I climbed over the balcony railing. I held on with both hands behind my back and arched my chest forward into empty space. The ground seemed far, far away. I was waiting for my survival instinct to kick in, but my body was unafraid. I let go with one hand and my body started to swing. Wind rushed in my ears. There was no one below, no one to stop me, no one to be traumatised by the sight of a fifteen-year-old girl hitting the ground.

The weeks following Mum's funeral were a blur. In the first few days, a river of mourners flowed to Detsi Chovka's house in Alkhazur village. There was always a ram in the backyard tied to a tree, ready to be slaughtered for a new group of guests. At night, I slept in the same room as my female cousins, sharing mattresses on the floor. The warmth and closeness of their bodies was reassuring, and allowed me to sleep. Several days later, my classmates and form teacher came to pay their respects. I accompanied different groups of guests to my mother's grave, which didn't have a tombstone yet. She was buried close to her father, Hussein.

In my dreams, Mum was alive. She seemed so real that I could feel the warmth of her skin when I touched her elbow. We'd be pottering about the flat or chatting in a brightly lit kitchen. It was always sunrise or sunset, and I could never see her clearly. But I could hear her voice, her laughter.

And then, I would wake.

Those first two seconds of disorientation were precious because in them she was still alive, until reality pierced me like a knife. *Mum is gone. Mum has been murdered.* My mind had lost its bearings, everything was upside down. Every night, I lived a normal life only to wake in a nightmare. I couldn't think about her at first, nor look at her photographs. My thoughts often turned to Greek heroes and villains doomed to excruciating fates: Prometheus chained to his mountain; Tantalus standing in a pool of water, unable to drink; Sisyphus pushing his boulder. And there I too was trapped in my own personal hell, day after day. I didn't know what to do with the abundance of grief and so I quickly taught myself how to bury it deep inside and to carry on.

Less than a month later, my Uncle Viskhan, Detsi Chovka's oldest son, came to the house to tell me that we had to go to the police station. A small kind-eyed man, he was always by my side in those days, guarding my interests and helping with bureaucracy. I changed into a long skirt, tied on a dark headscarf and off we went to Grozny.

At the police station close to our flat, I was introduced to the chief investigator, Igor Sobol. A tired-looking man with a professionally indifferent manner, Sobol was in charge of my mother's murder investigation. In those first weeks, the Russian authorities were under a lot of international pressure to bring the perpetrators to justice because of the high-profile nature of Mum's murder. President Dmitri Medvedev had promised the German chancellor Angela Merkel he would find the killers. But I didn't know that then. Wrapped in my village bubble, I didn't have access to the Internet and ignored the news on TV, only asking Mum's colleagues for updates.

Sobol asked about Mum's last day. A distrust of Russian law enforcement rose within me, but I decided to be polite, if I could . . .

It struck me then that I had been the last friendly person to see her alive. There was comfort in that. She was the first person I'd ever met and mine was the last friendly face that she'd seen. I composed myself and gave the investigator a mechanical minute-by-minute account of my mother's last day. *Don't you dare cry*, I thought to myself, and I didn't.

'One final thing,' Sobol added when we were done. 'We checked your mother's bank account and it is completely empty. Is there any chance someone could have broken into it?'

'No. The moment Mum was paid, she withdrew the money from the bank account in Ingushetia and handed most of it to those in need. We were never rich.'

I remembered the last time Mum and I went to a bank, a few weeks before her murder. There were still no banks in Chechnya, so she had to make the two-hour journey to Ingushetia to collect her salary every month. She had been wearing a belted cream top, a safety pin drawing its V-neck closer to make it more Chechnya-appropriate. After the bank, Mum and I boarded a crowded minibus back to Grozny, taking seats by an open window. Lulled by the sound of her making work calls, I placed my head on her shoulder and fell asleep. It was both comforting and exciting having her close after all those months apart. When I woke, I noticed an imprint of the beige foundation I had started to use on her left sleeve. I didn't tell her.

'Anything else you remember? Did she behave any differently that morning? Was she nervous?'

'No. It was an ordinary morning. She was supposed to meet me at the Memorial office later and take me to the village.'

To me, the investigation was like a children's play in which everyone had been given roles: Serious Investigator, Honest Policeman, Forensic Expert. It was just a performance, a pretence that something was being done. *If they don't make arrests in the first month, they will never arrest anyone*, I remember thinking back then, and I was right. So long as Ramzan Kadyrov remained Chechnya's ruler, there was no chance of justice: it was not in his interests or in the interests of the Kremlin. Kadyrov was involved, I knew it in my heart. By choosing not to have faith in the Russian justice system from the beginning, I saved myself disappointment but not heartache. And certainly not anger.

Auntie Sveta – so small in her modest black kerchief, dwarfed by the loud voices and alien traditions of Chechnya – was determined to take me back to Yekaterinburg. 'Natasha always said ... should anything happen to her, Lana must live with me. At least, until she finishes school,' she insisted in her quiet, determined way, pushing aside all other well-meaning but poorly thought through offers to adopt me.

I stayed in the village for the customary forty days after the funeral, waiting for the memorial event that marks the end of mourning. In Chechnya, those forty days are considered an important period during which the soul is still on Earth. At the end of August, Auntie Sveta took me back to Yekaterinburg. I had one final year of school, and then – who knew where I'd go. Somewhere far, far away from Russia. When she came for me, she brought along Sasha, my Uncle Andrey and Baba Klava. I took all of them to the cemetery, having memorised the way through the maze of near-identical graves. I silently pointed at the dark-brown mound, and Baba let out a heart-wrenching wail.

'Natashenka, why did you abandon us?' she cried. 'Those murderers, those villains have taken you! So young, so young ...'

She gripped my arm tightly with three splayed fingers, like a bird caught in a storm.

'Orphan, my orphan, no mother, no father ...' I heard her say through sobs, an eerie echo from all those years ago in Kamyshlov.

I stood next to her, motionless, not a tear in my eye because by then I'd no more to shed. At last, Baba snapped out of her state and asked to be taken to her run-away husband's grave. I stayed behind.

When we returned to Yekaterinburg a few days later, Auntie Sveta did everything to make me feel at home. She took me shopping. She allowed me to eat as much junk food as I wanted and didn't comment when I skipped science classes. We suffered together, in silence. Sometimes my grief draped me like a heavy ceremonial gown. There I was, the little queen of sorrow, in the middle of an absurd ritual of living on after everything was taken from me. They – Mum's friends, her colleagues and relatives – were all dealing with their own grief, but mine was the greatest. It was too cinematic. I squirmed in disgust, as if feeling sorry for myself was tasteless. Some days I wanted to leave it all behind. Everyone would keep looking at me, thinking I was there, and I would be sitting in a corner, present but absent, as though I were a single-celled organism with no feelings, no pain.

On the surface, I seemed to be coping. I laughed and made jokes, and got a terrible haircut with a blood-red, sideways fringe. My aunt enrolled me in a new, more accepting school. I even made friends and began to feel like an old version of myself. But at night I screamed into my pillow and cried until my eyes hurt. The past was unthinkable, the present was agonising and the future ... uncertain, distant and far too much work. Worst of all was the loneliness. I was getting used to it, but it was a chronic illness that flared up often, and at night, I succumbed. I was a distant planet without a satellite or signs of habitation, far away from the sun. I had no one to talk to because I didn't want to be a burden. And what was there to say? Some people called me, but rarely the ones I wanted to speak to. I would pick up and hear pained breathing on the other end.

'Hello? Please speak up!' I would ask in frustration.

'How are you holding up, Lana?' a voice would ask, and then the heaving breaths would resume. As soon as I started to speak, the voice would break into a cry.

'I'm sorry, I just can't, Lana. It's so tragic, I can't believe Natasha is no more.' I never knew how to respond.

'Do you need anything? Absolutely anything?' the voices would ask. I wanted to say, 'I need you to stop calling me all the time and offloading your grief onto me. I have enough to deal with as it is,' but was too polite to do so. I felt sorry for those voices. After a while, I stopped answering calls.

For months, the sound of a vibrating phone triggered panic in me. Reminded of *that* phone call, my muscles tensed, my forehead broke into a sweat and I would taste acid in my mouth. Sometimes my mind ambushed me with images of my mother being dragged into that white Lada, her resisting and screaming. There was no escape from them because whenever I shut my eyes, the scenes only became more vivid. I'd read so many accounts of torture by the age of fifteen, but back then I would have welcomed beatings and electric shocks over those visions of my mother's murder. And the sickest part was, they didn't kill her on the spot, like Anya and Stas, but kidnapped her first. They subjected her to the worst imaginable anguish for several hours. For several hours, she didn't know whether she would live or die. And then, they took her to her execution site and shot her like an animal. The thought of her in that car was so unbearable that I wanted to howl until my voice was hoarse. It made me want to crawl out of my skin. I didn't dare to ask God to reverse what had been done, but I would have given anything for my mother to have had a quick death right outside our flat. I would have taken the trauma of finding her first, of holding her lifeless body in my arms and wiping the blood off her head with the palm of my hand, just so she wouldn't be dragged into that car.

By February, it was all getting too overwhelming. The flashbacks, the numbness, the disorientation, the loneliness. The duality of my existence: a happy-go-lucky but stroppy teenager by day, a broken shard of a human by night. I wanted it all to end. I knew that if I waited long enough, the pain would subside and someday I might even, possibly, maybe, be happy again. But the road was so long; I was already so exhausted. And so, I found myself climbing over the balcony railing of the eighth floor. As I was swinging with one hand above the snow-covered asphalt, I felt almost liberated. Then, a violent gust hit my face.

But there is a hell, I suddenly thought. *If I do this, I will not end up in the same place as Mum.*

Suddenly the wind seemed fierce and cold and the fear returned. I became very aware of the danger I was in and my heart dropped. Snapping out of my reverie, I clutched the railings with both hands and climbed back to the safety of the balcony, heart pounding in my ears. My legs trembled. I leaned back on the wall and slowly slid down to the tiled floor. *What has just happened?* I slapped myself as hard as I could. As I massaged my burning cheek, tears streamed down my face. I felt a powerful surge of adrenaline pulsating like electricity through me. I hated myself for this moment of weakness, for my cowardice. For being so close to giving up the greatest gift that my mother had given me. *I'm alive! I'm alive! I'm alive! I will live to spite them all, I will live for both of us.*

12

The Investigation

It was around this time that my mother's murder investigation stalled and turned into a mockery of justice. Had it not been for the tireless efforts of her friends and colleagues, we would never have known what actually happened. Despite very few resources and limited access to the case files, they conducted their own investigation, for which I will be forever grateful.

At first, the state prosecutors considered four potential motives of the murder:

1. In response to her professional activities,
2. To discredit the Chechen authorities,
3. Due to personal hostile relations,
4. Murdered by members of the law enforcement agencies of the Chechen republic in relation to her publicising instances of human rights violations.

As Oleg Orlov from Memorial repeatedly pointed out, the first and the last theory were basically the same.

It was obvious that Mum had been killed because of her work, especially considering the final cases she was involved in, which mostly had one thing in common – the crimes had been committed by a group of policemen from the Kurchaloi District department of the Interior of Chechnya – Kurchaloi ROVD. The ROVD was no ordinary place; Kurchaloi is where Ramzan Kadyrov's fortified homestead of Tsentoroi is situated. The Kadyrovites from the ROVD were given 'special tasks' related to counterterrorism activities and were notorious for their brutality. They detained, tortured and killed hundreds of people; many victims disappeared and never returned.

Of all the 'red lines' my mother crossed, exposing their crimes was her most dangerous act. And she had been working on more than one case at once.

First, she had been investigating the abduction of Maskhud Abdulayev, the twenty-two-year-old son of Chechen rebel leader Supyan Abdulayev. Maskhud had been kidnapped as he landed at one of Moscow's airports. Shortly afterwards he appeared on Chechen State TV announcing he had come to Chechnya for a visit and was having a good time. But it was clear to human rights activists that he was being held hostage to draw his father out of hiding. Mum had filed a case at the Chechen prosecutor's office about his disappearance just a day before her murder.

Second was the kidnapping of four men accused of being linked to rebel militias. One of the parents of the disappeared boys had been brave enough to speak to Memorial and Mum had taken on the case, hoping their son – Nozha Dzhabikhadzhiev – might still be alive. The boy's father was then threatened by the ROVD who told him that unless he withdrew his missing person's report they would send him back his son's body. Despite following orders, he never heard from his son again.

Third was the dramatic kidnapping on 28 June of two men: Apti Zaynalov, who had been accused in the past of involvement in rebel groups, and Zelimkhan Khadjiev, who just happened to be driving Apti in a taxi when they came for him. Their parents had gone to Memorial for help, and Mum had persuaded them to file a report at the prosecutor's office. Just as they were leaving the office, Apti's mum found out that her son had been admitted to a local hospital with a serious head injury and signs of torture. She and Mum rushed there, arriving just in time to see him bundled into another car and driven away – kidnapped right before their eyes. They took down the car details and rushed back to the prosecutor's office, but officials there refused to do anything about it. Apti was never heard from again.

Fourth, and most public and provocative of all, was an interview Mum had given to the media outlet *Caucasian Knot* on 9 July 2009, concerning the public execution of a man accused of giving food to the rebels in the village of Akhinchu-Barzoi. Two days before that, Rizvan Albekov and his seventeen-year-old son, Aziz, had been kidnapped by the Kurchaloi ROVD. A few hours later the ROVD policemen returned to the village where the father and son had been taken and stopped their car in the middle of the square. They dragged the barely dressed and badly beaten Rizvan from the car and accused him, in front of the assembled villagers, of giving sheep to the rebels, which he repeatedly denied, before shooting him in the head. 'This is what will happen to anyone who helps the rebels,' was the message.

Threatened by the head of Kurchaloi ROVD, Rizvan's relatives were forced to publicly declare that he had died of a stroke, but Memorial was already on the case. Mum was working to try and locate Aziz, Rizvan's teenage son who was still missing. In her interview with *Caucasian Knot*, she hoped to draw attention to the case and secure his release. The following day, 10 July, her colleagues from Memorial were summoned to the office of Chechnya's human rights commissioner, Nurdi Nukhazhiev. News of the public execution emerging had enraged Kadyrov. Believing that everyone had a master, he ordered Nukhazhiev to reel in the human rights activists.

Visibly shaking as he relayed the message to Mum's colleagues Svetlana Gannushkina and head of the Grozny Memorial office, Shakhman Akbulatov, Nukhazhiev suggested that Mum should be on her guard. He told them that if Anna Politkovskaya had been more careful, she would still be alive to carry on her work.

The message was clear, and it was decided that Mum should leave Chechnya as soon as possible. 'I just need one week to sort everything out,' she reassured colleagues, but it was already too late. The truth was, after Mum's interview was published, an order was given and an invisible timer began counting down the days, hours and minutes to her murder.

Yet even in death, Mum continued saving lives. Following her murder, the taxi driver Zelimkhan was released, as was Maskhud, abducted at Moscow Airport to put pressure on his rebel father, and seventeen-year-old Aziz, whose father had been publicly executed less than a month before.

Any of these cases – and Mum's efficacy in pursuing them – was a viable motive for her murder. Kadyrov had ramped up his counter-terror campaign because it guaranteed continuous political and financial support from the Kremlin. In response, dozens of small-scale rebel attacks were carried out against Kadyrovites throughout 2009, but the Chechen authorities tried to block any information about them. Mum wrote about the increasingly sadistic methods that law enforcement used to punish anyone allegedly involved with the militants. The principle of collective responsibility impacted anybody even loosely connected with suspected rebels, resulting in the harassment, detention and enforced disappearance of distant relatives, neighbours and acquaintances. But the most 'innovative' tactic was the punitive house-burning. In Chechnya, home ownership is the foundation of the family. Traditionally, parents build homes for their first and middle sons so they can marry and have children of their own, while the youngest son inherits the family home. This is why the gutted and burnt-out homes of innocent people, brought to light by Mum, were such an affront to Chechens and why Mum increasingly drew the ire of the regime. She was becoming too loud, too inconvenient.

Kadyrov's regime broke every norm and honour code of Chechen society. Yet many of Mum's Moscow colleagues remained convinced that if anything were to happen to their Grozny counterparts, it would be the men who would be the primary targets. Back then, it was hard to foresee that the Kadyrovites would go so far as to execute a woman.

As for the official investigation into Mum's murder, many of her colleagues seemed to believe that in the first few months Igor Sobol and the Investigative Committee were genuinely making progress, even though the local authorities did everything they could to shield Chechen law enforcement from scrutiny. The investigators secured camera footage from the checkpoint 'Kavkaz' that captured the crossing of three white VAZ-2107 cars, which would make it relatively easy to trace the owners. According to the investigation, the assassins had planned to kill my mother and dispose of her body discreetly, so that the murder was never discovered, but on 15 July, because law enforcement was on high alert following the killing of a court bailiff, they instead shot her quickly and immediately left the crime scene. They didn't even bother clearing up the evidence. The only thing they took was Mum's work laptop.

THE INVESTIGATION

From the outset, the investigators failed to question eyewitnesses to Mum's kidnapping, citing the fact that people were too scared to talk. This was unsurprising since the witnesses weren't offered any state protection in return for their statements. Instead, it was Mum's friends and colleagues Katya Sokirianskaia, Tanya Lokshina and journalist Lena Milashina who managed to extract the truth from our terrified neighbours and then pass on the information to Sobol. Mum's colleagues shared everything they knew about her final cases with the police, as well as the potential involvement of Kurchaloi ROVD in her abduction. They were questioned again and again, and most questions seemed to relate to Mum's work and to Ramzan Kadyrov himself. But though Mum's last cases were crucial to establishing the murder motive and her link to any suspects, Sobol looked into them only superficially. His request for the exhumation of Rizvan Albekov's body was blocked by a court and he didn't probe any further. When Mum's colleagues came forward with their testimonies, the investigators advised them to be careful and warned that they were under surveillance. Just a month after the murder, one of Mum's colleagues had to flee Chechnya after being approached by Kurchaloi policemen driving the same car, a white VAZ-2107, that was used in the kidnapping of my mother. Their lives in constant danger, several Memorial employees from Chechnya were evacuated abroad.

Crucially, the Investigative Committee didn't arrange for the collection of DNA samples from Kurchaloi ROVD personnel. When Mum was being dragged into the car, she fought hard and scratched her abductors – at least three sources of foreign DNA were found underneath her nails and all over her clothes. These samples should have been used to either confirm or eliminate the suspects. But this wasn't done. Challenging Kadyrov's people was not worth the grief, whether you were a random witness or a high-profile government investigator. That's why in January 2010 a new official theory emerged, provided by the FSB – Mum was murdered by Chechen militants. Soon enough, this was accepted as the only theory by the state prosecution.

According to this story, the so-called Shalazhi Jamaat – a group of militants from the Chechen town of Shalazhi – had abducted and killed my mother in an act of revenge against a short Memorial article that mentioned eight people from Shalazhi who had gone to the woods. There was no way for the militants to know who from Memorial's sizeable staff of activists had written the unsigned article. Alkhazur Bashayev was the militant held responsible for her murder because he was apparently angry that his name was mentioned in the article. In January 2010, Chechen law enforcement searched Bashayev's house and discovered the gun that had killed Mum, as well as a fake police ID with Bashayev's photograph. A month later, the white VAZ-2107 used for the kidnapping was 'discovered' too, along with the silencer from the murder weapon. Conveniently enough, Bashayev couldn't speak for himself as he'd been eliminated during a counterterrorist operation a month earlier. He was merely a handy scapegoat.

Mum's colleagues set about proving this version of events to be untrue. Ballistic examinations unequivocally concluded that the silencer found in the car wasn't the one used for the murder. The forensics report showed that Bashayev's photograph, found in the fake police ID, was a botched Photoshopped image of his head on top of someone else's body, the photo having been taken from an FSB database. As for the vehicle used for the abduction, a detailed forensic analysis ruled that it was highly unlikely that it could have been this particular car. But the key piece of evidence that disproved Bashayev's involvement came from the independent investigation carried out by Mum's colleagues from Memorial, *Novaya Gazeta* and the International Federation for Human Rights (FIDH). They went to great lengths to locate Bashayev's brother, Anzor, now based in France, who not only cooperated with them but also provided a DNA sample. Bashayev's DNA did not match any of the samples found on my mother's clothes or beneath her nails.

Hopes of finding my mother's murderers were slipping away. Even if there was a genuine attempt to pursue justice, there would be no way to prove forensically who the real perpetrators were, because all the DNA samples extracted from my mother's body had expired due to their being improperly stored.

It wasn't hard to guess who really stood behind my mother's murder. Moreover, Mum's colleagues had heard it directly from the investigators. When Tanya Lokshina was questioned as a witness for the first time, the day after the murder, a member of the Investigative Committee asked her, 'So, who do you think did it?'

Tanya replied that she had serious reasons to believe that Kurchaloi ROVD policemen were involved. 'But I'm more interested in who gave them the order,' she added. 'Isn't it obvious to you?'

'Well, if you know it, do tell me.'

'It was done by Kurchaloi policemen and Ramzan Kadyrov gave the order.'

We might have believed that Kadyrov was involved but he of course denied it, even going so far as to claim he would investigate the killing personally. After Oleg Orlov accused him of being responsible for Mum's murder, the head of Chechnya successfully sued him and Memorial for defamation, though a criminal case against Oleg failed. Kadyrov later accused the rebels of her murder, which he claimed was a false flag operation designed to shift blame onto him and undermine his regime.

In 2015 we turned to the last resort, lodging a case at the European Court of Human Rights. Mum had helped dozens of people to file such cases and now she had become one.

Six years later, in September 2021, the court issued a ruling that was so weak it made me want to throw my laptop against the wall in anger, as if I was sixteen again. Instead, I composed myself and issued a measured but honest statement and gave comments to the press. It was ruled that Mum's right to life had been breached because Russia failed to investigate her murder and that the government hadn't provided the necessary case files to the court. However, the judges rejected the argument that government agents were responsible for her death, as it had 'not been established beyond reasonable doubt'. The burden of proof fell on the shoulders of our family lawyers, but how could they prove the involvement of state agents when Russia denied them access to the files?

It was an utterly disappointing judgment. My mother believed that the European Court of Human Rights was the last hope of justice for victims of state abuse, but when she became a victim herself the court failed her. Now, it was up to us – her loved ones and closest friends – to ensure that though my mother's murder investigation had been botched, her story was not forgotten. That her legacy lives on.

There is no doubt in my mind that Ramzan Kadyrov is guilty. But for years, I kept asking myself why the Russian authorities didn't prosecute at least one or two killers who were involved in the kidnapping and murder. After Anya was killed, five men were convicted of her murder. In 2018, after a prominent opposition politician, Boris Nemtsov, was gunned down near Red Square, five men were prosecuted. Of course, both investigations were rigged, but at least there was an attempt at a trial. For Mum, they didn't even bother with court hearings but simply blamed a dead militant. Why? Despite all the lives she saved, all the people she helped, all the articles she wrote and all the interviews she gave, why did they not prosecute a single person? My fists clench again in anger.

The answer was clear. Because she was shot within driving distance of Grozny rather than in central Moscow. Because she was, ultimately, a Chechen, and therefore her life was less valuable than a Russian life. Because the world had moved on to the next big story a few days after her murder. A year later, Russian president Dmitri Medvedev was having burgers with Barack Obama in front of TV cameras, announcing the 'reset' of Russia–US relations. My mother's murder, the Russian–Chechen wars, continuous human rights abuses – all were brief points on the bottom of the agenda, if they featured at all. Too few people cared, and when they finally did, on 24 February 2022, when Russia invaded Ukraine, it was much too late.

13

A Promise

Apart from the tenth-floor flat, Mum didn't leave me an inheritance. But what she did hand down to me was far more valuable than any trust fund. The incredible network of her friends and colleagues, from Memorial and beyond, not only carried out an independent investigation but also helped to fulfil my mother's dream of giving me a proper education. While we were in Oxford, Mum had befriended a woman with a daughter my age who attended an international school with all kinds of after-school activities. 'I wish Lanka could go somewhere like that,' Mum had sighed, as if she was dreaming of sending me to Mars. Her friends found a place for me somewhere just like it – St Clare's, a small independent school in Oxford, just a short walk from Norham Gardens where Mum and I had stayed. In 2010, aged sixteen, I moved to the UK – my new home.

'Aren't you scared of moving to a foreign country all on your own, where you don't know anyone?' everyone asked. I wasn't. I had been preparing for this moment all my life, moving further and further from Chechnya each year, seeing Mum less and less. Except this time, we would not be reuniting. Still, her presence was all around me, not least in the generosity of her friends and colleagues who raised money for my hefty school fees. To cover my education a fund was set up – grants, private donations, even book proceeds generously poured in.

And then there was Joy – my self-proclaimed English Mum – who managed the fund. Whenever I had a school break, she welcomed me back to her cosy yellow flat in north London, taking me on walks around Hampstead Heath and to her favourite sushi restaurant in Camden Town. Joy never tried to replace my mother, but she took on the more difficult parenting duties that no one else could. Had I done my homework? Did I need more help with maths? Did I want to take singing lessons, since I loved singing so much? Maybe now it's time to go to therapy, to process everything? Even holidays were covered – I often stayed with Mum's friends in Europe and became very close to one of her best friends, Sasha Koulaeva. 'You're my third child,' she told me upon our first meeting, as we sat drinking tea in her kitchen in Paris. In the summer, I went back to Auntie Sveta in Russia and, after a few years, she would often come to the UK for a visit.

When I thought of all the amazing people in my life, I imagined them as the beads of a priceless necklace that I had inherited from Mum. After her death, the necklace was ripped and the beads were scattered everywhere. I picked up the chain and repaired it, adding more and more beads year after year. Being around Mum's friends and colleagues made me feel closer to her. And seeing me was healing for them, too; she had left behind the part of herself that was most precious to her.

At St Clare's, I felt simultaneously too old and too young, not knowing how to fit in among my wealthy classmates. But I was no longer alone. One night, crying as quietly as possible in the dark, my roommate, Gintare, heard me. She climbed into my bed and gave me a hug. That's how our friendship solidified – I was encouraged to be vulnerable and talk about my past. We switched on fairy lights, listened to Pink Floyd and swapped stories, perhaps revelling a little too much in our 'not like other kids' energy. And as a true friend, she was unafraid to tell me, after I'd punched the wall because the Internet was too slow, that I needed to learn how to manage my anger. Soon my friendship group expanded and by the end of my time at St Clare's, I had gained a small circle of clever, funny, strong and emotionally intelligent girlfriends. We spent hours chatting, doing homework together, eating copious amounts of Chinese food and simply being teenagers. I learnt that fitting in did not mean giving up anything special and that, in the UK, social skills were more important than showing off your knowledge of Sartre. This school became a cosy, safe bubble that helped me to heal and express myself in creative ways. I always recognised how privileged I was to be able to attend such a place, and was looking forward to the moment when I could repay all the kindness that had been shown to me over the years.

When it felt right, I followed Joy's advice and went to therapy. All the suppressed emotions that I hesitated to share even with my closest friends poured out at every session. For years, people had been telling me, 'You're so strong! You survived something so terrible!' I didn't feel strong, but I did become better at hiding my vulnerabilities. Sometimes I looked around – at the beautiful, manicured Oxford parks; at my supportive teachers and amazing new friends – and thought them staging for a darker play. As childhood slipped away, my nostalgia for Chechnya intensified. I mourned everything: my mother, a homeland in the grip of a tyrant, our home, the little girl I used to be. But this was reality. My mother had been stolen and I had been gifted a good, new life. It made me feel somewhat guilty, as if it was a different Lana living this life, the real one having been killed on that sweltering July day. Losing my mother and my homeland at once shook the ground under my feet and triggered a prolonged existential crisis that often turned into melancholy and depression. I lost my sense of self and questioned every belief I had before. Growing up is traumatic enough, but coupled with personal tragedy, it became an impossible task. I often felt detached from the people around me and at points it seemed that I didn't exist at all, as though my body was functioning on auto-pilot. Whenever I noticed this, I tried to snap out of it and enjoy life almost aggressively – making new friends, contemplating the changing of the seasons, spending at least half an hour in the Rothko room at Tate Modern, going on a solo backpacking trip across the Balkans. Because somehow, all this pain coexisted with my unapologetic thirst for life and excitement for what was coming next.

I wasn't sure who I wanted to be but decided that I ought to study something serious and grown-up, like history. I dismissed the little voice inside me reminding me that I wasn't, in fact, a very serious person. That there was nothing that I loved more than reading a gripping novel and whenever I tried to read *Foreign Affairs*, my eyes glazed over. My friends encouraged me to keep writing, and I continued to publish poetry and rather gloomy short stories with shocking twists. But all Mum ever wanted was for me to have a proper education, and for me to be happy, and so in the end I chose to study international relations at the London School of Economics; to my glee, I was granted a full scholarship by the department. Rereading my acceptance letter for the hundredth time, I imagined how happy it would have made my mother. From sitting at an old desk in a bullet-ridden school with no doors and windows to attending one of the most prestigious universities in the world. I had done it for both of us.

And while I was fulfilling this wish of my mother's, her second, vaguer wish for my happiness came true too. It was Freshers' Week and I was nervous. Had everyone friended up already, as they had in that first year in Yekaterinburg? How do you even talk to British students? Having attended an international boarding school while in the UK, I'd barely spoken to British kids. On the morning I arrived at the student halls, I was greeted by a perky Iraqi girl who began introducing me to everyone. 'We can go to the boys' floor,' she insisted, as I shyly followed.

'Let's see who is awake,' she said, knocking on the first door. A hazel-eyed guy with unruly curly hair appeared in the doorway, wearing a blue and pink hoodie and a sleepy smile. In a sea of teenage freshers, he looked like a man.

'This is M. M, this is Lana.'

I smiled back. Later that day, we started chatting – he was always so easy to talk to. And he was intelligent. And he was kind. And for some reason, I felt safe around him. We became good friends. For the next two years, we shared student halls and cups of tea; views on politics, religion, constructivism versus realism, Chomsky, Plato, cats versus dogs, post-colonialism, Chechnya, Russia, the UK, the US military–industrial complex. Do you put the milk in first, or the teabag? What do you miss the most about your childhood? Does the future scare you? What *is* the point of it all? Shall we make some pasta? Are you okay? Do you want to go to this crazy protest in front of the Russian Embassy? What building is our lecture in? Do you know that you're the first person I ever told this to? And the most important question of all, asked one sunny afternoon when we were revising for finals:

'What's happening between us?'

'I don't know,' M replied. 'But I've been falling in love with you for quite some time now.'

A PROMISE

M and I were married in September 2016 in a picturesque botanical garden overlooking the Atlantic Ocean. Unsurprisingly, the wedding preparations were complete chaos, and being only twenty-four and twenty-two, M and I were in over our heads. But when the day came, everything was perfect. I walked myself down the aisle wearing a flowing, Greek-style dress, with flowers in my hair. When I reached my husband-to-be, I prayed that he wouldn't notice how much my legs were shaking under the skirt: it wasn't a case of cold feet but rather because I was wearing the most dangerously uncomfortable ten-inch heels. As I walked I saw dozens of faces, all of them watching me with joy. The faces of M's family who embraced me from the very first meeting. My friends from St Clare's and LSE. And in the front row, all my loved ones from my other life. My Auntie Sveta and cousin Sasha, who even bought a suit for the occasion. Mariana and Joy, whose bright-blue eyes matched the flowers on her dress. And in the corner, the rest of Mum's friends who had gradually become my own – Sasha Koulaeva with her family, Varya, and flame-haired Tanya, my dearest Tanya. 'Look at me,' I thought, looking back at them. 'I'm happy. I'm thriving. You've fulfilled your duty to her.' When I said my vows, I knew that everything and everyone that surrounded me that day – the slender palm trees and eucalyptus illuminated by the setting sun, the bandstand adorned with cheery carnations, all those people from every walk of life and most importantly my beloved, hazel-eyed husband who was putting a ring on my finger – they were all there for a reason. And at that moment, I felt another presence, as distinct as the gentle breeze which caressed my face, the presence of the person who had made it all happen.

When I took a trip to Chechnya in April 2012, I didn't think it would be my last. Grozny's city centre was unrecognisable with its glass buildings and symmetrical parks, built with Russian funds. It was an illusion of peace.

Fake, it's all fake, I thought, looking at the newly planted, scrawny trees which refused to grow in their patches of city soil. Just a few miles away, Kadyrovites continued to torture and kill. There was no one left to hold them accountable.

The only places that didn't appear to have changed were the villages. Even under the yoke of dictatorship, they continued their eternal rhythms. The next generation had grown up and were producing children of their own. My seventeen-year-old cousin, Malika, had a baby. She proudly fussed over her little boy and asked me: 'When are you going to have your own?' I was a whole year older.

My mother's grave had a neat headstone and was well looked after. Kneeling on the ground, I placed my palms on the dry soil, observing the movements of a small ant colony. It was quiet, but as my senses adjusted I began to hear multiple sounds: trees whispering in the wind; birds making that sweet, joyful music of spring; little insects bustling about . . . Life found its way even in this solemn place. Moved, I made three promises to my mother:

First, I would always live in safety and would never needlessly risk my life. My children would have boring, stable lives, far away from war.

Second, I would not succumb to bitterness but would fight darkness with light. I would see the beauty in everything, always, and never take my life for granted. And finally . . .

One day, when I'm ready, I will write a book about us. She will be remembered and her killers will fade like ghosts.

14

A Story Without an End
2016–17

I kept the second part of my promise.

Shortly after my wedding, I gathered all the notes and diaries that I had accumulated over the years and started to write a book. 'I should be able to finish it in a year,' I naively thought. M and I moved to Edinburgh, and because visa restrictions prevented me applying for a proper job, I started waiting at tables part-time in a Scottish-American diner. It will be so romantic, I thought: writing my book, living with my husband in a small Edwardian flat filled with second-hand furniture, clearing my head by walking to the top of Arthur's Seat, the basalt crag that dominates Edinburgh's skyline. But my memories had other plans.

After twelve-hour shifts, all that ever emerged when I sat down to write were three or four clichéd sentences. I'd just stare at the laptop screen, urging the words to reassemble themselves. I was opening wounds. All the healing I'd done over the past seven years was being undone in weeks, although it wasn't obvious right away. I'd thought I was ready but when I reread Mum's articles or spoke to her friends, my soul burned. It was isolating, like going down into a dark cave, tied to a rope, completely alone.

I sought out childhood memories, rummaging through my mind for something pure, something untouched by horror. There was the handmade book she'd made for my sixth birthday, *Mum's Fairy Tales*. In Edinburgh, I read it through, hearing her voice in my head. But one was missing, a story about a cherry stone. What had happened to it? Why wasn't it in the book? Was the story lost? It had been called 'An Endless Story', or 'A Story Without an End'. In my mind, it became the most important of my mother's fables.

I tried to shake off all the negative thoughts, but inevitably I would end up back in that dark place, overtaken with resentment:

What was it all for, Mama? Why did you sacrifice your time, your well-being, your life, for those who were too scared to fight for themselves?

I remembered how Mum and I constantly bumped into people that she'd helped in the streets of Grozny; how their faces would light up. On several occasions, women looked me in the eye and said in a serious tone of voice: 'Natasha is our hero. You are so lucky to have a mother like her. You must always take care of her.'

'Of course, I will!' I replied defensively.

But when the time came, did they?

There were no big demonstrations after Mum's murder, no calls for justice from the hundreds of people she had helped – bar a few. Cowardice has a thousand excuses, bravery has none. Cowardice hides behind euphemisms such as 'concern for the family', 'self-preservation'. Only Mum was daring enough to have principles; only she was willing to fight for others until the end. Everyone else was too clever to get themselves killed.

I could never forgive the men who executed my mother, or whoever orchestrated it, but nor could I forgive those who had watched her being abducted and hadn't told me. By 15 July, I'd been back in Grozny for nearly a month. I had popped out to buy groceries, gone for walks, had chats with neighbours. They knew me. I was never foolish enough to believe that finding out sooner would have saved her life. But it might at least have lessened her suffering.

Such thoughts kept me awake at night.

Soon, I was overtaken by a familiar numbness and sense of detachment. My eyes adjusted to the half-light of my Edinburgh life. Food had no taste and the sky was always grey. I couldn't even muster the energy to go for a short walk and slept through the day. Caught between the past and the present, I began to fade, haunted by questions: who was my mother, really? Do I even know her? Had she really given herself to others, leaving me only scraps? Before I could write about her, I had to find the answers to these questions for myself.

I leafed through family albums, my most treasured possessions that I lugged from flat to flat. I used photographs as prompts for my writing but couldn't help but get lost in the memories. I paused over photos of Mum, lightly touching the outline of her face with my fingertips. She was so beautiful.

Gazing at her high cheekbones, her green eyes, her skin marked by acne scars from her teenage years, the hair that she coloured chestnut with dye from a box to hide the grey, I began to understand that she was so much more than just my mother. She was a woman in her own right, imperfect, volatile, passionate, warm and endlessly kind. She was an extraordinary human being, a once-in-a-generation person, and I had been lucky to have her in my life, even if only for fifteen years. There comes a point when every child must forgive their parent for their failings. I forgave my mother for leaving me too soon. I embraced her in her entirety, with all her flaws and the mistakes she made along the way. I accepted her choice to live her truth until the end, knowing that it might result in tragedy. I accepted that she would always be a mystery to me.

My mum was a free person in an unfree place. She acted in accordance with her beliefs. Yes, one might ask where her beliefs got her, but with every year I learnt to see her life as a testament to freedom. Everything that is good in this world – democracy, justice, equality, civil rights – has been made possible because of people like her, people who refuse to place their comfort, safety and family life above fighting for what's right.

These thoughts were with me on a bleak June day in 2017 as I left the house that M and I shared in Edinburgh and walked towards Arthur's Seat. The wind was picking up, but it didn't look like rain. I had little energy in those days, but I began to climb the steep hill, indifferent to the familiar vista that unrolled before me. At the top, on the green cliff, everything looked drab, and the climb had exhausted me. The wind was growing stronger and stronger. A violent gust hit me so hard that I instinctively stepped back, although nowhere near the edge.

> There was an old cherry tree growing in a small orchard. Spring had only just set in, so there were no leaves or fruit, only small buds. A grey dishevelled crow landed on a branch and was preparing to nibble one of buds when she heard a noise.
> 'Who's there?' asked the alarmed crow.

'Me,' replied a tiny voice.

'Who are you?'

'I'm a flower inside the bud. It's very cramped in here. I can feel the warmth through the walls. I would love to be outside. It must be so much more fun out there!'

'Nonsense,' snapped the crow. 'It's cold, damp and there is no food around. I was going to eat you but since we're talking, that would be a bit awkward.'

'Please don't eat me, I would love to see the world outside!'

At that moment, the sun cut through the clouds. The air became warmer. The bud opened up.

'Oh, how beautiful it is out here!' she exclaimed, and then stretched and smoothed out her petals. Quiet sounds of cracking and rustling spread through the cherry tree. Little pink and green leaves climbed out of their buds. They trembled, overjoyed by light and warmth.

'Just you wait,' grumbled the crow. 'Let's see how you feel in the morning.'

Something happened to me after I was hit by that gust of wind. I glanced with astonishment at the world, at the rugged cliffs covered in heather, at the toy-like houses below and the perfectly blue sky. Everything seemed to have contours again. I felt light. The fierce wind kept slapping my body, but it didn't go through me as it might through a ghost. I could feel it now. I found myself squinting, as if someone had turned up the brightness. As I had when I first wore contact lenses.

So, this is how the world looks! I'd forgotten.

The night was cold. The little flower felt dejected. But in the morning the same sun came out and she cheered up.

'Hello, Crow! I'm alive!' she exclaimed, as she spotted the old bird.

'You'll see,' the crow grudgingly replied. 'The wind will rise and we'll see how tightly you can hold on to your stem. You won't survive until the morning!'

Indeed, the sky turned dark and the sun hid behind dark clouds. There was a strong gust of wind and the poor flowers held on to their branches as tightly as possible. One after another, they lost their petals, but the little flower held on.

The storm passed and the sun came out again.

'Look, I'm doing fine!' cried the flower to the crow. 'And it looks as if you've lost a few feathers.'

'Keep on laughing,' the crow replied. 'You don't have long. Soon your petals will turn to mush under foot and you will die!'

'No way,' disagreed the flower, assessing her pink petals. They didn't look so fresh anymore, but maybe that was because of the approaching dusk.

In the morning, the flower realised with horror that she could no longer hold on to her petals. One separated and was swept away by the wind, then another, and then another.

'I'm dying!' cried the flower. 'Soon my last petal will fall and I will be no more!'

'Don't be scared,' whispered the old cherry tree. 'You won't die, you will simply become something else.' The only thing now left of the flower was a small green bump.

'I'm so ugly,' she thought with sadness.

But the sun was shining so tenderly and there were so many other bumps just like her on the tree that her spirits soon lifted. She rotated and exposed both of her sides to the sunlight. Every day the bump grew bigger and bigger until one day it turned into a cherry.

'Oh, I'm big,' noted the cherry. 'Bigger than all my sisters!' And she blushed with pleasure.

'Isn't it time to eat you?' she heard the crow say.

'No, please, don't!' trembled the cherry. 'I feel so great, and I don't want to die!'

'All right,' croaked the crow. 'There's plenty to feast on, but beware, other birds won't listen to you – you are the brightest and the biggest of them all and you're very exposed.'

'I shall hide,' whispered the cherry as she saw a neighbour eaten by a sparrow.

I found myself in a Metaphysical Moment; everything swirled around me – the past and the future, the tragic and the joyful. Like a new-born, I greedily inhaled the pale Edinburgh air.

How could I betray the promise that I had made all those years ago? Always to see the beauty in life, to be excited about new things. In that moment, I embraced all the grief and the anger, all the happiness and the impossible love. Just because someone we love dies doesn't mean that your relationship with them ends. My mother had been taken but no one could ever take away the love that I continued to feel for her.

At that moment on Arthur's Seat, all that love suddenly pulsed through me like a spell and poured out into the universe like a bright beam of light. It was reflected back at me and in the murmur of the wind I heard a voice. I felt a connection to my ancestors and marvelled at the sequence of events that had led me to the top of that crag. Just like all those years ago, on the eighth-floor balcony, the voice whispered, *I'm alive! I'm alive! I'm alive, I'm alive, I'm alive*. I was finally myself again.

Many days passed and the garden filled with people. They picked apricots and cherries, filling baskets. One after the other, the cherries were taken, but our cherry hid well, and the baskets were taken away.

Suddenly, a small girl ran into the garden and upon seeing the fruitless cherry tree, she began to cry.

'I didn't get a single cherry and I love them so much!'

'She's so upset,' sighed the cherry. 'And only I can comfort her.' So she asked the tree to lower her branch towards the girl. The girl felt a gentle caress from the leaves, and on opening her eyes saw a wonderful dark-red cherry that looked as if it was going to burst from all the juice.

'Wow, how pretty!' marvelled the girl and carefully picked her. She'd never eaten such a delicious cherry. Her lips turned red. She spat the stone out on her palm, yelled 'Fly!' and threw it far, far away.

The stone flew high, higher than the old cherry tree, then fell on the ground and vanished into a small burrow a worm had dug.

'Your time's up, silly,' scoffed the crow. 'Now you will disappear forever!'

'So what?' thought the stone. 'I regret nothing. I just want to sleep.' Summer changed to autumn, then winter covered the earth with snow. Our little stone kept sleeping.

Then spring came once again. The snow melted and a trickle of water poured into the burrow. The stone felt damp and turned over on its side. Then she decided to see what all the fuss was about. Her hard shell had grown thin during the winter and it now split open, revealing a green sprout. It grew taller and taller until finally it climbed out of the ground.

'And who do we have here?' croaked our crow. 'Get back inside the earth, it's cramped out here, the garden is full of trees. If you don't listen to me, you will die! It's freezing out here.'

'I don't believe you, Crow!' laughed the sapling. 'You keep trying to scare me with stories of death, but I keep living and not dying – only changing!'

'Well done,' smiled the old cherry tree. 'Indeed, you will not die. But my time has passed, and this year I will not bloom and put out leaves. I give you my strength.'

'Does that mean you will die?' the sapling cried.

'No. I will live on inside you. And you will give life to many leaves, berries and trees. And life will never end.'

'Never!'

On the way home, I threw shy looks at passers-by. Suddenly, strangers meant something. I passed a brown building shaped like an octagon. Beside it was a small pond in which white water lilies bloomed – how beautiful the contrast between the brutalist, stone architecture and the flowers. I passed identical rows of grey apartment blocks, made of rain. Home, where M was waiting for me. I had so much to tell him. But first, I had to write down a thought that I had carried down from the mountain like a precious bucket of water that couldn't be spilled. A very simple revelation that I'd been waiting years for. Still in my shoes, I hurried to my desk, grabbed the nearest notebook and a pen and hastily scribbled in the margins:

Happiness is a true victory.

Acknowledgements

This book has been my companion throughout my twenties. Sometimes we parted ways, only to ferociously entangle again until it was finished. Writing it has been a beautiful, devastating, maddening, profound, challenging and religious experience. It would not have been possible without the many people who have cheered me on over the years.

Thank you to Jocasta Hamilton and the rest of the John Murray team for taking on *Please Live* and paying it such careful attention from the start. You've handled my story with much respect and consideration, for which I'm eternally grateful. Thank you to my editor Kate Craigie for working closely with me to ensure that *Please Live* became the best version of itself without compromising my vision and style. I will never forget the mad dash to complete the final edits before my baby's arrival – and finishing with just two weeks to spare! Thank you to Katharine Morris for her insightful comments. Thank you to Dave Watkins and Hillary Hammond. I feel I am a better, more confident writer having absorbed all your feedback and suggestions.

I'm very grateful to Tom Parfitt for putting me in touch with Patrick Walsh, who became my agent. Patrick, thank you for seeing the potential in those first chapters and working hard to make sure *Please Live* became a reality. Your words of encouragement spurred me on. Thank you to the entire team at PEW Literary for all your support.

I would like to say a special thank-you to Mary Lawlor for believing in this book right from the beginning and to Denis, who provided the grant that allowed me to get started. It might have taken longer than expected, but delivering on my promise to the two of you has been one of my biggest motivations.

ACKNOWLEDGEMENTS

Thank you to Maria Ordzhonikidze and the rest of the Justice for Journalists team for supporting me, and the book, while leaving the door open for me to return. Being given free reign over my podcast Trouble with the Truth got my creative juices flowing, turning me into a better interviewer and a more productive writer, and making finishing *Please Live* a much easier job.

Words can't describe how grateful I am to my mum's friends and colleagues for not only helping me with the book but making me the person that I am today. I'm in awe of your bravery, wit and composure in the face of adversity. I've always said that despite everything, I'm lucky to have grown up on the right side of the barricades. You are my heroes. Thank you to everyone at Memorial – Katya Sokirianskaia, Sasha Cherkasov, Oleg Orlov, Svetlana Gannushkina, Elisa, Shamil, Usam, Shakhman, Dokka, Taisa, Zarema, Milana, Akhmed and the rest. Thank you to Sasha Koulaeva and Varya Pakhomenko for always being there for me when writing this book was weighing me down.

Special thanks to Tanya Lokshina, who's judgment and advice I trust wholeheartedly. Your remarks on those first chapters were invaluable. Thank you for always being available and replying to every question – be it a translation query or a memory check – over the past two years.

Thank you to friends who are no longer with us. To Joy Watkins, my English fairy godmother who inspired me to write and gave me a safe space to be myself. Joy, you are greatly missed. Thank you to courageous Alik Mnatsakanyan for his warmth, his stories and his jokes about Mum.

Thank you to my relatives, the ones whose identities are hidden and those I wrote about openly. Auntie Sveta, you are the glue that holds our family together and one of the strongest people I know. You fulfilled your promise to your sister and took care of me in those darkest days. You never ask for thanks but I'm grateful for all your help over the years and the memories we share, including the painful ones.

Thank you to my friends for their unwavering faith in me and my book. I know how long you've been waiting to read every sentence and I'm grateful for your patience and encouragement.

ACKNOWLEDGEMENTS

Thank you to my husband for being my biggest champion and go-to for everything – my first reader, editor, advisor, sounding board. Thank you for aggressively believing in me and not letting me drown in self-doubt and hesitation. You have been there for me from the moment I told you my idea for the book over a cup of tea in Hoxton. This would have been impossible without you. Thank you for the beautiful life we've built together.

Although this entire book is written in memory of my mum, I want to finish by thanking her. Mama, I owe everything in my life to you. Everything I do is dedicated to you, one way or another. The least I could do was ensure that your memory lives on and that people around the world get to meet you long after you've gone. One of them will be little Natasha once she's old enough to read. You live in her too.